COLLABORATIVE LEADERSHIP

We all live in an interconnected world and for business leaders the last decade has seen a dramatic rise in the speed and scale of this interdependence. But while increased connectivity is inevitable, increased collaboration is not. To succeed in today's environment, leaders need to be able to build relationships, handle conflict and to share control in order to promote effective collaboration where it is needed most.

Archer and Cameron have been working in this field for over ten years and were amongst the first business authors to define and explain collaborative leadership in their 2009 book. This second edition draws on interviews, examples and additional cases studies of the new collaboration challenges that leaders face, such as: working together to deal with the consequences of financial contagion in the Eurozone or elsewhere; responding to the growth in the use of social networks by their staff and customers; and managing global supply chains to reach new growth markets.

This fully revised, updated and restructured text provides an easily accessible 'how-to' guide for leaders in today's interconnected world. It will give both experienced and aspiring leaders the techniques and confidence to manage complex collaborative relationships in a sustainable way. It also acts as a guide for leadership development professionals, coaches and consultants who have to build leadership and collaboration capability within organizations.

David Archer and **Alex Cameron** are founding Directors of Socia Ltd, a company which has an international reputation for advising leaders of large organizations on how to get more from their critical business relationships. Their clients include leaders from sectors such as the central government, transport, oil and gas and finance who face particularly significant collaboration challenges.

'Today's toughest complex challenges facing business and society need bold leadership across boundaries and many different organisations. Archer and Cameron's latest book shines a practical light on examples of collaborative leadership in action across private, public and voluntary sectors, and on the key leadership capabilities needed by not just one but many leaders who need to work together.'

Dr Keith Ruddle, Associate Fellow in Leadership, Oxford University

'The world's most dynamic businesses have one thing in common – they're boundaryless. They work naturally and happily with others. If you want to know the secrets of becoming boundaryless, this book is your best choice – wise, authoritative and extremely useful.'

Robert Jones, Head of New Thinking, Wolff Olins

'The benefits of collaboration are irrefutable; the evidence overwhelming. But it remains counter cultural in many business environments. The real value of this book is in its combination of practical tools that leaders can deploy and inspiring case studies to keep you on track when the going gets tough.'

Andrew Haines, CEO Civil Aviation Authority

'The world is looking to technological innovation to help solve its biggest problems. It is only by bringing people together from different disciplines and organisational backgrounds that we can build lasting solutions. In this book David Archer and Alex Cameron address practical lessons on how to make such collaboration work.'

Tony Ridley, Emeritus Professor, Imperial College London

'This new edition of *Collaborative Leadership* could not be more timely. The recession and ongoing austerity are forcing the pace on partnership working between organisations and across sectors. Archer and Cameron brilliantly demystify what collaborative leadership is, and how to do it, in an accessible and engaging way. Anyone involved in commissioning, joint ventures and not for profit collaborations will benefit from reading this book.'

Linda Holbeche, former Research and Policy Director CIPD and author of *Engaged: Unleashing Your Organization's Potential Through Employee Engagement*

'The British summer of 2012 was like no other before: showers of gold medals, 20m spectators, sideburns, Union flags and an impeccable Games delivery. This didn't happen by chance. Seven years of collaborative leadership across and within the public and private sectors made it such a stupendous success: that's why this book should matter to leaders.'

Hugh Sumner, Director of Transport, Olympic Delivery Authority

'This is a practical book grounded in fertile experience. In a complex and highly interdependent and increasingly densely connected world, proven practitioner tools are vital to the leader seeking sustainable, collaborative success. David and Alex capture the wisdom of all of it.'

Gary L. Mann, Global Lead, Talent & Organization Capability, Pfizer Primary Care

'This book is a timely reminder that we live in an increasingly interdependent world and the problems we face can rarely be solved by one organisation acting on its own. This puts a huge premium on leaders who are good at working across boundaries; at identifying a common purpose and reaching solutions. Collaborative leadership requires energy, determination and different behaviours. It isn't a guarantee of success. But it is essential in today's tougher climate. Alongside the theory (from evolutionary biology to slime mould), there are practical tools and real world examples. A great read for those who are looking for inspiration at the end of an eventful year.'

Bronwyn Hill, Permanent Secretary at the Department for Environment, Food and Rural Affairs

'Originally published in 2009, the new edition provides an important update in thinking about collaborative leadership and its importance in this global, interconnected and rapidly changing world. I enjoyed reading this book – it is very accessible, interesting, and provides a useful source of ideas and points to reflect upon. It is clearly located in the "real" world and everyday best practices of business and management. As an educator, I will recommend it to students – particularly those with aspirations to become global leaders.'

Professor Barbara Allan, Dean, Westminster Business School

'This is the age of collaboration, survival and success demand it. Technology enables collaboration across geographies, but the biggest challenges remain those of culture and leadership. This book grasps the nettle of where leaders go wrong and is the user manual to survive and thrive in complex organisations facing 21st-century challenges that demand a new type of collaborative leader.'

Clive Grinyer, Director of Customer Experience, Cisco

'Alex Cameron and David Archer have been pioneers in articulating the advantages of collaborative leadership. Leadership styles vary, from the autocratic and dictatorial to the consensual. The authors, though, make a compelling case for a different approach in a fast-changing world – one which embraces the ability to build relationships; to handle conflict; and to share control. There have been plenty of examples, some well-documented in this book, of alternative styles less suited to the contemporary world, with all its complexities and inter-dependencies. If you read this book, it will at the very least provide you with much food for thought; and at best, you may be encouraged to act on its wisdom.'

Sir Ian Magee CB, Senior Fellow, Institute for Government and Senior Adviser Booz & Company

'Archer and Cameron have again proven their expertise in new world of interconnected relationships. Technology may have increased and changed dramatically, however, the second edition of this landmark book shows the foresight the authors possessed in understanding how collaboration is the key to deal with conflict, share control, and serve stakeholders, all while maintaining the bottom line.'

Dr E.S. Wibbeke, author of *Global Business Leadership*

COLLABORATIVE LEADERSHIP

Building relationships, handling conflict and sharing control

Second edition

David Archer and Alex Cameron

Routledge
Taylor & Francis Group

LONDON AND NEW YORK

First published 2009 by Butterworth-Heinemann, an imprint of Elsevier
This edition published 2013
by Routledge
2 Park Square, Milton Park, Abingdon, Oxon OX14 4RN

Simultaneously published in the USA and Canada
by Routledge
711 Third Avenue, New York, NY 10017

Routledge is an imprint of the Taylor & Francis Group, an informa business

British Library Cataloguing in Publication Data
A catalogue record for this book is available from the British Library

Library of Congress Cataloging in Publication Data
Collaborative leadership : building relationships, handling conflict, sharing
control / David Archer and Alex Cameron. – 2nd ed.
    p. cm.
Includes bibliographical references and index.
1. Leadership. 2. Strategic alliances (Business) 3. Business networks.
4. Public–private sector cooperation. I. Cameron, Alex, 1957- II. Title.
HD57.7.A73 2013
658.4'092–dc23   2012032165

ISBN: 978-0-415-53948-7 (hbk)
ISBN: 978-0-415-53949-4 (pbk)
ISBN: 978-0-203-06750-5 (ebk)

Typeset in Bembo
by Cenveo Publisher Services

MIX
Paper from
responsible sources
FSC® C018575

Printed and bound in Great Britain by MPG Printgroup

CONTENTS

ILLUSTRATIONS

Figures

Tables

FOREWORD

Some think that the trajectory of human progress has been fuelled uniquely by competition and creative destruction. For me the human capacity to relate, co-operate and collaborate has been just as fundamental a driver at the heart of our progress as a species. Indeed, as the world we live in becomes progressively inter-twined and interdependent our continued prosperity depends increasingly on our willingness and ability to collaborate effectively.

In business, collaboration has been at the heart of our organisations for centuries. Joint stock companies evolved to enable individuals to combine intellectual and financial capital to pursue ventures that required collective action and shared respon-sibility for risk to be successful. In today's economy the confines of a single organi-sation often does not provide sufficient capacity to make progress. In the global beverage business, where I have worked for more than 35 years, this need for effec-tive and efficient collaboration has never been more apparent. But the need for leaders to work together across organisational and cultural divides is a growing phenomenon in all industries and is arguably even more of an imperative in the delivery of public services, particularly since the advent of the financial and eco-nomic crisis. Often the requirement is to be able to quickly mobilise a team, har-nessing resources from several disciplines to find a solution. While the technology helps, it is the attitude of the individuals, their willingness and ability to collaborate that determines that speed of response and the capacity to resolve the problem.

Collaboration is not the soft option

I've known David and Alex for more than a decade now and they have been pio-neers in this field for even longer – long before concepts like collaborative leader-ship became fashionable. The first edition of their book was my own initiation into the emerging consensus from biology, social psychology and behavioural economics of the human capacity to collaborate. It also introduced me to a set of skills that facilitate collaboration, practices that have become even more critical and relevant since that edition was written in 2008.

The rhetoric of markets can make words like collaboration, partnership and co-operation sound like soft options in a world that can seem increasingly competitive, uncertain and hostile. But the reality is that collaboration is demanding, relying on a set of sophisticated skills to be successful. Collaboration is initiated by leaders who see an opportunity and who are determined and capable to do what is required to bring it to fruition. It is not simply about people getting on better or having more fun working together – it's about aligning disparate interests into a common purpose, it's about building trust, it is about working with each other to create something new together. It's also about managing conflict and often ceding control. Unless leaders are willing and able to see beyond their immediate self-interest the default position can easily become competition and conflict. Successful collaboration requires difficult conversations with partners you can't control. People who don't think like you, don't have the same history as you, and don't have all the same objectives as you – but partners you depend on and who depend on you to make progress.

One example from my own career may help to illustrate the point. For Diageo, water is a critical resource. It is a primary ingredient in the company's products, a critical component of the production processes and a fundamental requirement for the provision of the agricultural raw materials on which the company depends. Diageo recognises water as central to the sustainability of its brands and its business and is collaborating more and more with a range of stakeholders to address the challenges of availability. Conserving water and using it responsibly in all geographies is important but this is particularly true in areas of high water stress such as parts of Africa. In Kenya, Diageo's Guinness business is growing rapidly in a region that faces long-term water supply issues to meet the needs of a burgeoning population and rapid economic growth. To safeguard its own interests and support the needs of the community and environment in which it operates, Diageo has been working in partnership with NGOs, local governments and other large commercial water users to develop a sustainable water supply infrastructure. But the relationships required to make a real difference can take years to build – you've got to sustain the focus on the long-term gain, and be prepared to work at the pace of the collective. And that brings its own tensions with managing the levels of internal impatience and the need for year on year results within your own organisation. But as David and Alex would advise – 'you can't hope to collaborate successfully with external partners unless you can build the necessary coalitions within your own organisation'. In the end we often have to accept that we may be taking a lead but we are not in control.

It's human nature – one way or another

Human nature has evolved to be tribal; we band together and imitate those with whom we identify. At the same time we are intensely competitive with those we see as different from us in some way, even those in very close proximity. You can see these dynamics at play in football grounds up and down the country every week – and you can see it in business life too. People like to stick with their own, look after their own, and beat the competition where they can. But tribalism at the small group level is no longer sufficient to address the challenges we face in business, far less at the level of society. Like it or not we are dependent on each other in more and more ways. And leaders need to enable their 'tribes' to see beyond the confines of what they can achieve alone – inspiring individuals to look beyond their own boundaries and work collectively to maximise the benefits for the whole system. This will ultimately be the best for their own tribe too.

In this book David and Alex address this fundamental human dilemma head on. They combine their own expertise developed over many years of working in a range of sectors with the latest thinking about human motivation that has emerged from academic research to paint a path forward for leaders. They see people as having the intrinsic capability to both collaborate *and* to compete conditioned largely by the environment they perceive themselves to be in. And it's the actions of leaders that can create and shape that environment. Leaders have the job of analysing the many relationships they are in to find the situations where the greatest needs for collaboration lie, and then building the right framework of behaviours, processes and rules to enable collaboration by stimulating our natural ability to find common cause given the right circumstances.

Why read this book?

For those of us who forage for our living in organisations, this book provides us with the tools and skills required to develop and deploy some of our most critical skills. So if you are a leader who has to break down internal silos or to build coalitions of common interest in environments where you don't have control you should read this book.

Working as a collaborative leader is challenging – but there is an emerging body of knowledge of how to make collaboration work and many of the skills and capabilities are explained in the pages that follow. I encourage you to read it and, more importantly, to learn the lessons it offers to enable us all to prosper.

Gerry O'Hagan
Global Technical Director
Diageo

ACKNOWLEDGEMENTS

This book is a distillation of our experience working with many leaders over the last ten years at our consulting company, Socia. We want to thank everyone who has collaborated to make Socia such a successful business over the last ten years: our chairman, Julie Baddeley, our advisory board (many of whom are quoted in the book), and of course all our clients.

We couldn't have written this second edition without the first to build on – and we couldn't have written the first edition without the help of Sandra Greaves.

Thanks also to our families who have had to put up with all our moods as we've managed the ups and downs of writing and editing this book. Their support has been great and they've been as glad to see the finished product as we were.

And finally we want to thank all of the collaborative leaders whose stories form the lifeblood of the book and who are quoted throughout. It's their success that we want to celebrate and their experience that we offer to you, the reader, to learn from.

ACKNOWLEDGMENTS

INTRODUCTION

A lot has happened since we wrote the first edition of this book in 2008. The sub-title of that edition was *How to succeed in an interconnected world* – but, as the financial crisis hit, we soon saw that for many leaders the challenge was simply how to survive.

Back then we worried about the early days of the credit crunch and the knock-on effects of the collapse of Lehman Brothers. But now we fear 'contagion' may force a radical restructuring of the Eurozone. Wherever their business is based, leaders can have no doubt that they have to manage in a world of financial interdependency.

In the technology world the increasing speed and scale of interconnection has been enormous. The growth in the number and power of smartphones since 2008 (the worldwide sales volume has gone up four fold to over 500 million) means that now more people are buying mobile devices to connect to the internet than PCs. We want to be connected anytime anyplace anywhere and connected in new ways, especially through the growth of social media. Facebook may have started as an exclusive club for members of Ivy League universities but it rapidly spread to the general population and is predicted to pass 1,000 million users. People clearly want to share details of their lives on-line with networks of friends. The business consequences of this social media trend are still to be worked through but it is one of the new topics we discuss in this second edition.

In the UK, there has been another significant development since 2008 that has affected the way people think about co-operation and leadership. In 2010, we were faced with the outcome of a general election where no party had an overall majority. During five long days in May the Conservatives and the Liberal Democrats had to work out how they were going to govern in coalition and write a coalition agreement which would bind them together for the next five years. Never in a generation has an incoming UK government needed more access to collaborative leadership skills.

Collaborative leadership goes mainstream

Our own consultancy business Socia celebrated its tenth anniversary in 2012 and that caused us to reflect how the conversations with our clients have changed over the years. We wrote the first edition of this book when many of our clients were struggling to make relationships work – mostly in formal partnership situations. At that time if you came across the term collaborative leadership in management literature at all it was usually to do with the challenges of PFI (Public Finance Initiatives) and other public–private partnerships.

Since then the concept of collaborative leadership and the growing body of knowledge and practical experience around it have gone mainstream. (It may be a trivial example but tracking the number of viewers of the Wikipedia page on collaborative leadership has climbed from virtually nothing to over 2,000 hits a month – not up there with cute kittens or dancing babies on YouTube but nevertheless some measure of increasing interest.)

Today we see leaders in all walks of business and political life talking about the need to break down silos, build collaborative relationships and deal with the challenges of not being in direct control. The questions we get asked are not just about the need to deliver results through contracted partnerships anymore – the need is much wider than that. And in our view that need is not going to go away. Most forecasters seem to agree that we are facing a very tough economic climate for many years to come, in Western countries at least. In these tough times the temptation for leaders can be to turn inwards to try to isolate themselves and protect the interests of their own group or organization. That may win some short-term popularity – but whether it's leading a business or a country the lesson of the last few years is that this tribal approach just doesn't work in the long run. If interdependence is here to stay then the only successful response is to develop your own collaborative leadership capability to deal with it.

It's not all about being nice

We've never thought that collaborative leadership was an overwhelmingly intellectual subject – it doesn't require any fancy mathematics or an encyclopedic knowledge of legal precedents before a collaborative leader can decide on a course of action. But it does require a depth of understanding of people and the values that guide them, a willingness to build support across many different constituencies and a maturity of temperament to deal with the conflict that will occur along the way.

It's not all about being nice to your business partners either. Of course interpersonal skills are important, but in all the interviews we've conducted with leaders for this book one message is very clear – collaborative leadership is hard and it's certainly not for the faint-hearted. Sharing control and putting the future of your company partially in the hands of others, who have different ways of working and skills to your own, is tough work.

How this edition works

Collaborative leadership may be difficult but that is no cause for despair. There are plenty of well-developed tools and techniques and a growing body of experience from leaders to draw on.

The structure of this second edition reflects these two sources of support.

- Part 1 (Chapters 2–6) contains a set of tools that aspiring collaborative leaders can use to analyse, to create and to maintain effective business relationships, with lots of checklists and examples of how to use them in practice.
- Part 2 (Chapters 7–12) focuses on the lessons leaders can learn from others working in the field and how they manage the risks and conflicts associated with collaboration at all levels from front-line services to the boardroom.

Each chapter has a box at the end which summarizes the main messages and then a checklist with key lessons for leaders.

As part of the research for this second edition, we conducted additional interviews with collaborative leaders from many different industry sectors to learn from their most recent experience. All the unreferenced quotes in Chapter 7 and throughout the book are from these personal conversations and from similar interviews undertaken as part of the research for the first edition.

And finally

In the midst of one of the many all-night sessions where European politicians were trying to decide on the next step to take to fix the problems of the Eurozone, the Luxembourg finance minister Jean-Claude Junker said 'We all know what to do, we just don't know how to get re-elected after we've done it.' And in a way that is a neat encapsulation of the dual challenges we face as collaborative leaders. Standing alongside our partners we have to work out what it is we all need to do – but then we need to work out how to win support for that shared solution amongst many different interest groups with many different concerns, any of whom could derail our plans.

When one organization is dependent on others their actions are bound to interfere with one another. And as the illustration on the cover of this book shows, that interference can be constructive, creating bigger waves and more impact, or destructive with their actions cancelling each other out. The successful collaborative leader has to accept the fact that interference will happen and work with their partners to minimize destructive risks and maximize the constructive impacts.

It's hard work – but it's worth the effort. And we hope this book will help you along the way.

David Archer and Alex Cameron
London 2012

1

INTERDEPENDENCE AND ITS CONSEQUENCES FOR LEADERS

Past performance does not guarantee future success

For Fred Goodwin growth was all about making deals. As Deputy CEO of the Royal Bank of Scotland (RBS) he had already played a major role in carrying off what was then the biggest deal in UK banking history when RBS bought the National Westminster bank in 2001. Three years later, and now as CEO, he led the acquisition of Charter One which propelled RBS into the top ten of US commercial banks. The biggest deal was yet to come. In 2007, RBS bought Dutch banking group ABN Amro and briefly became the largest bank in the world by asset value. And yet within a year he was out of job and the bank he had grown so spectacularly had come 'within hours' of running out of money altogether, according to the Governor of the Bank of England.[1] To a large extent Fred Goodwin's rapid growth strategy for RBS was undermined because the number of businesses involved made the system too complex to fully understand. But it wasn't just the complexity of the system that was at fault, the suitability of leadership style was also part of the equation.

Hindsight is a wonderful thing, but the Financial Services Authority was raising concerns back in 2004 about Goodwin's leadership style and saying that 'the challenging management culture led by the CEO raised particular risks that had to be addressed'.[2] You might have thought that this would have been a sufficiently important warning sign to investors. But Sir Fred was building a bank that he and many others seemed to think would be 'too big to fail' – and exploring the impact of his personal leadership style was probably not high on his agenda. How wrong he was and what an enormous cost his shareholders and the British public paid to learn the lessons. Fred Goodwin lost out too. He lost his Knighthood as well as his reputation – joining a small group of disgraced political leaders including Robert Mugabe and Nicolae Ceausescu in having that honour revoked.

Or take another leader whose rise and rapid fall from grace has been well documented in recent years, Tony Hayward at BP. In February 2010, he reported another good year-on-year increase in profits with good prospects as the company continued its industry-leading 17-year run of increasing reserves. Under John Browne's leadership BP had developed into a major player in deep water oil exploration and Haywood was seen as a straight-talking, enthusiastic and above all safe successor to a CEO who had become increasingly controversial in his later years.[3] But two months later came the explosion on the Deepwater Horizon rig and the start of the most costly oil spill disaster in the world.

Drilling for oil at depths such as those found in the Gulf of Mexico is a technically very difficult operation – and one that calls for close collaboration between the many different experts working for different contractors. The chain of events that led to the explosion of the Deepwater Horizon platform was complex and involved people working for BP's partners Halliburton and Transocean as well as their own staff. But although the cause of the accident was technically complex it was not inevitable. The reports from the Presidential Oil Spill Commission clearly trace the causes back to leadership failings on the rig and in the chain of responsibility reaching right back through the management of BP. To quote from the Chief Counsel's report, 'The Chief Counsel's team concluded that all of the technical failures at Macondo can be traced back to management errors by the companies involved in the incident. BP did not fully appreciate all of the risks that Macondo presented. It did not adequately supervise the work of its contractors, who in turn did not deliver to BP all of the benefits of their expertise.' And they also found that 'What the men and women who worked on Macondo lacked – and what every drilling operation requires – was a culture of leadership responsibility.'[4]

In the immediate aftermath of the explosion Tony Hayward's leadership response was to 'circle the wagons', to try to gain control of all crisis operations and communication about the incident. His instinct was to defend his own organization at all costs in the belief that they had all the expertise and resources needed to stop the leak and fix the problem. Ultimately this approach didn't work. BP needed to reach out for help from lots of other organizations and agencies to deal with sealing the well and reducing the amount of damage to the Gulf Coast. And Hayward himself was replaced by BP's US Chief Bob Dudley who quickly set about a different leadership approach, listening to stakeholders to try to address their concerns.[5]

Goodwin and Hayward show how the leadership characteristics that had smoothed their progress to the top of their own organizations may not be what is needed to succeed in a more complex world – with multiple stakeholders and many interdependent relationships. And this lesson doesn't just apply to business leaders. Let's take one more example of a leader that couldn't adapt – ex-Prime Minister Gordon Brown. After three years as PM (and 13 in cabinet) his Labour party government lost its overall majority in the 2010 election. The polls in the run up to the vote were inconclusive but an outcome where no one party had an overall majority was always a high probability. In these circumstances for the Labour party to stay in power they needed a leader that could take them into a successful coalition with the Liberal Democrats. When the result was announced and the negotiating for a coalition began, it became clear how ill-equipped Gordon Brown was for that task.

His leadership style had been described by his predecessor, Tony Blair, as 'a great clunking fist' – and it was clear that the Liberal Democrats just weren't going to work with someone like that. We'll never know exactly went on in the various negotiations but it was widely reported that 'Mr Clegg said it would be impossible to work with Brown because of his attitude towards working with other people.'[6] For four days from 6 to 10 May, Gordon Brown resisted the inevitable and then eventually resigned in order to try to pave the way for another leader to take the Labour party into coalition. But by then it was too late and the Conservative–Liberal Democrat coalition was formed with an agreed joint programme of work and with all the news channels commenting on the excellent chemistry between their two leaders David Cameron and Nick Clegg. Now the reality of setting up a coalition government may well have put all sorts of strains on a Cameron–Clegg relationship, but the point is that in the minds of the public and the media the perceptions were clear – here were two people that could adapt to the realities of coalition and have a positive relationship. That perception of leadership adaptability and collaboration certainly helped to pull their parties together and also helped give the public (and the financial markets) confidence that their coalition could work – at least in the short term.

In contrast, whatever his capabilities when he was Chancellor of the Exchequer or Prime Minister, Gordon Brown couldn't adapt to the demands of a collaborative situation, and within a few weeks he had pretty much disappeared from public life.

These are just a few examples of leaders who struggle to adapt to the challenges of interdependence and complexity – but there are many others, from Jurgen Schrempp, who presided over the disastrous merger of Daimler-Benz and Chrysler, to Bernie Ebbers, whose passion for deal-making built WorldCom into the world's largest telecom company but couldn't translate this into the savvy necessary to run such a complex business in a tough market. Leaders respond to change in different ways but the biggest message is that their past performance does not guarantee future success – as it says in the small print of all your investment brochures!

Like it or not, we live in an interdependent world. Creating coalition governments, managing mergers and partnerships are just some of the specific examples of how we may have to adapt to today's reality of interdependence but one thing is for sure, as leaders we can't ignore it.

But, as the next section shows, that may not be such a new realization anyway.

The rise of interdependence

On US Independence Day 1962, in a speech delivered in the hall where the American constitution was created, John F. Kennedy chose as his subject not independence but interdependence. Or, as he said, 'not the individual liberty of one but the indivisible liberty of all'.

At the time he was trying to engage his audience in the creation of a new transatlantic partnership, and the need for America to support the emerging consensus in Western Europe against the Warsaw Pact. To do so he drew by analogy on the long tradition of checks and balances in the United States constitution between state and federal power – a system 'designed to encourage both differences and dissent'.

But in a rather prophetic way his speech looked ahead to the wider challenges facing political and business leaders across the world in this twenty-first century. As Kennedy put it: 'As the worldwide effort for independence inspired by the American declaration of independence now approaches a successful close, a great new effort – for inter-dependence – is transforming the world about us.'[7]

He saw that however strong the desire for independence might be, the prosperity and the security of one country (even the most powerful and wealthiest on earth) was dependent on the well-being of all its trading partners and neighbours.

Some 46 years later in a speech at the DAVOS World Economic Forum in 2008, former British Prime Minister Tony Blair quoted from JFK and echoed the theme. He said 'Globalization is forcing changes in how people collaborate in a fundamental way - if we are interconnected and the world is interconnected, the only way for the world to work is to have a set of common values. We have no option but to work together.'

And this is not just political rhetoric; we believe there are many financial and technical forces which will continue this drive to increasing interdependence and this drive has consequences for business leaders as much as for politicians in the years to come.

There are many forces that drive interdependence. Whether it's oil, the supply of credit or specialist skills, if there is a limited resource and multiple calls on its use, interdependence of one form or another is inevitable. In addition to resource constraints, there is the growth of networked technologies. As these technologies grow, so do the interconnections of the people who use them – and in turn the technology provides faster and more extensive ways for people to be connected. Leaders cannot ignore the consequences of networked technologies for the way they communicate and manage their business. But the speed of global communication has major consequences for the way leaders feel that they have to behave. And finally there is the impact of regulation, especially in utilities, transport and telecommunications. Whilst the main job of the regulator could once have been seen as achieving value for money for the public by ensuring competition between the various players in the system, they now have the task of enabling collaboration, often to achieve cost reductions required by the government.

The leadership response

In today's world, interdependence is inevitable but collaboration takes lots of leadership effort.

That doesn't mean you need to collaborate everywhere but you must know how to decide where to collaborate and how much to collaborate. And then you need to build the collaborative leadership skills and capability across your organization to sustain those relationships in the areas where it brings the greatest benefit.

Interdependence can have its advantages. When there is an urgent global problem such as an imminent pandemic, organizations from many different countries and cultures can see the need to collaborate and pool large resources to innovate at surprising speed. For example, when the World Health Organization needed to combat a deadly outbreak of the SARS virus, it was able to bring together teams from 11 research labs around the world to collaborate on isolating the virus – they managed this incredibly demanding and complex task in just one month.[8] Collaboration between organizations with different knowledge bases and traditions can be immensely creative – if it works.

But all leaders need to find a strategy to respond to the reality of interdependence – you can't go it alone anymore.

The significance of this was perhaps best expressed by the CEO of Nokia, Stephen Elop, as he launched their partnership with Microsoft in 2011. At that time Nokia was still the biggest mobile phone manufacturer in the world with over 23 per cent market share but it was losing out in the growing smartphone market, primarily to the Apple iPhone but also to Blackberry and Google Android devices. Elop saw it wasn't just his rivals' design quality that was attracting customers away, it was the whole set of add-ons, downloads, covers and other highly fashionable items that were tying customers in. Nokia were being beaten not just by better products but by entire ecosystems – a universe that customers would enter when they bought an Android or iPhone that they would never need to leave. By entering a partnership with Microsoft, Elop was taking a bold leadership step to respond to this new threat. He said: 'Today, the battle is moving from one of mobile devices to one of mobile ecosystems ... Ecosystems thrive when they reach scale, when they are fuelled by energy and innovation and when they provide benefits and value to each person or company who participates.'[9]

Elop makes the case for collaboration as a leadership response to this business challenge of a complex world – but that brings with it the need to bring about a change in leadership style. Away from style of a charismatic or heroic individual leading their team or their organization to glory, and towards a more co-operative style where leaders have to work together to build the relationships they need to ensure mutual success. Towards being more of a collaborative leader.

So before we go any further, we need to define what we mean by collaborative leadership.

Defining collaborative leadership

John Kotter in his classic 1996 book *Leading Change* discussed the difference between leadership and management. Leadership he said 'creates the systems that managers manage'. And he defined the key tasks of leadership as:

- Creating vision and strategy;
- Communicating and setting direction;
- Motivating action;
- Aligning people.[10]

In 2012, the inevitability of interdependence means the leadership task is more complicated than this. Leaders do still have to create strategies, build systems and align people, but they have to do it across many different organizational boundaries – and in co-ordination with their partners who are probably trying to do the same (but different) to them at the same time. This challenge of leading and delivering results with others across a boundary is at the heart of the task of collaborative leadership.

Traditionally leaders have looked at their role within an organization managing their own teams very differently to their role outside their organization where they have to deal with their stakeholders, supplier's competitors or customers. Within an organization the leader's role is to build strong teams – possibly even high-performance teams – or self-organizing teams that can function when the leader is not present. Outside the organization the leader's role is often that of the transactional deal maker – they negotiate and broker agreement, they outmanoeuvre competitors and they fight hard for a good deal with suppliers.

But the world of interdependent relationships and partnerships, created to be mutually beneficial, muddies these waters. The boundary between what is done inside an organization and what is done outside is less clear – and shifts over time. Leaders need to be able to shift their ways of working in response.

Three capabilities of collaborative leaders

Put simply, collaborative leadership is the leadership required to get results across organizational boundaries. And that also means the leadership required to get value from the differences (in culture, experience, or skills) that lie in the organizations that sit either side of that boundary.

To meet those requirements leaders need to be able to do three things:

- build relationships – especially with leaders in other organizations;
- handle the inevitable conflict that these situations create; and, most importantly,
- share control with others.

There is an old adage that the best time to make friends is before you need them. And there is a truth in that for all collaborative leaders. The most successful collaborative leaders are all interested in other people and invest time in building wide and diverse networks. Some may do that because they are born networkers and others because experience has taught them that they need to consciously develop their contacts and their reputation. But whatever the motivation, it's clear that good personal relationships between senior people, based on shared values and common concerns, are an essential foundation when it comes to creating successful collaborative relationships between the organizations that they lead.

Skills in handling conflict are important because in any collaborative relationship there will be some points of tension. Different parties will always have somewhat different objectives to each other. If the relationship is well founded these will be reasonably well aligned but as time moves on there is always the likelihood of different objectives bringing people and groups into conflict. And some conflict arises because one or more individuals simply can't, or choose not to, collaborate whatever the situation. Successful collaborative leaders need to be able to recognize the early signs of conflict as useful warnings of hidden differences in objectives or priorities. In that way the visibility of conflict and criticism in a collaborative relationship is like the first signs of a muscle strain for an athlete, a useful warning that mustn't be ignored. Collaborative leaders need to listen for the signs of conflict and respond quickly. Once a leader has noticed the signs of conflict they must then be confident in handling it – in ways that result in increased understanding from all parties about the needs of their partners rather than a bloodbath! And key to this is the ability of a leader to be an effective mediator when the need arises.

Being able to build relationships and handle any resulting conflict doesn't quite capture all the skills of a successful collaborative leader. If handling conflict is a reactive response to a hidden problem, the third area of capability is much more proactive – sharing control, often with other leaders.

Sharing control is central to collaborative leadership because in an interdependent world no one can succeed on their own – nor can they succeed by dominating their partners and controlling all they do. Across that boundary are other leaders who will fight back if they feel over-controlled. There needs to be a mutual understanding of what sharing control means in each specific context.

It's important to understand that sharing control is different from empowerment. Sharing control in a collaborative relationship doesn't mean giving power to others so they can function without you. It means recognizing where and when you have to be completely aligned and taking decisions together – and being able to act independently (within agreed limits) outside those points. It also means recognizing that you cannot achieve your individual objectives without each other and are tied together by long-term overarching concerns – particularly your shared reputation with customers. Because the ability to share control is so important you could perhaps say it was the number one defining capability of a collaborative leader.

So there we have the three components of our definition: *Collaborative leadership – building relationships, handling conflict, sharing control.*

It's also worth saying a few words about what collaborative leadership is not.

What collaborative leadership is not

In our view collaborative leadership is not about the leadership skills involved in building a collegiate culture of collaboration within a single organizational unit. Several successful leaders have built their careers on being able to bring together groups of creative individuals, motivating them to focus on a shared vision and building an organizational environment where their combined talents can thrive. You could see the success of Steve Jobs in his second phase in charge of Apple as fitting this mould. By all accounts, Apple under Jobs' leadership was a very closed organization. A creative hothouse where innovative individuals were challenged to 'push for perfection' and famously to 'stay hungry and stay foolish'. But, by and large, the creative collaboration stopped at the walls of Apple's HQ in Cupertino – and Steve was always in charge! Apple was and is extremely controlling in its dealings with suppliers. As one its managers was quoted as saying 'There is no such thing as partnership with Apple – it's all about Apple.'[11]Nor is collaborative leadership about building communities of common interest by pulling people together from across the world using the internet to collaborate on a shared project. Wikipedia is often cited as a great example of collaboration – an encyclopaedia with 21 million articles in 284 languages, with 365 million readers, written largely for free by volunteers who have rarely met. What sort of 'Wiki-leadership' is required to create that? Well the answer may be very little. The beauty of the concept that Jimmy Wales and Larry Sanger launched in 2001, is that it is largely self-organizing. Anyone can amend an entry, and policing comes from vigilance by other interested individuals. Although Wikipedia has many flaws, factual errors tend to get ironed out fairly quickly by lots of individuals acting independently. There is not much need for collective leadership because there is not much connected action – one article is very largely independent from another. In a Wiki world individual contributors have great freedom of action – with the knowledge that whilst what they do may have a lot of impact on a particular entry, the effect on the total Wikipedia product is small and contained.

And finally, whilst we are talking about 'nots', collaborative leadership is not about being altruistic or subsuming your own views/needs for the good of others. The most effective collaborative leaders are good at expressing the needs of their own organization clearly and succinctly and also good at listening hard to understand the needs of others.

Collaboration is not a moral choice, it is a business necessity.

Why this is hard – an evolutionary parallel

The sad fact is that many collaborative efforts fail and many leaders find the personal challenges of sharing control impossible to overcome. Research by the authors of a 2004 *Harvard Business Review* article found that 48 per cent of alliances between American firms ended in failure in less than two years.[12] Collaboration is difficult – it takes much more energy and effort to deal with the complexity and frustration of working with others than the amount of effort required to operate independently in competition with others. And so for every management text expounding the benefits of collaboration there are many more extolling the virtue of competition and the rigour of the market as the best way to produce the most efficient goods and services. So why bother trying to be a collaborative leader? This is a question of belief. Are human beings by nature just competitive animals? And are the organizations that they develop always governed by a version of Darwin's law of the survival of the fittest – so any attempt at collaboration is doomed from the outset? Or, over centuries of human development, have we learned to live together in co-operative groups to the extent that collaboration is now a natural part of our make-up?

In trying to resolve this dilemma of whether or not human beings have an in-built capability to co-operate many commentators have gone back to arguments about evolution. Certainly many species have evolved to be able to carry out collaborative activity as part of the survival strategy – and we're not just talking about ants, bees and other social insects. Many organisms also form wider social groups that offer greater protection and allow roles such as food gathering or looking after young to be shared.

Lessons from slime mould

One of the most powerful examples of collaboration comes from one of the world's most primitive life forms – it's called slime mould, the sticky, reddish jelly-like stuff you sometimes find under half-rotted bark.

Slime mould has been hard to classify as it's not really a mould at all. Cellular slime mould is a single-celled, amoeba-like organism where each cell spends most of its time minding its own business un-connected with any fellow slime mould cells in the vicinity. But when resources are scarce (specifically water and nutrients), individual slime mould cells start to join together and co-operate to form something that resembles a more complex organism that behaves as one and can even move over the ground to reach food. What's more, when slime mould cells get together, they can display surprising levels of apparent 'intelligence' – like solving the puzzle of a maze by stretching between two food sources at either end. And then, perhaps most amazing of all, when the crisis is over, the individual slime mould cells split up and go back to functioning as single cellular organisms once more.

Steven Johnson tells the story of slime mould brilliantly in *Emergence: The Connected Lives of Ants, Brains, Cities and Software.*[13] His point is that slime mould displays emergent behaviour – the 'intelligence' it demonstrates comes about from aggregating a mass of relatively simple elements. No one element is directing the show: rather, this complex behaviour emerges from the level of individual cells. The reason we reference slime mould is slightly different. It's because it illustrates that you don't need a complex organism to work out when and when not to collaborate. Slime mould cells 'know' when to be independent and when to work together as a simple response to the environmental conditions they find themselves in. They don't spend all their time together as some sort of team – each single cell manages perfectly well on its own for large stretches of time. But when (and only when) the environmental conditions require it, slime mould cells have the capability to get together, and together they can do extraordinary things for their collective benefit.

Martin Nowak, a Professor of Biology and Mathematics, in his book *Super Cooperators* has taken this further and developed five mechanisms at work in the natural world that assist the evolution of co-operation in particular circumstances.[14]

The mathematics is complex but he makes a convincing case for why and how species have evolved collaborative strategies for survival. Some of these such as reciprocity and kin selection have direct parallels in human relations, but extending this argument to use the same natural mechanisms to explain the 'evolution' of collaborative organizations to govern human behaviour is quite a big leap.

However, to help us make this leap from the life of slime mould and social insects to the behaviour of groups of human beings, we can turn from evolutionary biology and look at some interesting discoveries in the discipline of anthropology and the study of how tribes and communities have developed ways of managing scarce resources such as grazing land, water supplies or fishing groups over centuries.

Avoiding the tragedy of the commons

Elinor Ostrom won the Nobel Prize for economics in 2009 for her work in this area. Over a lifetime of study she has set out to understand and eventually disprove what has been called by earlier writers 'The Tragedy of the Commons'.[15] That was the belief that any shared or 'common' resource, such as a village green on which everyone could graze their sheep, would always be overused – and therefore eventually ruined – by individuals acting in their own self-interest. According to this theory the only way to prevent this was by having an external authority to enforce rules for 'fair' shares.

But Ostrom observed that some societies had managed to evolve ways of managing scare common resources and had evolved institutions for dealing with disputes without the need for external authority. She studied systems as diverse as alpine meadows in Switzerland, irrigation systems in Valencia and Alicante in Spain, coastal fisheries in the Philippines and rain forests in Nepal. These were systems that had maintained stable governance of what was often a precious and vulnerable resource over many centuries. From these very detailed studies she distilled a small number of variables which affected the likelihood that collaborative systems would evolve in a community. She then tested these variables in game theory experiments with her own students to see how different factors affected their collaborative or competitive behaviours.

These field studies and the results of the game theory experiments led her to a number of design principles for the evolutions of long-term stable collaborative institutions, and these hold important lessons for business leaders today. In summary, her studies show that stable collaborations are more likely to form when: the community has clearly defined boundaries, reliable information about the costs and benefits of collaboration is available to all, graduated sanctions are applied by the community to those that don't play by the rules, people have access to rapid conflict resolutions mechanisms in the case of disputes, and the community's right to organize itself is recognized and respected by external authorities.[16]

She went further and in her later research developed a mathematical formula to try to solve the problem 'Why do some communities manage to devise self organised collaboration while others do not?'[17] You can debate the details of the mathematics but her conclusion is clear – collaboration is not a fixed ability – a product of the human mind which some of us can do and others cannot. Her research shows that when it comes to sharing resources collaboration emerges from the conditions in which we live. It is the physical and social environment; the resources that are available to us, the proximity to others, and the way that the local society has set rules for behaviour, that determine the likelihood of a collaborative outcome.

Evolutionary lessons for collaborative leaders

Retracing our steps slightly and going back to slime mould, what does all this tell us about the role of the collaborative leader? Well in the right environmental conditions slime mould cells can self-organize and work together for the common good. In a different context the work of Elinor Ostrom and others shows that environmental conditions are the key to whether human communities manage to evolve ways of sharing scarce resources.

Human beings are tribal animals – our evolutionary history has given us the drive and the ability to both collaborate *and* to compete with others.

Down the centuries we have used these dual abilities most often to collaborate within our own tribe and then to compete with other tribes that we come into contact with. You just have to go to any Premier League football ground on a Saturday to see that we haven't come very far from this tribal past – feeling part of one tribe and celebrating victories over a rival tribe is an experience that runs deep.

However, the way we apply these collaborative and competitive abilities in our business life can be, and should be, a matter of conscious choice. Partly this is a choice about who we regard as being within our tribe and who we regard as outside it. There are plenty of business examples, such as outsourcing arrangements, where the same people can quickly move from being labelled as being part of your own organizations to part of another, which show how fluid these ideas of who is inside and who is outside can be.

But more than that, we have seen that the environment leaders create – the way they set the rules, the language they use to describe the game they are playing – has an enormous effect on whether the organizations that they run are able to collaborate successfully with others or not.

If this evolutionary digression tells us anything it is that environments shape individual and collective behaviour and that business leaders can shape the environment in which those around them operate. The dual competitive and collaborative nature of human beings will always cause a dilemma for a collaborative leader and it is finding ways to resolve that dilemma – to decide where and how much to collaborate and how to motivate others to join you in that endeavour – that is the work of this book.

Applications of collaborative leadership

There are a number of specific areas in which leaders have had to apply their collaborative leadership skills over recent years. The different situations (three of which we highlight here) each have their own particular characteristics but the key challenges remain; building relationships, handling conflict and sharing control.

Public–private partnerships

The number and scale of public–private partnerships (PPPs) have grown phenomenally across the world. The UK is still considered the largest and most mature market but there are significant PPP programmes in most countries in the EU and Canada, the USA, and more recently South Africa and New Zealand have put large high-profile projects into a PPP structure.[18]

Originally conceived as a way of getting private finance for large-scale public sector infrastructure projects and transferring risk from the public to the private sector, PPPs (and their close cousin in the UK the Private Finance Initiative) have run into a lot of criticism. It is clear from well documented cases like the collapse of the London Underground PPP contract that, however much effort public officials may put into creating watertight legal agreements, at the end of the day the public purse will still have to bear the ultimate financial risk. So there is a greater necessity than ever to understand what helps to make the difference between PPP success or failure. Much of the analysis points in one way or another to a failure of leadership as a key causal factor.[19]

From our experience based on working in many different Public Private Partnerships, leaders typically face three particular challenges in these situations:

- Managing and motivating staff across a public–private cultural divide. Many of the staff working in a PPP have been transferred across from the public sector and bring with them fears that their terms and conditions are going to be downgraded and their skills de-valued by private sector management.
- Developing cost-effective ways of managing risk – so that responsibilities for mitigating strategic and operational risks are allocated to the organizations with the best capabilities for handling them at the right price.
- Governance of decision making. So often we have seen the creation of excessively cumbersome or adversarial decision-making structures across a PPP which just don't reflect the need for speedy and transparent decision making that most of these projects require.

Private sector alliances and joint ventures

The private sector has been distinctly creative in its approach to collaboration, spawning many different structures for joint working. First, there are transaction-based partnerships – which can range from outsourcing a particular service such as HR or IT to managing a whole global product supply chain. Then there are alliances of various kinds, from the informal to the contractual. In consortia each partner retains legal independence but agrees to share the profits of joint activities, whereas equity-sharing joint ventures create a separate legal entity for the duration of the partnership.

A *Harvard Business Review* article estimates that more than 5,000 joint ventures (JVs) were launched worldwide in the previous five years, with the largest 100 JVs representing $350 billion in combined annual revenues.[20] But success is tough to sustain. An Accenture study produced some pretty gloomy figures: of every 100 alliance negotiations studied across all industries, 90 fail to reach agreements and only two survive more than two years.[21]

'Mistakes made during the launch phase often erode up to half the potential value creation of a venture', say McKinsey consultants James Bamford, David Ernst and David G. Fubini. 'Launching a world-class joint venture is complex and demanding. Research shows that it can, in fact, be more resource intensive than post-merger integration or internal business start-ups.'[22]

In JVs and alliances, leaders face the particular challenges of building trust between parties who may well have been vigorous competitors in the recent past – and in many cases will be again at some point in the future. In our experience this sort of high trust JV relationship calls for a particularly mature leadership style. One that can look to the long term for the success of their own organization and also take decisions for the benefit of the whole alliance which may count against their own organization in the short term.

Trust based collaborative arrangements take time and effort to make work and in recession it gets even harder to trust your partners to deliver. When *Harvard Business Review* surveyed its readers in 2009, it found that more than one-fifth of respondents admitted that their trust in suppliers had been shaken over the past 12 months.[23] When times get hard, maintaining trust in relationships becomes more important than ever for the collaborative leader.

Not-for-profit collaborations

Third sector organizations have a long history of working in partnership with each other. And they're frequently involved in partnerships with central and local government too. The Citizens Advice service, for example, is part of a partnership examining how to tackle poverty in retirement led by the Department for Work and Pensions. And many local authorities rely on charities to deliver large parts of their social care provision.

The difficulty with collaboration between the charity sector and government is often one of scalability, particularly with smaller, less centralized charities. At a local level, collaborative relationships can be built up on the ground between committed voluntary sector workers and local public sector officials. When the same approach is scaled to a national level, the dozens of individual relationships that held together local partnerships can stand in the way of strategic decision making and long-term planning.

Collaborations between third sector organizations are also common and becoming more so – in fact joint working is being strongly encouraged throughout the sector. In an attempt to drive efficiency and reduce duplication, the Charity Commission advised in 2003 that 'all charities should consider seriously and imaginatively whether there are ways in which they could do more and better for their users by working together'.

It's not always easy for voluntary organizations to work together like this – passion for individual causes and detailed questions of policy may get in the way – but where charities can achieve common purpose, it's a powerful way to make things happen. At the heart of such collaborations is clear self-interest. Not only do participating organizations achieve a louder voice through uniting, they also share and dilute the reputational risk of any negative messages.

But this means that for collaborative leaders in the not-for-profit sector the biggest challenge is often finding that common purpose with people in other organizations that they want to work with. This means not letting their own loyalty to a cause (or group of staff) get in the way of delivering the greater goal.

Whatever your own experience of leading in complex situations where collaboration is required, this book can help you. There are two main parts, the first of which contains a set of tools that aspiring collaborative leaders can use to analyse, to create and to maintain effective business relationships with lots of checklists and examples of how to use them in practice. And there is a second part that focuses on the lessons leaders can learn from others working in the field and how they manage the risks and conflicts associated with collaboration at all levels from front-line services to the boardroom.

Chapter summary

Collaboration isn't a moral choice – today it's a business necessity

We live in an interdependent world. Resource shortages, networked technology and in some cases regulation can contribute as drivers of increasing interdependence, but, whatever the cause, leaders have to adapt to the new leadership challenges that interdependence brings.

There are lots of high-profile examples of leaders, from Fred Goodwin at RBS to ex-Prime Minister Gordon Brown, who have struggled to make this adaptation and have paid a high personal price. But there are also plenty of counter examples of leaders who have embraced the concept of interdependence and indeed entire new industries (such as the market for smartphone apps) that have grown from the creation of a new and very interdependent business ecosystem.

Many organisms (from slime mould to social insects) have evolved collaborative strategies for survival but these examples seem to depend on quite specific environmental conditions. In the business world, the work environment has a big impact on whether we collaborate or not – and leaders can play a big part in creating the environment that their staff experience.

We define collaborative leadership as the leadership needed to deliver results across organizational boundaries. And it has three core components which we develop throughout this book; building relationships, handling conflict and sharing control.

The principles of collaborative leadership can be applied in many varied leadership situations such as: public–private partnerships, joint ventures and mergers in the private sector, joining up the public sector including working with third sector organizations and in internal collaborations.

Lessons for leaders

- Human beings are tribal animals and much group behaviour is a product of that heritage. We have within us all the skills and the instincts to compete and to collaborate. The easy thing to do is to collaborate with those that we define as being part of our own tribe and compete with others outside.
- As a collaborative leader you need to create the environment where people will collaborate with those around them that can best help to achieve agreed joint goals – whatever tribe they appear to belong to.
- To be a successful collaborative leader you need to be able to:

  - **Build relationships** – prioritize relationship building activities and build shared values and trust with others – before you need to call on them;
  - **Handle conflict** – you need to recognize the early signs of conflict and use these warnings to uncover hidden differences in objectives between others; and, most importantly,
  - **Share control** – recognizing that you can't achieve your objectives on your own – knowing where you have to be completely aligned with your partners – and being able to act independently (within agreed limits) outside those points.

PART 1

Tools for collaboration

This part of the book contains a set of tools that aspiring collaborative leaders can use to analyse, to create and to maintain effective business relationships.

The craft of collaborative leadership builds on many of the foundations that leaders have learned down the years from experience and from conventional leadership development programmes. But some of the techniques that work well when leading people in your own team can be less effective when it comes to dealing with the challenges of leading across interdependent organizations. These tools focus on the needs of leaders who are facing the specific challenges of collaborative leadership. These are leaders who have to build lasting relationships, handle conflict and share control.

These five chapters draw on our own experience of working with successful collaborative leaders over the last ten years. Each chapter contains a number of 'How to' checklists and re-usable examples that you can tailor to your own situation and each chapter ends with a 'points to remember' summary box and a set of lessons for leaders.

A note on language

Every business relationship is different and in these chapters we use examples that range from formally contracted partnerships with enormous budgets and clear delivery goals, to much looser informal relationships between organizations that aim to collaborate out of a common sense of mission or a need to get more from scarce funds.

When it comes to summarizing the lessons learned, we've chosen to describe them in the language of partnership and so you will see references to *partners* where in your own organization you might be used to talking about colleagues, alliance members or stakeholders.

In this part

Chapter 2: The collaboration spectrum

This chapter explains how to determine the amount of collaboration a particular situation requires by assessing the points of interdependence between the parties involved. Collaborations can range on a spectrum from those functioning like a close-knit team to a much more distant, customer–supplier, type of transactional relationship. Use this chapter to help you and your partners define what type of collaborative relationship is required. The answer to this question, and the direction of travel for the future, will have big consequences on the leadership approach required to make your relationship a success.

Chapter 3: The three-legged stool – governance, operations and behaviours

Every collaborative relationship needs a solid and stable leadership framework. This chapter is based on a three-legged model for defining the right governance, operations and behaviours to make the relationship work. Combining this model with the collaboration spectrum in Chapter 2 gives you a way to work out where you need to focus your leadership efforts and how to build a stable platform for any long-term collaborative venture.

Chapter 4: Measuring collaboration

Measurement can make or break a relationship. Many leaders use excessively detailed and backward looking measures in an attempt to over-control a partner – often with unintended negative impacts on trust and delivery. Use this chapter to produce a balanced set of measures based on the governance, operations and behaviours framework in Chapter 3 to track the health of the relationship. And then use this set of leading indicators to drive improvements in overall performance.

Chapter 5: Analysing different organizational cultures

Clashes of organizational culture are one of the biggest obstacles to making collaborative relationships work. But trying to avoid these clashes by making your partners clones of your own culture doesn't work either. You need to understand the differences and use them to bring new perspectives on problems and to create value that neither of you could achieve on your own. This chapter gives you a tool for analysing organizational culture, dealing with its impact on the contribution different parties can make to a relationship, and spotting where possible points of future conflict may lie.

Chapter 6: The partnership roadmap

One type of collaborative relationship, contracted fixed-term partnerships, tend to follow a fairly similar pattern. Their lifecycles go through a number of distinct stages each with its own specific risks and warning signs. This chapter lays out a roadmap with four stages – selection, transition, maintenance/improvement, and ending – for you to use to navigate through the lifecycle of your own partnership. In each stage there are signs you can use to check whether you are approaching a danger zone and advice on how to get a partnership back on track.

2

THE COLLABORATION SPECTRUM

Quantifying collaboration

There is little doubt that in the second decade of the twenty-first century the business world is becoming increasingly interconnected. The era of the vertically integrated corporation is over (at least for the foreseeable future). Companies now rely on global networks of suppliers for all aspects of their value chain, customers become key elements of marketing strategy through the use of social networks and customer-review websites (like Trip Advisor).

In the public sector too, the last 20 years have seen the continuing fragmentation of monolithic Departments of State and the growth of a complex delivery landscape of multiple agencies tasked with implementing government policy (the numbers are large, of the 520,000 civil servants in the UK 78 per cent work in these executive agencies).[1] At a local level, long-term partnerships with private sector service providers are becoming the norm to deliver core council services such as refuse collection or road maintenance. More innovative collaborative arrangements are being set up to bring commercial and third sector expertise to bear on complex social issues such as probation services or drug rehabilitation, often with the added uncertainty of payment-by-results type contracts.

A collaborative leader may find themselves having to manage many of these relationships, each with their own demands and risks. This chapter sets out a key tool for analysing and handling this range of different relationships by thinking of each as lying somewhere on a collaboration spectrum.

The myths of partnership

Entering any kind of long-term business relationships means you're going to need to collaborate. But just how much collaboration do you need, and when? Some leaders may be attracted to the idea of always working in close collaboration with their partners just because that is their preferred leadership style but, as we'll see, if you try to manage your partners as you would a team of direct reports you'll quickly run into problems. On the other hand, if you treat a collaborative relationship as purely transactional, where you're the customer and your partners are the suppliers, that's exactly what it will become – and you'll miss out on the potential value and innovation that could have been created in the space between the two organizations.

Thinking of collaboration as a binary process – a relationship is either collaborative or it is not – is a dangerous over-simplification. Instead leaders need to start to think about the amount of collaboration required in a particular relationship to make it effective and what specific aspects of a relationship need a collaborative working style in order to succeed.

One of the things that gets in the way of understanding here is the word partnership. We have all seen workers wearing a shirt with the slogan 'working in partnership with …', but one day visiting the UK Ministry of Justice we saw that same slogan worn by the delivery driver from the company that supplies paper for the office photocopiers as one worn by someone working for G4S, the private company that runs some UK prisons and the electronic tagging system that keeps tabs on many thousands of offenders! The same word, 'partnership', was being used to describe radically different sorts of relationships – and ones that need different amounts of collaboration and a very different focus of leadership attention to be effective. We need a mechanism for understanding and discussing these differences.

Transactional, symbiotic or mutual

To put some order into all this, we'll start by making a distinction between three different kinds of relationship on the collaboration spectrum: *symbiotic, mutual* and *transactional relationships*. The collaboration spectrum diagram (see Figure 2.1), is a simple depiction of how the amount of collaboration required changes in different kinds of relationship laid out along a spectrum. In this and the next chapters we will look at the implications of where a relationship sits on the collaboration spectrum for leaders and how they need to act.

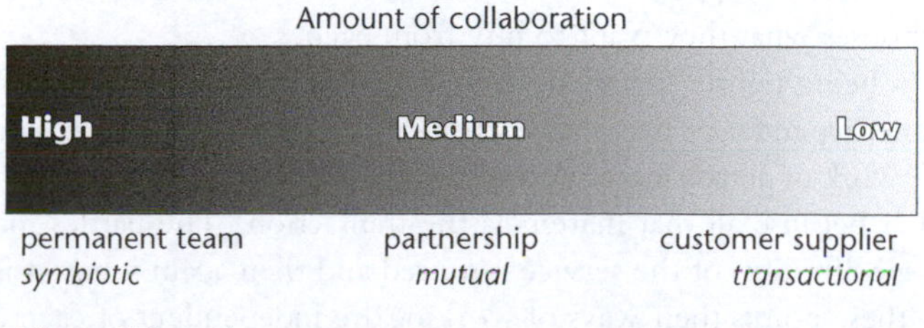

Amount of collaboration

High	Medium	Low
permanent team	partnership	customer supplier
symbiotic	*mutual*	*transactional*

FIGURE 2.1   The collaboration spectrum

Symbiotic relationships

At the far left of the spectrum, those relationships which require the greatest amount of collaboration are symbiotic, where each party is heavily dependent on the others for their success or failure. These are usually long lasting relationships (and may feel permanent to participants), and to perform well have to be highly collaborative. A symbiotic collaboration functions, and can be led, very much like a conventional team, even if the members wear different shirts. Team members are very close, they depend on each other, their objectives are the same or at least closely aligned, and they tend to spend a lot of time together both inside and outside work. These symbiotic collaborations frequently generate strong loyalty.

National sports teams sit at this end of the spectrum. The players may all come from different clubs but when they come together to play for their country success depends on them being tightly aligned. Military task forces drawn from the armies of many nations also fit this model of a close symbiotic 'live and die together' relationship.

Contracted partnerships sometimes have to (and can) work at this extreme end of the spectrum as well – the PPP created to upgrade and maintain the London Underground network could be seen as an example of this. But even these examples of groups of people drawn from two or more organizations are not a true team. Leaders need to recognize that the different objectives and organizational heritage of the different parties involved will sometimes bring them into conflict. For the individuals involved this can be quite unsettling – people they thought of as team members are suddenly acting to serve different interests. When you hear phrases like 'but I thought you were one of us', it may be because partners have had misplaced expectations of a symbiotic relationship being the same as a permanent team.

Nevertheless it's fair to say that many of the lessons of team leadership do apply at this symbiotic end of the spectrum.

Transactional relationships

Contrast this with relationships at the transactional end of the spectrum (see Figure 2.1). Here relationships are relatively straightforward and clearly defined, boiling down to a simple transaction: I buy, you sell. The relationship works if we both feel we get a good deal. The typical customer–supplier relationship, for example, is transactional – the client specifies exactly what's needed and the supplier delivers it, or a set of suppliers each set out their stalls in the market place and the customer chooses what they want to buy from each.

As well as being tightly specified, these relationships are characterized by a low degree of interdependence between each party. Whether the purchase is an office desk or a network of personal computers, buyer and seller don't need to spend much time together because all that matters is the transaction. The parties may meet to discuss the specification of the service required and then again when it is delivered but outside these points their ways of working are independent of each other.

Things get a bit more complicated in situations when a customer has entered into a long-term deal with a single supplier. Here the amount of choice is reduced and the dependence on that supplier begins to grow. The relationship starts to move from right to left along the spectrum. But the interaction between the parties is small and each could choose to find another partner – albeit, at a cost. The relationship between Apple and its suppliers sits at this transactional end of the spectrum. Apple is a notoriously secretive company and they guard their relationships carefully but in a book by Adam Lashinsky from *Fortune* magazine one Apple manager is quoted as saying 'the way to get integration is to control everything … down to what kind of saw you are going to use [to cut] the glass' and another says 'There is no such thing as partnership with Apple – it's all about Apple.'

Just as there is much written about team leadership that can be applied to collaborative relationships that lie at the symbiotic end of the spectrum so there is a wealth of information about managing a set of transactional customer–supplier relationships – indeed you could say that the whole field of supplier relationship management has developed from analysing relationships at this end of the spectrum.

Mutual relationships

The relationships that we're mostly concerned with in this book fall somewhere between these two extremes. The foundation of these relationships is a belief that there are mutual benefits to be gained from two or more parties working together collaboratively and that these benefits are greater than you would get by merging the organizations to become a single integrated entity. These mutual relationships require a degree of collaboration between the parties, but not total loyalty to the combined unit. In fact, too much close collaboration can create an unsustainable leadership overhead on all involved. Many relationships in the centre of the spectrum depend for their success on partners working in a more or less independent manner for much of their day-to-day activity, otherwise the management overhead of being involved in each other's business would get in the way of efficient operations.

These periods of separation are enhanced by clear points when the parties need to come together, solve problems, learn from each other, take collective decisions, and then move apart again.

Individuals in mutual partnerships have to divide their loyalties between their own organization and the whole collaborative relationship – or as management guru Charles Handy puts it, they must manage the dilemma of dual nationalities or 'twin citizenship'.[3] It's something we should perhaps be good at in the UK. Someone born in England may support England against Wales in the Rugby World Cup, but root for Great Britain in the Olympics, and even support the European Ryder Cup team. It's much the same for people working in a mutual collaborative relationship – leaders must balance loyalty to their own employer with the good of the whole joint enterprise.

Sometimes this can create tensions and real conflicts of interest. However, the difficulties are balanced by the potential prize: mutual relationships allow leaders to achieve joint successes that would be hard or impossible to deliver on their own.

Leaders in this sort of collaborative relationship (at the centre of the spectrum) have to realize that the tools used to run a conventional team or to manage a set of transactional customer–supplier relationships aren't going to suit the needs of their new situation. They need to develop different ways of working for the middle of the spectrum – occasionally borrowing from the leadership tools that work at each end. It's a dynamic process. But all parties need to be clear about what is required of them and when.

One way to help leaders determine how to act is to start by assessing where different relationships fit on the collaboration spectrum. The best way to do this is to look for the number of points of interdependence between the parties and to map out where responsibilities intersect.

Points of interdependence: look out for the platform edge

As a rule, the more points of interdependence in a relationship, the more collaborative that relationship needs to be and the further to the left it will lie on the collaboration spectrum. So what are these points of interdependence? For some organizations it's not easy to see where intersections of responsibility lie but one good analogy for mapping points of organizational interdependence is illustrated by a picture that will be familiar to many people across the world – the London Underground Tube map.

The management of London Underground is organized around its different lines. People who work on Piccadilly line trains or stations are managed by a different organization to those who work on, say, the Jubilee or Victoria Line. And at one level that works just fine. For most of the time on most of the network, the two lines are quite distinct and staff don't need to bother themselves much with what is happening on another line. Just looking at the map you can see that the number of points of interdependence is different between different lines. For example, the linkage between the Circle, District and Metropolitan lines is very high, they share many stations and lots of track. And indeed this group of lines is managed as one integrated network.

The number of intersections (and hence the linkage) between other lines is less. But even here at an interchange station – Green Park, for example – what happens on one line has clear implications for staff working on the other. Staff at Green Park need to know how the Jubilee, Victoria and the Piccadilly lines are running and to be kept up to date with information on all three. The points of interdependence between the London Underground line organizations leap out from the Tube map – and these have to be managed accordingly.

The notion of points of interdependence goes deeper still. Within each line, some staff are employed by a part of the organization that runs stations, and others by a part that runs trains and signalling. Again, for most of their working day the two parts of the operation can get along quite independently. But if a breakdown happens somewhere on the line, and trains and stations start to get very crowded, a vitally important point of interdependence comes into play – the platform edge.

The platform edge is one of the points of greatest risk in the system. If a train crammed with commuters pulls into a station where platforms are already full to overflowing and opens its doors, people could be seriously injured in the crush. In those conditions, the trains and stations organizations have to work very tightly together, with all the relevant people given access to enough information and paying minute-by-minute attention to managing the boundary between their two domains.

Defining and managing points of interdependence is a sophisticated operation. Too much sharing is as bad as too little. At London Underground, train managers don't want or need to know the congestion state of all the stations all the time. The sophistication lies in working out when to share information appropriately, and in being a tight-knit team only where it matters.

Leaders have to pay a lot of attention to points of interdependence, because these are the areas they simply can't control on their own. Instead they must share responsibility, and trust in the skills of their partner. Flagging up these points, making them explicit and working out ways to deal with them together cuts down on headaches – and minimizes potential disasters.

In any partnership, then, leaders have to pinpoint your 'Green Parks' and look out for your platform edges. It helps leaders decide where to focus management time and effort – and, just as importantly, where to leave individual partners to do their own thing. As a partnership becomes more collaborative, it doesn't do it uniformly; rather the number and significance of these points of interdependence increase across the relationship. And the more points where leaders have to share control, the better they need to get at collaboration.

The collaboration spectrum in practice

The collaboration spectrum has many uses. At the start of a new collaborative relationship it can be used as a tool to help leaders from different partners to understand what the nature of the relationship between them all needs to be in order to achieve the stated goals. It can help to resolve conflicts where one partner is feeling let down by others because their expectations of the degree of collaboration or teamworking are not being met, and it can help a busy leader to decide which relationships to focus their time and effort on building – and which to keep at arm's length.

With the help of the collaboration spectrum, it is possible to plot the characteristics of each relationship at a moment in time, examine how those characteristics are likely to change in the future, and explore where the relationship needs to be in order to deliver its business goals.

Working out where each partner thinks the relationship needs to be positioned on the spectrum can usually help to resolve initial differences in perspective and approach. Often, though, it's the debate generated from this process that is of the most value. We've found it useful in stimulating conversations between parties that begin to answer some critical questions, such as:

*   How much does each party want to collaborate? Do they want to operate as independently as possible or to interact closely?
*   Where do parties disagree about the ways of working?
*   Are there potential areas of conflict that are easy to predict?
*   Are the answers to the first three questions driven by an understanding of the needs of the joint enterprise or by the preferences of each of the partners?

At the right hand side of the spectrum, you are working with straightforward transactions with low interdependence and a minimal need for collaboration. These may be quite short-lived relationships where each side takes what they need and moves on. As you move along the spectrum, from right to left, interdependence and the demand for collaboration increase. Each step along the way represents greater involvement and commitment. By the time you reach the left-hand side of the spectrum, the relationship has moved a long way from dating – you're well and truly married! And while this commitment can pay huge dividends, at the same time the amount of choice available in the relationship decreases. The consequences of changing your partner are far greater, more disruptive and costly. Divorces are rarely anything but messy.

Find your place on the spectrum

Where do your relationships fit on to the spectrum? Partnerships vary widely: some are more transactional, some more collaborative. It's important for leaders to analyse their own situation dispassionately and honestly – the data is only helpful if it reflects the reality of the leader's situation rather than the way that they would like things to be. It's also worth remembering that high levels of collaboration aren't always desirable – in fact highly collaborative relationships come at a considerable cost in time and leadership effort.

The two most important issues to consider are whether there is a dominant player, and what are the measures of success.

Is there a dominant player in the relationship?

If one party has all the power and is perceived to dominate the relationship and control the output of the partnership, it's easy to assume that there are low levels of interdependence, and therefore a lower requirement for the parties to collaborate. In such situations the contract often dominates the relationship.

However, take care when identifying the dominant party, as it may not be the obvious candidate. One partner may be larger and financially stronger, with more resource to bring to the partnership. Their way of working may also reflect their perceived power. But if leaders look hard at the critical skills in their partnership, they may be surprised at where the power really lies.

The creation of a national computer network for the NHS was one of the largest IT projects in Europe. It was managed as an interconnected set of contracts between the public and private sector – and on the private sector side many of the organizations involved were themselves consortia with numbers of powerful players coming together to provide the capacity and range of skills required. But a small software house, iSoft, emerged as the most significant player in the whole network – because they supplied a key component on which the whole edifice was built. When iSoft hit financial difficulties, all the financial clout and perceived political power of the big players could do nothing to stabilize the situation, and a lot of time and money was lost as a result.

It pays for leaders to understand where all their partners lie on the spectrum. Just because one player is small, they can't always afford to treat them as an anonymous and easily replaceable commodity supplier. In fact the smaller player may be the real dominant power in the relationship. But until the larger partner truly sees the need to collaborate actively, the effective functioning of the partnership is at risk.

What are the measures of success?

The other key to finding your place on the spectrum is for leaders to examine their measures of success. Do those measures drive greater levels of collaboration, or do they ensure that the parties involved can deliver their part of the bargain independently from each other?

If there is a large number of output measures and a stringent auditing process to police them, this will drive the nature of the relationships towards the transactional. If, on the other hand, the measures adopted address the wider objectives rather than the detail – how the relationship will be sustained through the life of the partnership, how added value is shared, and so on – this will tend to move the leader towards a more collaborative style, and they'll need to find effective ways of incentivizing collaboration. What gets measured gets done – but *the way* things are measured also affects the way things are done. Measure a lot of outputs in a very transactional way and you're likely to get a transactional relationship whether you wanted it or not. We'll look at measuring success in partnerships in far more detail in Chapter 4.

So using the collaboration spectrum can help leaders to understand what kind of partnership they're getting themselves into. But first, a word of warning.

Don't fight shy of complexity

Neither individuals nor organizations like complex relationships if they can be avoided. This means that leaders will often plump for one or other extreme of the collaboration spectrum shown below – either a close-knit team approach or a straightforwardly transactional customer–supplier relationship – and try to drive that approach through in the relationship. It may look simpler, but unfortunately it ignores crucial aspects of the relationship that are likely to come back and bite the partners later.

Amount of collaboration

High	Medium	Low
permanent team	partnership	customer supplier
symbiotic	*mutual*	*transactional*
close		*distant*
same objectives		*separate objectives*
loyal to the group		*loyal to my employer*
lots of time together		*little time together*
They're really one of us		*They give us a good deal*

FIGURE 2.2 Finding your place on the collaboration spectrum

The first mistake: 'one team' rhetoric

Imposing a 'one team' ethos on a complex collaborative relationship can seem appealing on the surface. With many of their models adopted from sporting or military environments, teams can have heroic, do-or-die overtones. For these teams performance depends on each of the team members working in a highly integrated way. People rely on each other and often can't play their own role without the support of the rest of the team.

The vision of becoming a 'high-performance team' is often talked about within organizations, and many groups aspire to this vision in their cross-organizational relationships as well. But the truth is that a partnership is not 'one team' – individuals must respond to the needs and pressures of their own 'home organization' as well as the partnership. Pretending to be a team can be misleading at best, and at worst dangerous and damaging to morale.

Using 'one team' rhetoric when in fact the leader has their own separate reasons for entering into the relationship may also mask important differences in culture and approach. In particular it can prevent people from airing problems early and store up conflict for later on. Effective collaborative relationships aren't about ironing out difference or simply pretending it isn't there – the last thing the partners want is to be clones of each other. In fact the most successful collaborative leaders tap into their different skills and approaches of their partners to create something that goes beyond the individual players' capabilities – an area we'll explore in more detail in Chapter 5 when we looking at the challenges of leading across different organizational cultures.

Consider the case of a public–private partnership where staff are transferred over to work for a private sector organization. A mix of public and private sector managers now leads the partnership. But if this group tries to take a traditional 'one team' approach, it risks losing much of the value civil servants were trying to gain by bringing in a different management style in the first place.

The second mistake: transaction-like control

Seeking simplicity by trying to drive a collaborative relationship to work at the transactional end of the spectrum isn't a recipe for success either. Much has been written about supplier and customer relationship management, but these techniques don't really apply to situations that sit in the middle of the collaboration spectrum. As a powerful customer, treating your partners as a string of independent suppliers may seem attractive, but can result in each party simply doing what they are told, nothing more and nothing less.

Equally, specifying the processes and procedures of a partnership too tightly can choke a relationship if in fact there are multiple points of interdependence. The trend towards service level agreements for just about everything certainly hasn't made partnerships run more smoothly. And although the urge to control is understandable, it can cause frustration and resentment, and may even encourage subversive game-playing behaviour. In the end it's likely to lead to a blame culture, with each party pointing the finger at the other for poor performance.

The same risk of seeking to apply too much control is true in mergers. When a small company is taken over by a large multinational, for example, the temptation is to absorb the small business into the culture and corporate processes of the larger player. All too often the value of the smaller business is lost as morale dips, creativity declines, and key players leave. In the end the value of the merger is lost.

In both cases, opting for a simple operational model at either end of the collaboration spectrum can destroy the potential value of the relationship. There's no simple rule of thumb. Most partnerships contain elements from both extremes of the spectrum, but actually sit somewhere between them. And within the broad expanse of mutual partnership, different relationships require different degrees of collaboration. As a collaborative leader, you shouldn't rush towards straightforward models of teamworking or transactions. Leaders need to get comfortable with shades of grey.

Be forensic about who you collaborate with and why

The collaboration spectrum can also help prioritize how leaders work across different partnerships. When they're working with many different partnerships at one time – as we know is the case for many leaders – they can't afford to collaborate closely with everyone. It's expensive and often it's downright counterproductive. So leaders need to be forensic.

Take, for example, the case of a government department charged with encouraging people to save for their retirement. The department can't do it alone – it needs partners from both the private sector and the third sector. It will also have to work closely with other departments – not least the Treasury. Finding the external partners is not difficult, but sustaining the right relationships over time definitely is, because suddenly everyone wants to talk to the department.

Keen to develop close relationships, departmental officials are concerned to find that all their time is swallowed up in endless partnership or stakeholder meetings. They don't have a map of what all these relationships are really for or how to get best value from them all. It's high maintenance and it requires a high level of communication – often to no purpose. Meanwhile the private and third sector partners are becoming more and more dissatisfied because they don't feel their views are being heard. Quickly it becomes clear that the 'one team' approach is unsustainable.

Finally the department realizes that 'one size fits all' won't work in managing a complex set of partnerships like this. Each relationship needs a different amount of collaboration and a different approach. The collaboration spectrum helps them negotiate the right approach with each partner – and in turn manages those partners' expectations of airtime with the department.

As a collaborative leader, then, you need to exercise discretion. Each partner won't necessarily require the same level of investment of time and effort – and shouldn't be given it. Leaders need to select where it will be most beneficial, and put their effort into building collaboration only where they get the best return.

The aspiring collaborator's checklist

As we've seen, indiscriminate collaboration doesn't help a partnership. You need to choose where to focus your efforts on collaborating, and where to back off.

The following questions can help you determine just how much effort to give each partner:

- **How certain can you be of the outcome?** Can you define the product or service you require clearly? And are you confident that your potential partners are fully capable of delivering it with little help from you? If so, then high levels of collaboration are a waste of effort, and you'll often be better advised to go for a productive customer–supplier relationship driven by a clear contract. In a longer-term situation where the product being delivered is dependent on contributions from many parties, the investment in higher levels of collaboration may be justified. Do you and the other parties have similar assessments of the needs of the situation?
- **Where does your partner think you are on the collaboration spectrum?** Do the other parties involved assume that you will operate either in a highly interdependent or highly contractual manner? What are the signals that you and your organization are sending to your partners about the type of the relationship that you want? Are the assumptions made by your partners explicitly stated or are they implied? What evidence do you have for your assessment? And are the demands of others realistic given the objective of the relationship and the other pressures on you?
- **What is the direction of travel?** How are the demands on the relationships in the partnership changing, and how might you need to change to meet the future needs of the situation? Instead of aiming for a close relationship at the outset, it can be better to start with lower levels of

collaboration, until all parties prove they can deliver. Demonstrating that partners keep their promises helps to build high levels of trust, which, in turn, help enable the parties to collaborate more closely. Most successful collaborative relationships grow by moving form right to left along the collaboration spectrum. Start by delivering reliable transactions and build a closer relationship from there.

- **What will help you get there?** What processes, organizational structures and ways of working will inhibit your relationship from developing? What will enable it? If you want an effective contract-driven supplier relationship, then this demands a particular skill set and is likely to be distracted by a series of 'team-building' meetings! Building relationships requires skill and the right attitudes along with the right structures and processes. What needs to be developed to help create the relationships that are required? And is this realistic?
- **What have you learned from past relationships?** Have you worked with this partner before? Does this situation require the same or a different level of collaboration, from past experience? What about your own style when it comes to cross-organizational working – do you tend to work more effectively in close highly interdependent relationships or in looser more distant relationships? What is most challenging for you in working with others? And when do you need to challenge yourself more in order to get the most from a relationship?

All this work to define your terms may seem a burden, but it cuts out much bigger problems down the line. Entering a relationship with a clear idea of what you're getting into prevents wasted time on the wrong approach – and saves everyone time and money in the end. It's no use setting up expectations of high levels of collaboration if this is not going to benefit all parties – after all, collaborative partnerships are a big investment, and have to be worth the effort for everyone involved. And realistically, no leader can expect to influence a dozen or more highly collaborative partnerships at the same time – yet half the directors questioned in our Ipsos Mori survey said they are running up to 15 concurrently, and a third said they were running more than 20.[4]

Working out where a partnership sits on the spectrum helps all parties focus on what they need to achieve their objectives. Just because one party wants a close relationship doesn't mean it should be granted: there has to be a mutual recognition of the need and the potential value in working closely together.

The spectrum also helps define where you as a leader should direct the greatest attention – not to the groups that make the most noise, but where it adds value to the partnership. By reflecting on the objectives the leader is trying to achieve, and on what is needed from each party in order to deliver it, they may be surprised at the critical relationships that have been overlooked.

Finally, understanding the type of relationship needed makes it clear what kind of language should be used. 'Team' talk instead of 'customer–supplier' language and vice versa can be deeply frustrating for the people involved who know the reality all too well. Categorizing the partnership properly lets the leader tell it like it is – and that's a whole lot healthier for everyone.

Chapter summary

Only collaborate when and where you need to

Collaboration costs. It costs in financial terms but it also costs in leadership time and commitment and so as a leader you should only invest in collaboration in proportion to what you see as the potential return.

Successful business relationships aren't black or white, collaborative or non-collaborative; it's about shades of grey – getting the amount of collaboration that the situation requires. To help work out how much collaboration is needed in a particular relationship it's useful to look at the number (and significance) of the points of interdependence between the different parties. These points of interdependence are the key places in the overall business processes where the action (or inaction) of one partner can have a critical impact on the work of others – at these points alignment is essential.

To start a discussion with your partners about the amount of collaboration that you are each looking for in a relationship you can plot it using a tool we call *the collaboration spectrum*. This shows relationships ranging from a symbiotic (with many points of interdependence and therefore a high degree of collaboration) at one end, to transactional (with relatively few points of interdependence and therefore a low degree of collaboration) at the other. Partnerships and mutually beneficial relationships sit somewhere in between in the middle of the spectrum.

Lessons for leaders

* Ask yourself if you are balancing your time appropriately between the different business relationships you are involved in. Are you giving those that require a higher degree of collaboration the time they require?
* Collaborative groups or partnerships are not conventional teams, even if they sit at the symbiotic end of the spectrum. People in collaborative groups have different loyalties and have to be led and motivated accordingly.
* Ask your partners where they think your relationship needs to sit on the collaboration spectrum. Is this different from your own view?

- Where do you both think the relationship has been in the past and is at the moment on the collaboration spectrum? And what does that tell you about the necessary direction of travel for the future?
- Don't send mixed messages. If you are used to running customer–supplier relationships are you falling into the trap of using this language to describe a more collaborative partnership? Or if you are used to leading and building close teams does your style confuse suppliers who expect to work at more arm's length?

3

THE THREE-LEGGED STOOL – GOVERNANCE, OPERATIONS AND BEHAVIOURS

The foundations of successful collaboration

Collaborative business relationships come in all shapes and sizes. Some require a little more close cooperation than a typical transactional customer–supplier relationship to deliver their objectives – but others look much more like a traditional team and have to be led accordingly. The collaboration spectrum as discussed in the previous chapter is a useful tool to look across a range of different relationships and to pick out their similarities and differences – and the consequences of this for how they need to be led. But in this chapter, we focus on the areas that collaborative leaders need to address in order to build these complex business relationships.

We've seen successful collaborative relationships built on many different foundations – some place the emphasis on 'creating a watertight contract', others favour a 'process-based' approach to creating common ways of working, and still others cite a common set of 'values and behaviours' as the most vital underpinning. But as we analyse what each of these have in common, and what their leaders pay attention to, three critical elements emerge: governance, operations and behaviours. Get these three right and you have the foundations for a long-term stable relationship.

In this chapter we'll explore what we mean by these terms, introduce a simple model which ties them together, and flesh out this framework by breaking down the broad headings into three further components that help to define what is important under each one.

Setting leadership priorities

It's all very well laying out a comprehensive framework, but for many senior people the challenge is leading across a large number of complex relationships when they only have a finite number of hours in the day. They have only a limited amount of time or management bandwidth to devote to any particular relationship – so where should they focus their efforts? Faced with this question, the risk is that leaders do what comes naturally – or what they've always found to work in their own organization – but that may not be what their partners need. So we also go back to the collaboration spectrum and look at how a leader can use this tool to prioritize the amount of attention they give to each of the areas of governance, operations and behaviours depending on where a particular relationship lies on the spectrum.

Governance, operations and behaviours – a case study

Let's start with a story that illustrates the dilemma one leader faced; the difficult task of collaborating across several functions and organizations. It is based on a combination of the real experiences that leaders typically face at the start of a new partnership or when taking over a collaborative leadership role and wondering where to focus their efforts.

Eleanor's story: IT isn't working

Eleanor has just been appointed chief information officer of an NHS Trust. It's a challenging post – the Trust wants to bring in new infrastructure, as well as trialling new ways of working, such as remote laptops for district nurses. With 40 IT staff, she's responsible for 10,000 IT users on three different sites. At the same time she's expected to bring in several new systems – without disrupting care services. All of this is complicated by the NHS setting up central contracts for new IT infrastructure as part of the national Connecting for Health programme

On her first day she's faced with a barrage of urgent tasks. Two IT suppliers who've just been awarded major new contracts are jostling for position. Both want to have the key relationship, and both want meetings straightaway. Meanwhile there are already signs of dissent among the hospital consultants who are due to get a new 'consultants portal' to give them all the data they need through one screen. The overall reliability of the systems isn't high, and is forecast to get worse in the short term as old infrastructure is ripped out and new cables are installed. To top it all, her own department is in permanent crisis mode, and its reputation is falling fast. As Eleanor walks through the corridors to her office, she sees that someone has put a big handwritten sign on one of the notice boards which simply says, 'IT isn't working'.

Sitting down at her desk to review the situation, Eleanor could adopt any one of three classic responses. She could decide that the supplier contracts are the most important thing, take a couple of days to understand them inside and out, and then bring in the legal department to see what room she has

---

for manoeuvre. She could concentrate on processes, hiring management consultants to map out every step from supplier to end user, benchmarking against best practice, and designing an ideal workflow. Or she could take a team-building approach, starting with the problems in her own department and moving on to try to build a common IT vision throughout the trust. But the truth is that in a network of complex relationships like this, none of these classic responses taken on their own will get Eleanor very far.

Instead, the first thing she should do at this point is identify her critical issues and then map out her key relationships and work out how much attention they really require – the stuff of Chapter 2. Understanding the interdependencies in each relationship and plotting them on the collaboration spectrum (see Chapter 2) will uncover which ones require high levels of collaboration and which can be tightly specified and then left to run with minimal involvement. For example, the provision of office and mobile PCs, including the ones being trialled by district nurses, is a fairly standard contract, with low dependence on other systems, and can be run in a transactional way. This means Eleanor can keep one of the demanding suppliers at arm's length, and put in place an account manager to handle the relationship.

The consultant portal, however, demands close attention. It gives consultants access to patient records and specialist information about their job – and it is both highly interdependent and highly significant. First of all, it is new technology, which means that even the supplier is anxious, while the consultants are downright jumpy. If they're unhappy with the delivery of service, Eleanor's staff – and quite possibly some patients – will suffer. And as a project, it is at the centre of a web of other significant IT systems and organizational relationships – its perceived success or failure will have knock-on effects in all sorts of places. Eleanor needs to focus on involving the consultants and making this system work.

Mapping out the significance and degree of interdependence of each project gives Eleanor a clear sense of what she personally needs to tackle first. The consultant portal scores highly on both – and it's an area she needs to prioritize.

Eleanor's next step should be to look closely at each relationship, and check that all partnerships are built on solid ground. Over the rest of the chapter, we explore a simple but effective model for doing this. As we examine each part, we'll come back to Eleanor's story, and look at what she should do under each heading.

The three-legged stool

Any collaborative relationship needs a strong and stable framework to see it through the bad times as well as the good. The model we use is simple, but highly effective, and it helps you plan where to focus your leadership time and effort in situations like the one Eleanor is facing in our example. It's called the three-legged stool.

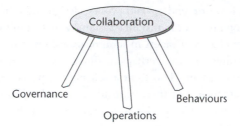

FIGURE 3.1 The three-legged stool – governance, operations and behaviours

The three legs of the stool are the three areas to focus on: governance, operations and behaviours – and as we'll see each is important. But first some definitions:

- By **governance** we mean the formal ways in which the overarching purpose of the collaborative relationship is agreed, objectives are set, accountabilities are defined and joint decisions are made.
- By **operations** we mean the process by which things get done, resources are allocated, progress is measured and communicated, and information and learning is shared.
- By **behaviours** we mean the way leaders at all levels in different organizations act with each other to solve problems, work across different cultures and produce joint results.

We use the analogy of a three-legged stool because when we've seen relationships built on only one or two of these three legs, they may show signs of short-term success but they tend not to be resilient – something changes and they become vulnerable and liable to fall over.

- **Governance:** A collaborative relationship built solely on strong contracts and formal governance is often inflexible and slow to respond. People stick to the letter of the contract – there are often penalties in place if they don't and so they are unwilling to put themselves out to help their partners. That means that new opportunities can be missed – or the competition gets there first. This focus on playing by the letter of the contracts also encourages game playing. A supplier may sign up to a tight contract that doesn't look too profitable at first knowing that as soon as anything changes in the client specification they will be in a very powerful position to negotiate high fees for any work that wasn't identified in the original contract. And the client can be in a very weak position if they've not got anything other than a legalistic contract-bound relationship to rely on.
- **Operations:** A relationship built on slick processes and operations can be more adaptable – especially if the feedback and improvement processes are strong. A lot of the success of manufacturing and supply chain partnerships has

come from a focus on end-to-end process design and efficient operations. But a pure focus on process can produce systems which aren't good at dealing with more strategic change. Leaders in such relationships find it difficult when they need to shift direction and perhaps to throw away many of the old hard won systems and start again. Too tight a reliance on processes can mean that the strategic governance isn't there to force a re-evaluation of the situation, and the right behaviours haven't been encouraged to make people feel that they can raise the awkward questions that inspire change.

- **Behaviours:** A collaborative relationship that focuses primarily on getting the behaviours right might look ideal at first glance – but it's only sustainable if the other two legs of the stool are in place as well. Truly collaborative leadership behaviours and great relationships between people at all levels can get you a long way. But although people may start off with the best intentions to work closely with their partners, contracts and incentives drive behaviours, and if these are wrong, the tensions will build up over time. And what happens when the key people move on or fall out with each other? We've seen many collaborative relationships that have been over-reliant on a highly trusting relationship between two people at the top to set norms of behaviour right through their own organizations. But if those key individuals leave suddenly there can be nothing left to fall back on and the relationship can feel remarkably hollow.

The results of our Ipsos Mori survey showed that the majority of directors questioned had put most of their efforts to date into operations – closely followed by governance.[1] However, over half thought that the greatest additional value was to be gained by focusing more on behaviours.

What do leaders need to pay attention to and why?

Whilst the three areas of governance, operations and behaviours are important to any collaborative relationship it's difficult to pay equal attention to all three at once. Different relationships seem to have different priorities, so how can leaders decide what to focus on in particular situations – perhaps at the start of a new relationship or one that is hitting difficulties? The collaboration spectrum described in the previous chapter is a useful way of analysing the needs of a relationship.

To recap, you can map any relationship on a spectrum based on the amount of collaboration it requires to be successful. The spectrum ranges from highly symbiotic 'one team' relationships that require a large amount of collaboration for all their interactions, through to transactional, customer–supplier, relationships that require much less collaboration or only at very particular times.

We can then extend this figure to show the degree to which a leader needs to focus their attention on each of the three legs of the stool in a particular relationship.

Starting at the right-hand side of the diagram with a focus on governance and contract, transactional relationships typically rely on well-defined specifications and contracts. It's by having the rules well defined and understood that all parties can

Finding your place on the collaboration spectrum

Amount of collaboration

High	Medium	Low
permanent team	partnership	customer supplier
symbiotic	*mutual*	*transactional*
close		*distant*
same objectives		*separate objectives*
loyal to the group		*loyal to my employer*
lots of time together		*little time together*
They're really one of us		*They give us a good deal*

FIGURE 3.2 The collaboration spectrum

get on with their own work most of the time in a relatively independent way. Contrast this with symbiotic relationships. If a leader works in a close team environment the last thing they want to be doing is continually referring to the formal governance to get things done. Indeed when people start getting the contract out of the drawer it's often a sign that a team is running into problems. With these as the two extremes we can produce Figure 3.3. You could argue about the shape of the curve but even in a purely transactional relationship you can't have a 100 per cent focus on governance and similarly this doesn't go down to 0 per cent for a totally symbiotic relationship.

Now let's look at what happens with another leg of the stool, behaviours. Here the percentages are rather reversed. In a transactional relationship a leader need not put a lot of time into defining common values and re-enforcing behavioural norms. The different parties don't spend much time together anyway – and when they do meet they are likely to be negotiating a deal or testing a product. Of course people need to behave in a civil manner with each other but this is unlikely to need a major leadership focus. However, in a symbiotic team-based relationship building a common set of values and codes of behaviour is always a high priority. You see this

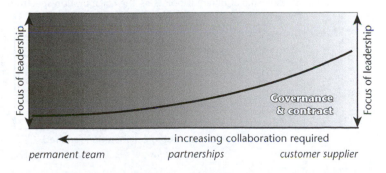

FIGURE 3.3 Governance on the collaboration spectrum

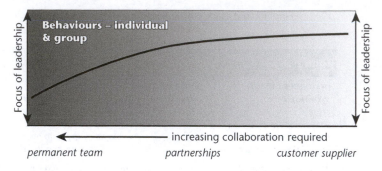

FIGURE 3.4 Behaviours on the collaboration spectrum

in military and sporting collaborations where the emphasis on 'team building' is paramount.

Plotting this on the same collaboration spectrum you get Figure 3.4 below – but note this time we have measured the percentage of leadership focus down from the top of the y-axis. We'll explain why in a moment.

Again you could argue about the precise shape of the curve – but the direction of travel from one end of the spectrum to the other is clear. Symbiotic relationships need a large focus on behaviours but not 100 per cent, their transactional relationship needs are much less, but it's not 0 per cent.

We can now combine these two figures and add the third leg of the stool, operations.

Having combined the three areas of governance, operations and behaviours on one figure you can see the consequences for the aspects of a relationship that a leader should focus on and how they should divide the finite time they have to give.

In the most symbiotic relationships a leader should perhaps put 80 per cent of their attention on the behavioural aspects and maybe 10 per cent each on governance and operational processes.

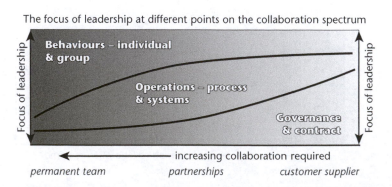

FIGURE 3.5 Governance operations and behaviours on the collaboration spectrum

In purely transactional relationships the numbers are reversed: 80 per cent of leaders' attention could usefully be spent looking at governance issues and only 10 per cent each on operational processes and behaviours.

But in mutual partnering relationships, where value is created by constructively harnessing the differences between the parties, leaders need to pay roughly equal amounts of attention to governance, operations and behaviours. That may sound straightforward but it doesn't come easy.

Challenge your own habits

All leaders have preferences for where they like to focus their efforts. Some of these habits will be innate and others learned over the years from studying what works in their own organization. The message of these two tools taken together, the three-legged stool and the collaboration spectrum, is that leaders need to challenge themselves and their own leadership habits.

The questions a leader should ask when faced with a new or difficult collaborative relationship is, first, where does this relationship lie on the collaboration spectrum and, therefore, what balance of leadership focus on governance, operations and behaviours is likely to be required for success. Then to ask – so what are my habits, what do I normally focus on and is this right for the particular situation. And of course a collaborative leader needn't use this tool in isolation. Working through these questions with your colleagues and partners can often help build understanding about what is really going on in a troubled relationship and how to work together to put it right.

The first leg: governance

By governance, we mean the formal and informal joint governing structures of the collaborative venture, from the contract through to management and steering groups, reporting lines, accountabilities and decision-making structures.

Governance
Clarity of purpose
Quality of decision making
Clarity of accountabilities

Governance is the skeleton of a collaborative relationship – the supporting frame that holds everything together. And it's important to get it right – and to be prepared to change it if it's not working. While some governance structures may be specified in the contract from the start of a relationship, leaving these set in stone may not necessarily be the way best to manage a relationship over time. As the relationship progresses and matures, you may need to alter and simplify some of the structures. And in times of crisis, you may need to put in extra layers of governance. To help, it's useful to examine some of the key components within a successful governance arrangement.

Clarity of purpose: know what you're both after

One of the most important success factors in any collaborative relationship, according to executives in our Ipsos Mori survey, is having a common purpose and shared objectives.[2] This has to go well beyond a bland statement like 'delivering value together' – you need to know what the value is, and exactly why it's worth working together. If you don't understand each other's objectives in detail, you won't know what success looks like to each other, and you're likely to get in the way of that success. Even more dangerous, you may find your motives are actually in competition with each other.

London Underground's public–private partnership with Metronet to modernize the Tube infrastructure is a case in point. One of London Underground's main objectives was to minimize the costs of renewing track, power cables and trains. However, Metronet, one of the two firms responsible for the upkeep and upgrading of the Tube, was largely owned by companies that were part of its own supply chain – the people that built the trains and supplied the power systems. It's a bit like expecting that if supermarkets were entirely owned by farmers they would keep down the cost of milk. This was a partnership that always had a conflict at its heart – the two organizations' objectives were incompatible. And in the end this was probably one of the causes of Metronet going into administration in 2008.

This is not to say that success has to look exactly the same for each party. It doesn't – in fact, it's pretty unlikely that everyone's motives will match. Leaders don't need to find a clone of their own organization – but it's important that individual partners are transparent about their motives for entering a partnership. That way, each can consider from the outset whether it's possible for them to contribute fully to their partner's success.

When Alan Braithwaite, a widely respected authority on supply chain partnerships, named his Seven Laws of Logistics, the sixth law was entitled 'the Law of Supply Chain Asymmetry'. It reads: 'The commercial interests and strategic priorities between partners in the supply chain are never symmetrical and working to share mutual interest is an unreal proposition – [therefore] defining trading or functional relationships to work to co–operative self-interest is the objective'.[3]

For example, a construction firm appointed to build a new hospital wants several things from the partnership. They want the project to be profitable. They want recognition of their abilities in the market. And in the end they want their stakeholders to demonstrate their satisfaction publicly.

The hospital trust, meanwhile, has its own separate set of objectives. It wants the building finished on time and on budget, stakeholders to see it as a good investment, staff to find the new building an attractive and efficient place to work, patients to be impressed, and for the overall building to contribute to healthcare outcomes.

Interestingly, the joint objective – building a good hospital efficiently – doesn't tell you very much. It's only meaningful when you separate it out into individual components for each member of the partnership.

Knowing what you're both after is crucial. As a leader, you need to be honest about your motives from the start – otherwise, how can you expect your partner to help you achieve them? We advise prospective partners to take the time to map out three statements of purpose: I'm in it for x, you're in it for y, and we're both in it for z. Make sure you understand them fully, and that they're not in conflict. Because without clarity of purpose, you're fumbling in the dark.

Quality of decision making: get the right people in the room

The principles of good decision making are straightforward: leaders need the right people to make decisions at the right time and to adhere to them. The reality is more complicated. If the leader's steering committee only meets once a quarter, it can't act as the gatekeeper for every operational decision. There's no use waiting for an agreement on buying new gritting lorries if the meeting isn't until March and the snow has been and gone.

Criticizing decisions from hindsight is always easy. But some structures are a format for failure. Having a small number of like-minded people in the room may make it easier to come to a decision, but it increases the risk of that decision being severely flawed. Sometimes you need to allow the devil's advocates in there too, and put up with the friction they create, because it makes for a better decision in the end.

Thankfully, collaborative business ventures don't have to decide whether or not to go to war. Nonetheless, the decisions they make can still have major conse-quences for the public or for stakeholders. Leaders of partnerships need to make sure they get everyone in the room when decisions really matter. And even though the process is time-consuming, it helps considerably to know as much as possible about each partner's views on any important decision.

The complexity of many multi-party relationships makes decision making much harder than in single organizations or structures. Leaders need to allow for that and not rush the process unduly. Sharing information – and concerns – is vital, because you may not realize until it's too late that some elements are interdependent and make a difference to the quality of the decision. Yes, it can be a drawn-out process. But good decisions consider all the consequences and getting all the parties in the same room is usually the place to start.

In fact we often describe this step 'as getting all the parties in the same room AND speaking the same language' – because a pre-requisite for good decision making is a common language to describe the terms of reference for the decision and to understand the joint evidence. Usually this means helping all parties to break down any barriers of in-company jargon but sometimes it has a more literal meaning. We worked with a group of the most senior civil servants in the govern-ment of a Central European country who wanted to reach some joint decisions about how they could strategically re-organize work between their different ministries. Getting everyone prepared to attend the key two-day workshop in the right frame of mind required a lot of one-to-one preparatory work. All of this had been done perfectly well in English but when it came to the nitty-gritty of joint decision making it was clear that everyone needed to be able to express themselves in their own language – which much to our initial surprise they did. So we quickly had to learn how to facilitate a workshop with a very light touch in a language we really didn't understand. But it worked – all the time we had spent persuading the right people to be in the same room at the same time – all focused on an inter-connected set of challenges that had to be solved together – paid dividends. And all the time they spent together over the two days in formal discussions and lots of informal conversation in the margins of the meeting enabled them to reach signifi-cant decisions and helped to cement some important cross-ministerial relationships. For us as consultants, working in a different language showed us that in terms of facilitation less is more!

Clarity of accountabilities: stop the turf wars

Clarifying roles and accountabilities is another element of governance that requires close attention. In a typical television crew, for example, most of the people will be on freelance contracts, and some may meet for the first time on the day of filming. Yet each person is entirely clear about their role, right down to the runner, whose job it is to fetch and carry, and feed and water the rest of the crew at regular intervals.

Everyone turns up punctually on location (lateness is rarely tolerated because the cost of a single filming day is so high), they get on with their own specialist jobs independently, follow the director's instructions, waste no time, and collaborate only when necessary. Most of the time, it's a well-oiled machine.

Yet this tight definition of roles also allows the crew to respond rapidly to changing circumstances. Things often go wrong during filming – the weather takes a turn for the worse, one of the subjects doesn't work out, or a hoped for event doesn't materialize. At this point, the crew goes into overdrive, rejigs the filming sequence, and often pulls new content out of thin air. The goal for the crew is to come home with useable footage at the end of the day, and though they have a firm plan at the outset, they're highly flexible in how they achieve it – and quite prepared to throw that plan out of the window if necessary.

At first sight this tight-role, open-task approach doesn't appear to fit other types of collaborative relationship – it seems counterintuitive. Surely spelling out the approach to the task matters more than fixing the roles for each team member? Won't you ensure a greater interplay of ideas and contributions, and greater innova-tion, if you leave the roles loose?

The answer in collaborations is absolutely not. Research by Lynda Gratton and Tamara J. Erickson has shown that what matters in a collaborative team is for each team member to know exactly what their role is and be able to fulfil a large part of it inde-pendently.[4] They call it 'role clarity and task ambiguity' – and it's essential in partnerships because it cuts down on distrust, time-wasting and turf wars. Leaving the definition of the task relatively open also leaves room for creativity in the collaboration.

Failure to define roles sufficiently can have a big impact on costs. It's not just financial risks that are increased by lack of clear accountabilities. The report by General Counsel to the US Presidential Oil Spill Commission into the BP Gulf of Mexico disaster identified that 'the blowout occurred in large part because the companies diffused knowledge, responsibility for, and ownership of safety among groups of people … They did not recognize the need for individual leadership in addressing the multiple anomalies and uncertainties that they observed. Instead, they relied on many ambiguous dotted line relationships within and between the companies and personnel involved.'[5]

Collaboration is difficult enough without blurring the lines of accountability. Being crystal clear about people's roles cuts out overlap and waste, but it also reduces risk and makes people happier about their competence and sphere of influence. It lets them get on with their jobs. And that certainty of role makes it possible for them to get creative when it really matters.

Governance and Eleanor's story

So how does a consideration of governance apply to Eleanor's situation as a new CIO? First of all, she needs to deal with the question of aligning objectives. The hospital consultants, managers and ward staff all want different things from the new systems, and her own staff and the two suppliers clearly have different views about what the new contracts should provide. In terms of decision making, she faces multiple layers of steering groups and user groups for each separate project, all of whose decisions can apparently be overruled by the hospital trust's finance committee, which often gets bogged down in details of approval of changes to IT budgets at its monthly meetings.

Eleanor's response is to simplify the governance process, dramatically slimming down the number of steering groups, and creating clear terms of reference for each that specify which are discussion groups and which have real decision-making authority. She also sets up a single IT portfolio management board for the whole trust, with responsibility for setting priorities across the full range of projects and user groups – and presenting a single view to the finance committee if new funds are needed.

In addition, Eleanor runs a series of workshops for suppliers, customers and IT staff to reach agreement about 'what success looks like'. This isn't easy, but over time they begin to understand each other's viewpoint and accept that the IT portfolio management board has the authority to set priorities and targets for them all to work to.

The second leg: operations

By operations, we mean the processes that have to work across the whole relationship, from communications and information sharing to joint learning and staff development, to ensure that the relationship thrives and grows. Operations within a successful collaborative

Operations
Aligned systems and processes
Effective communications
Capability improvement

relationship should be like jigsaw pieces – they have to fit together properly if the partnership is to run smoothly.

If good governance is like a skeleton supporting the structure of a living relationship, good operations are its blood supply, pumping information to all parts of the body. And like the bloodstream, operations are dynamic. What works one day may not be right for the next. So a healthy partnership or other collaborative relationship is always reviewing and improving its operations and learning as a result.

The problem is that the individual parties involved all want to use and hone their own efficient systems and processes. So why can't they just combine operations or pick the best for use across the partnership? The answer is distinctly human: people are used to doing things the way they have always done them. In addition, sharing the intimate details of your own company's processes with a partner can feel uncomfortable. It may take months or years of inefficiency, frustration and crisis before fundamental processes are linked together. Get them right at the beginning, though, and your relationship is off to a solid start.

Aligned systems and processes: make sure the plug fits the socket

It's the little things that get in the way. Data that has to be re-entered to fit your spread sheet package, invoices that don't get paid because they're in the wrong format, timesheets that don't tally with the number of hours you're apparently supposed to be billing. They can drive you mad – and they erode faith between partners remarkably fast. As one partnership director put it, 'It's like trying to put a UK plug in a European socket – you can only push so hard and then someone is going to get a nasty shock.'

One of the basic questions that needs to be addressed at the outset of a collaboration is whether everyone is looking at the same data – a much bigger problem than it might seem. A single source of truth can be hard to find if each partner is sticking rigidly to their own systems.

Trust is the essence here. Misunderstandings often occur when partners don't have enough faith in each other to keep score without supervision. A roads department at a local authority, for example, is frustrated that none of the 27 complaints received by its call centre have been dealt with. The private contractor insists that in fact it's doing a great job because it's been charged with 12 jobs and closed all of them. Who is right? The only way to sort out the confusion is to make sure the systems fit together properly – or, better still, to make everyone use the same system.

One warning sign that a lack of alignment is causing problems is people having to re-enter data at every stage in a process: the customer service desk sends a written request to the council works department, which rekeys it to generate a works order, then prints it out for the people who mend the road, who in turn rekey it for jobs scheduling. At every point there's a huge opportunity for errors to creep in.

An obvious example of the need for process alignment is in HR, and particularly in performance management and incentive schemes. When these are badly out of kilter – for example, when there are hugely differing pay-scales for the same job – it's a recipe for resentment. And if the rules are different across a partnership, people may see staff in their partner organizations 'getting away with' things they would

never be allowed to do, or being rewarded in ways that seem unfair or dispropor-
tionate. There is no easy way around these issues – policies and practices that have
been negotiated over years with staff can be thrown into sharp relief by a partner
that does the opposite. In our experience the most important thing is to get these
issues out into the open and to not let them fester. We've seen partnership relationships soured for many months by something as seemingly trivial as the policy on
what to do with air-miles earned on company business trips.

The hard truth is that if systems and processes are to be aligned then somewhere
along the line people are going to need to compromise. It's certainly a pain to fill
in timesheets when you never had to before, but if it means everyone's working
from the same set of figures, it's worth doing for the sake of the relationship.
Solving these sorts of system problems is not easy but leaders need to strive for as
much simplicity in the process as they possibly can. A multi-party relationship with
its systems and processes working well together has sorted out the petty stuff which
in turn can free up leaders to concentrate on the big picture.

Effective communications: cut the propaganda

Good communications across a partnership or other collaborative relationship are
like communications in any organization: they have to be timely, targeted and
effective. But above all, they need to be believable. Trust is far more of an issue in a
multi-party collaboration than in a single function or organization, so a monthly
newsletter stuffed with self-congratulatory articles just won't wash. People on
the ground know the reality, and a lot of the time it tells a different story. Put
out too much propaganda and people are likely to suspend their belief in the
collaboration – and quite possibly to stop collaborating at all.

Although it's tempting to treat cross-partnership communications as a PR
exercise, leaders have to resist the urge. Instead they need to take a deep breath and
start sharing the downs as well as the ups, allowing the critical voices an airing,
and holding their hands up when they get things wrong.

When the world's largest cement manufacturer, Lafarge, entered a sponsorship
agreement with global environmental charity WWF, it seemed an unlikely match.
Yet both had much to gain from the partnership – not least by demonstrating that
big business could work successfully with NGOs. Despite facing major challenges
to their relationship (in particular over the proposed siting of a superquarry on the
Scottish island of Harris), the partnership was 'open, straightforward and inclusive'.[6]
Sceptical voices were invited to meetings, there was no attempt to hide major
disagreements, and Lafarge even published both sides of the argument on the
superquarry in its sustainability report.

This unusual level of frankness helped the partnership scale some steep obstacles.
According to Michel Picard, vice president of environmental issues at Lafarge
Group: 'The permanent dialogue with WWF challenges our beliefs, our strategies,
and our practices, and produces tangible results. I am convinced that through this
process Lafarge is gaining a competitive advantage for the future.'[7] For Picard, the

partnership has become the company's 'environmental insurance', allowing it to address environmental issues before they become urgent, and way ahead of the competition. Meanwhile, for WWF, it's an effective way to deliver their mission by engaging with business from within – and a model for other NGOs.

When communicating externally, it's not always possible to be quite so frank. However, taking joint responsibility in all communications is vital – even when things go wrong. Having a single person in charge of communication for the relationship helps, so long as they take care not to favour one party over another. But if partners end up presenting separately to stakeholders, or briefing journalists on their own, they need to honour the partnership and hold the party line. Without this discipline, it's all too easy to descend into back-stabbing and mutual recrimination.

The essence of good communication in collaborative relationships, then, is to behave as one. All parties have to drop their guard and accept that they're in it together, for better or worse. This doesn't mean ignoring differences in culture, skills or contribution. Those still matter, and failure to acknowledge them can throw a relationship off course. What it does mean is sharing good news and bad across the whole partnership, being honest with each other, and standing together when it counts. A little solidarity goes a long, long way.

Capability improvement: build together for the future

Our Ipsos Mori research found that the length of an average partnership is around six years, outlasting most management appointments.[8] It's inevitable, then, that good people are going to leave before a partnership runs its course.

The implications for leaders are clear. You need to look at the capability needs over the whole length of the relationship and to invest in skills and capacity long before you're likely to lose them. Succession planning is a necessity. Equally important is the need to develop staff all through the life of the partnership so that they stay motivated – you can't afford to let a partnership become a graveyard for ambition.

Some manage to do this in imaginative ways. One county council's partnership with its consulting engineers, for example, was a model of far-sightedness. When the council realized its quantity surveyors were all going to reach retirement age at around the same time, it knew it needed to address the issue fast. It's not easy to recruit experienced quantity surveyors and the council didn't want to be at the mercy of the market. In an ideal world, they would take on new graduates immediately and train them up, but with a headcount freeze, this wasn't going to be possible. The solution was unexpected but inspired. Their partners agreed to step in and recruit the graduates, and set up a joint training programme that saw people moving between public and private sector posts as their career developed so that when the time came they would have opportunities to work either for the council or the contractors.

It's not always about planning for the future – joint leadership development programmes are also a great opportunity to bring people together from different parties to learn how to use common tools and leadership techniques and get the added benefit of building some personal relationships around the coffee machine and lunch table at the same time. The relationships between Network Rail who own the majority of the UK rail infrastructure and the Train Operating Companies (TOCs) who manage the train services that run over it have had a long history of challenge and conflict. The industry has tried to use all three legs of governance, operations and behaviours to address these issues. But one particular example has been for Network Rail to invite TOCs to send some of their high potential young leaders on to the Network Rail Senior Leaders Programme run by Warwick Business School. This six month modular programme gives people a chance to build their understanding of the interdependencies in the whole rail system and to learn where closer collaboration may bring opportunities for cost saving or improvements in customer service. Warwick also runs a similar programme for the Highways Agency (the Roads Academy Masterclass programme) which brings together leaders from all the major highway maintenance companies in the UK.[9]

Building capacity and leadership capability together in this way is highly collaborative – a marriage rather than a cohabitation. It's not for the faint-hearted, but the mark of a mature and sophisticated relationship. When partners are prepared to put in time or money to help each other out of a dilemma that hasn't yet happened, it sends out a clear signal. They're in it for the long term, and investing for the future – together.

Operations and Eleanor's story

The biggest issue for Eleanor in the field of operations is getting everyone to work from a single version of the truth about IT performance. She is regularly berated by angry hospital consultants and managers about the poor performance of IT, with people demanding that she should extract penalty charges from the suppliers as compensation for their problems. Yet her own teams tell her that although they aren't satisfied with what is happening, the suppliers seem to be hitting the majority of performance targets.

The trouble is that there are dozens of ways to measure performance formally, and dozens more anecdotal measures. It's clear that users aren't happy, so no number of bar charts demonstrating on-target performance will make a difference. On the other hand, a high percentage of help desk complaints are actually caused by users who don't understand some of the new features of the system.

Eleanor puts her effort into two immediate short-term initiatives. The first is to use the newly formed IT portfolio management board to develop a simple performance scorecard that reflects the day-to-day reality of the system, and that contains measures of user satisfaction with the service. As everyone reviews and acts on the same data month on month, they gradually begin to see the real (and perceived) performance improve.

Her second initiative is to start a programme of user communication and education to help people get the most out of their existing systems. By training her own staff to improve their communication skills, and then sending them all out for a day each week to train groups of users at their desks, she not only improves perceptions of IT, but also the relationships between IT staff and clinicians.

In a longer-term initiative, Eleanor conducts a skills inventory to see what skills she has in-house and what skills are available through her suppliers. With this she is able to build a long-range development plan so that as the current contracts draw to a close, she has the right skills in place to tender for the next ones.

The third leg: behaviours

> **Behaviours**
> Role modelling
> Cross-cultural awareness
> Joint problem solving

Many leaders of collaborative relationships – particularly those of formally contracted partnerships – address at least some aspects of governance and operations, but forget all about behaviours. They spend all their time sorting out the contract, pinning down the processes and dreaming up penalties for if things go wrong. Yet if they don't concentrate on behaviours, there's every chance that things will go downhill rapidly.

It's rare to see managers trained in how to behave collaboratively. Some firms, however, have taken a lead on training their employees in relationship skills. May Gurney, a construction firm based in East Anglia, runs an induction programme for all new staff to explain the company's approach to partnering and collaboration. All its managers go through development programmes to build their skills in coaching and holding difficult conversations, and when it starts a new partnership contract they hold joint leadership development workshops for their own staff and managers from the client organization.

Similar capabilities are needed to run internal partnerships. When Lloyds bank group was moving to a corporate shared services model, it needed to set up a network of internal business partners to cover functions such as HR, IT and finance. In order to prepare the people appointed to these new business partner roles for the behavioural challenges of working in a shared service environment, it defined a development programme to build the core capabilities of: managing the customer relationship, developing strategy, delivering business results, influencing, leading others, using information effectively, making good decisions, and making change work. The aim of this corporate programme was to mitigate the risks of different parts of the shared service organization not working together to meet the needs of their internal customers.

Role modelling: walk the talk

Collaborative leaders need to model the kind of behaviour that they know they need to see throughout a relationship. It's not enough to say the words, staff will judge you by your actions. Sometimes that means standing by your partners through thick and thin, even if it may be seen by some as 'letting your own side down'. The trouble is that when things go wrong, it's easy to find fault and to dish out the blame to those outside the fence. And if you succumb to that temptation, so will everyone else. Backbiting is like an aggressive cancer – left unchecked it spreads rapidly throughout an organization.

Leaders need not only to model good behaviours themselves, but to stamp out carping when they see it, and to challenge staff when they avoid personal responsibility. Even when you have true cause to complain of a partner, you need to hold back wherever possible, seeing it as an opportunity to address the issue constructively and to improve the relationship for the long term.

When the world press broke the story that high street clothing chain Gap was accused of using child labour in India to hand-embroider fashion tops, Gap didn't immediately strike off the Indian supplier that had sub-contracted the work.[10] Instead they took a financial hit by preventing these products ever being sold in stores, and convened a meeting of suppliers to reinforce their prohibition on child labour. Their aim was first and foremost to protect their own reputation – but also to try to tackle the causes in an attempt to stop the same thing happening again. It's not enough to stop working with an individual sub-contractor that is using unethical labour – Gap needed to ensure that its first-tier suppliers understood why they must monitor the ethical practices of their own sub-contractors and take responsibility for the way the work is carried out right down the supply chain.

Apple took a rather different approach when reports started emerging about the treatment of workers in their partner Foxconn's factories in China that made iPads and iPhones. Apple's approach was much more contractual. The *New York Times* reported that 'Apple has a supplier code of conduct that details standards on labor issues, safety protections and other topics. The company has mounted a vigorous auditing campaign, and when abuses are discovered, Apple says, corrections are demanded.' [11]

Truly collaborative leaders look for contribution, not blame. In other words, they examine what both parties have contributed to make the problem arise in the first place. It's a technique that allows people to stop judging each other, and instead try to disentangle what happened between them so they can do better next time.

John Yard, a former CIO at the Inland Revenue, is a strong advocate of mapping contributions to a problem instead of dishing out blame. Early into a massive IT outsourcing contract with EDS, there was an issue with their underperformance. While the Inland Revenue board wanted to press for penalties, John Yard realized this could not be an effective solution for either party. Instead he argued the case for readjusting the deal to make it more commercially viable for EDS in return for improvements in service.

Cross-cultural awareness: get beyond first appearances

Some collaborative business relationships are like love at first sight. 'Many executives use romantic analogies to describe the enthusiasm that accompanies their discovery of a new corporate partner', says Rosabeth Moss Kanter. 'The best intercompany relationships are frequently messy and emotional, involving feelings like chemistry and trust.'[12] In other words, some deals depend on a strong personal rapport between chief executives, and on similar cultures and philosophies in the partner organizations.

Similarity of outlook will take a partnership a long way. But we'd argue that it's not essential to the success of the collaboration. In fact, most partnerships – even cross-functional ones within organizations – are likely to bring together differing cultures. And part of the sophistication of leading a collaboration is getting under the skin of a partner who's different.

The sociologist Richard Sennett makes the distinction between what is involved in co-operating within your own tribe and the much greater challenge of seeking out and co-operating with other different tribes. In his book *Together* he contrasts the growth of communities of common interests (or prejudices) on the internet – with the much greater challenges that political and religious leaders have to over-come to find ways of helping different communities and cultures to live together and contribute to the growth of great cities down the centuries.[13] In his definition, building communities is about creating islands of similarity – and the internet is an ideal environment for that because the connected population is so large and the means of searching it so efficient. Typically these on-line communities have little reason or inclination to interact with other communities. Whereas for a city to thrive, different groups and cultures need to live in proximity with one another, trade goods and services and share common resources.

Working across different cultures is easy to say but much harder to do. All too often differences in culture breed suspicion and mistrust. The first warning sign is hearing stereotypes being bandied around: a partner is overly bureaucratic, brash, slow, slick, corporate, American, French, whatever. The slogans are a smokescreen for a more basic misunderstanding: they're not like us.

We'll cover the subject of understanding cultural difference in more detail in Chapter 5. Here, though, it's worth noting that to get beyond first appearances, partners need to start looking at not just each other's output but at their approach. What motivates them? What gets them riled? What upsets them? What ways of behaving do they find easy or difficult?

If partners can work out what makes each other tick, they can start to figure out how to accommodate each other's preferred ways of working. Where there are strong cultural differences, they may need to invest in tools like the Organizational Partnering Indicator (described in Chapter 5) to analyse how best the relationship can function. Social events help break down barriers too, although it's important to make sure that the content of the event isn't skewed heavily to fit one culture rather than the other.

So while some marriages may be made in heaven, most require a little more work. Taking time to understand what your partner is really like pays off. What's more, it can spark creative dialogues that simply wouldn't happen if everyone was just like you. If a collaborative business relationship is to reach beyond the skills and capabilities of individual members and create something new, difference may be exactly what it needs.

Joint problem-solving: fix it fast

Finally, the vexed question of how to deal with things that go wrong. Any relationship will have its fair share of problems especially when the relationship is new – but the way those problems are managed is a strong indicator of the health of the collaboration.

When a problem surfaces, do the different parties flag it up and get together to try to solve it? Or do they close ranks? Worse still, do they moan about their partners' apparent deficiencies rather than helping out? This can emerge at first in petty squabbles and stalemates – one party won't pay invoices, for example, because they're not presented properly, and rather than showing their partner what 'right' looks like, they fail them for getting it wrong. Although such behaviour looks harmless enough in isolation, it bodes badly for a time when the partnership faces more difficult challenges, and leaders should take care to nip it in the bud early.

When things go wrong in the healthiest of relationships, groups quickly come together to find innovative solutions. Of course this is more likely to happen – and be easier to facilitate for a collaborative leader – in close relationships that are at the 'permanent team' end of the collaboration spectrum where people typically spend lots of time together and share common values and behaviours. But even in transactional relationships, you can promote a culture of joint problem-solving by putting it in the contract and setting a budget aside to cover the costs.

One example of innovative problem-solving can be seen in a partnership between London Underground and a construction project team involving Costain Taylor Woodrow, Ove Arup, the Department for Transport and English Heritage, to build new ticket halls for King's Cross station. The difficulty they faced was in digging holes – an activity which in London is fraught with problems. At any point you may turn up something unexpected – from ancient ruins to unexploded bombs. To deal with this, the partnership contract stipulated that whenever workmen turned up something unknown, they had to fill in a method statement on how to solve the problem. This statement went to all the other parties involved, including English Heritage.

London Underground recognized that Costain Taylor Woodrow had a serious problem with the length of time allowed for parties to respond – they couldn't ask their workmen to lean on their shovels for three weeks until all the paperwork had been dealt with. So they brought all the parties together to hammer out a solution.

It soon emerged that English Heritage was the bottleneck – as a charity it was low on administrative resource, and on top of that, the method statements were far too complicated for their needs. But a creative solution was found. Costain Taylor Woodrow would send them only the documentation that was essential, and in addition they agreed to supply them with an administrator for the course of the project.

Solving problems jointly takes creativity and courage. It means opening up. It means washing your dirty linen in public. It means asking for help when you need it, and offering it where you can. For most organizations, this doesn't come naturally – it's easier by far to resort to carping and insularity. However, finding a joint solution speeds things up, and usually saves money. What's more, joint solutions are often more creative, more ambitious and longer-lasting than those made – or ignored – in the comfort of one's own boundaries.

Behaviours and Eleanor's story

Let's look for a last time at Eleanor's story and see what she pays attention to when it came to behaviours.

First and foremost, she acts as a role model. She invests time in making good relationships with key customers and suppliers and makes it obvious to all those around her that that is what she is doing. She also runs a series of workshops that look at the different cultures of her two suppliers and her various user groups. From these workshops the leadership group jointly defines a charter of behaviours to which they expect staff across the partnership to sign up. It lays some basic ground rules such as 'never knowingly let colleagues fail' and 'explain decisions openly and transparently'.

The leaders also agree to meet regularly to review progress, not just on the delivery aspects of the contract, but also on how people perceive the state of play. As part of this they plan to set up a 360° feedback process measuring perceptions of governance, operations and behaviours of people across the partnership on an annual basis.

Finally, Eleanor tackles the short-term problems early by bringing together the groups concerned, airing the issues, and helping them to find solutions that benefit them all. These end-of-the-week lunchtime problem-solving sessions soon become part of the new culture. They even get their own name: 'fix-it Friday lunches'. And the sceptical consultants are also starting to come around and engage in constructive debate with the IT department. Several of them offer to collaborate on the design of the next update to the 'consultants portal' to make sure it meets their needs. Eleanor begins to feel that she has turned a corner and the chaos of her first few months is behind her.

Conclusion

Of course this is a fictitious example but it is drawn from a combination of real-life events. Many leaders describe their first few months in a new role as just a struggle to keep their heads above the water. Walking in to a new organization means having to build relationships from scratch and not being able to rely on your informal networks to find out what is really going on. It's often a disorientating time, and the pressures can push some people into acting in their least collaborative style – over-controlling everything as a means of minimizing the risks and establishing your presence. But as Eleanor's example shows, using the three-legged stool framework of governance, operations and behaviours – and analysing how much attention you need to spend on each depending on where relationships lie on the collaboration spectrum – is a way of prioritizing your leadership actions and avoiding the pitfall of over control.

Interactions between governance, operations and behaviours

We have highlighted the importance of building a strong framework of the right governance, efficient operating processes, and joint standards of behaviour, as though these were separate leadership activities. But of course in most practical cases progress in one area has a positive influence on another – and vice versa.

The way leaders behave in a formal governance meeting will affect the likelihood that others will abide by the rules that are set. A well-defined set of end-to-end processes will only operate smoothly if people in different organizations understand and accept their own accountability for each step in the process. And people will only behave freely and constructively in joint problem-solving or innovation sessions if they believe that the contracts for sharing out the benefits of their work are fair and will be followed by all.

So, as well as understanding what makes up the three legs of the stool, collaborative leaders need to think about the way to use interactions between them most effectively.

For example, much has been written about ways to nudge people to contribute valuable social activities like donating blood or saving for their retirement. This involves not just governance changes such as setting legal rules or giving financial incentives but finding ways to make it easy to do the right thing usually in the form of simple process. In their book *Nudge*, Richard Thaler and Cass Sunstein describe an experiment they carried out to encourage more US employees to save more towards a retirement pension through their pay check.[14] The scheme called Save More Tomorrow first helped people identify the contributions they would have to make to receive the sort of pension they needed in retirement. In most cases this involved making a large increase in contributions and in turn most of the employees in their study felt that they couldn't do this immediately because of the consequential drop in take-home pay. But what the scheme then did was to offer people the choice of committing to set an extra percentage of their salary towards their pension but only when they got a pay rise. By synchronizing the increases in contributions with the timing of an annual pay rise the company was able to ensure that employee pension contributions increased but individuals never felt the negative effect of a drop in take home pay. Understanding the interaction between governance and process, and the impact that would have on behaviour, was key to success.

The importance of naming the game

Or take another example of the way communication and rules affect behaviour – the importance of naming. The prisoner's dilemma game is a classic tool of experimental economists. There are several rounds of the game and in each round pairs of players can each choose to co-operate and both win a small prize or to defect. If one person chooses to defect and the other co-operates the defector wins a big prize and the co-operator nothing. But if both defect they both face a penalty. Of course seeing what you do in one round will affect what your partner (or opponent depending on how you choose to think of them) will do in the next. The question is over many rounds can both players learn to adopt the optimum strategy. Or do they just take it in turns to punish each other for defecting. In 2004, a psychologist from Stanford University, Lee Ross, decided to look at the impact of the name of this game on the behaviour of the players.[15] He divided his students into two groups. He told the first group that they were going to play a game called The Wall Street Game then gave them the rules, put them into pairs and watched the result. The second group were told they were playing a game called The Community Game and given exactly the same set of rules.

For the group told they were playing The Wall Street Game, 33 per cent evolved a co-operative strategy but for the group told they were playing The Community Game this rose to about 70 per cent. The result although very striking is perhaps not surprising to a collaborative leader. People entering a new business relationship often start by trying to figure out 'what sort of game we are playing here', they look for clues in the incentives in the contract, the way work is organized and other people's behaviour and they put a name to what they expect to find – 'It's a private sector rip-off', 'It's a bureaucratic nightmare' – and then they behave in a way which is most likely to bring just what they expect to find about. Naming and framing a relationship is a powerful way to influence behaviour.

If leaders can understand some of these subtle interactions between governance rules, operational process and people's behaviours they can help to set the right framework for a successful and resilient collaborative relationship.

Chapter summary

Collaboration is not just about being nice to each other

Successful collaborative relationships are built on a framework of three things: the right governance structures, efficient joint operations, and collaborative behaviours. Together these act a bit like a three-legged stool. With all in place the system is stable in a range of different environments but take one away and it rapidly becomes unstable and liable to fall over.

Leaders can decide how much attention they need to pay to each of these areas by combining the governance operations and behaviours model with the collaboration spectrum introduced in Chapter 2.

In a highly collaborative, symbiotic, relationship the emphasis needs to be on behaviours – understanding and working with each other's culture to get value from difference. Whereas in a transactional, customer–supplier relationship the biggest thing to pay attention to is the governance – get this specified correctly and you can let the other parties get on with their own tasks without too much interference.

In relationships that sit in the middle of the collaboration spectrum you need to pay as much attention to the efficiency of joint operations and the processes for communicating and learning across all parties as to the governance arrangements and behavioural norms.

The collaborative leader's job is to assess the situation, identify the extent of interdependence and choose the right level of collaboration required.

Lessons for leaders

- Beware of your own habits – base the balance of time and attention that you pay to the areas of governance, operations and behaviours on an analysis of the needs of the situation and not just on you own leadership preferences.
- You will be a role model for your own staff – what you personally pay attention to in the management of a collaboration will set the tone for the whole relationship.
- Whilst transactional relationships can rely a lot on good governance and symbiotic ones on supportive behaviours, in neither case can you let your focus on the other legs of the stool drop to zero.
- Watch the interactions between governance, operations and behaviours, and look out for unintended consequences. Your governance actions will affect the behaviours of your partners – and setting the wrong expectations for the way people behave can break the most well-designed process.

• Be careful about how you frame or name a relationship to your staff – it sets powerful expectations that you've then got to live by. So if you choose to christen it 'A partnership of equals' you must be prepared to act and be judged by all that that implies – otherwise cynicism and the roots of failure will start to grow.

4

MEASURING COLLABORATION

You get what you measure

Ever since Frederick Taylor published his *Principles of Scientific Management* in 1911, measurement in business has proved its value. Taylor's time and motion studies focused on getting the most out of individual activities – 'the science of shovelling', for example, determined the optimal shovel-load a worker could lift. The answer – 21 pounds – delivered a three- to four-fold increase in productivity.[1]

Today scientific management has morphed into the strongly held conviction that you get what you measure. Every organization, from the police force to Wal-Mart, employs a range of measures to run its business. We no longer just measure productivity, but also customer satisfaction, process improvement, people development and many more. And the pressure to deliver value, either to shareholders or to the public, has given rise to a slew of measurement techniques, from service level agreements to the balanced scorecard. All of these have duly made their way into partnership contracts and other collaboration agreements.

The adoption of formal measurement can vary widely. A study by Accenture found that only half of business alliances were using formal performance measures.[2] In the world of public–private partnerships, however, the picture is very different. Intense public scrutiny means the output of every project is closely examined – not just by the organizations in question, but by a confusing range of elected and appointed bodies. In the UK for example, public–private partnerships are regularly examined by the National Audit Office, the Public Accounts Committee, the Treasury and of course the national press too. In particular, a massive industry of measurement has grown around the use of Private Finance Initiative projects, PFIs, to build roads and hospitals, because politicians have needed to prove that outsourcing to the private sector can provide both good service and value for money.

The problem for many leaders is that lots of the measures employed for the purpose of political and public scrutiny don't actually evaluate how well a partnership or other collaborative relationship is delivering the long-term objectives of the deal. What's more, they rarely show leaders how to improve the way they run things over the life of the arrangement. In the Accenture study, only 20 per cent of executives thought that the performance measures they used were reliable predictors of success.[3]

The rear-view mirror only looks one way

Traditional measurement is all about delivery. It relies on Key Performance Indicators (KPIs) or other metrics to determine outputs and quantify improvement or decline – anything from 'average revenue per customer' to 'number of potholes mended per week'. These indicators are easy to read and easy to specify, so they're well loved by accountants and solicitors. Because of this, they get written into 'output-specified contracts', and used to incentivize and punish alike. Unfortunately, while they give an accurate picture of the past, they're not much help in predicting the future.

Delivery measures tend to come in droves. Often there are hundreds of KPIs in each contract. Gathering the data and checking it all becomes a huge task in itself – and individuals and organizations soon learn to play the game of manipulating and maximizing KPIs even at the expense of other important (but non-measured) things. Meanwhile, if the indicators get too complex, there's a danger that people lose sight of why something is being measured, and end up working against the objectives that inspired the KPIs in the first place.

On the other hand sometimes the measures aren't there at all. Although every-one has an impression of what they should be, the parties involved haven't agreed them. This is often particularly true of internal partnerships such as shared service arrangements. We've worked with a number of HR and IT business partners who say that although they have been given their own personal objectives and targets by their own line management, they don't have a clear set of joint measures of success for the relationship they are meant to be managing with their internal clients. And without this, the whole shared service relationship is built on shaky foundations.

But even when they exist, output-based targets and measures can only ever show half of the picture. Imagine building an extension to your house using an architect and a construction firm, and relying only on final output measures. Your indicators would probably include the extension being built to budget and deliv-ered on time, meeting building regulations, and having heating, lighting and plumbing systems that work properly. Each week you could check on progress against these measures. But with the best will in the world, they wouldn't in them-selves prevent the usual litany of disasters: budget overruns, late delivery, and quite possibly an extension that doesn't match what you had in mind at the outset. The measures are important, but they're not all that you need. At worst, all they do is give you the basis for a row with your builder. Ensuring the work gets done to time, budget and quality is about performance management not just performance measurement. And effective performance management of any collaboration depends on having the right foundations of governance, operations and behaviours that form the three legs of the stool we discussed in the previous chapter.

Bulldozing with detail

Contracts that tried to specify every detail of future performance were a feature of early public–private construction partnerships. The theory was that all the risk should be transferred to the private sector, but in actual fact, there was little trust in this happening. The consequence was that public sector officials (and lawyers) tried to control the risk by specifying from the start in incredible detail exactly what had to be delivered. Of course, this approach didn't take into account the fact that client needs would change over time. It also meant that by legally enforcing contractors to do exactly what they were told in the contract it took away any incentive for them to seek out new and innovative lower cost solutions as the work progressed.

Over-specification is still an unfortunate characteristic of many public–private partnerships. To take one example, the *NHS Healthcare Cleaning Manual* runs to 215 pages, including appendices.[4] Written for hospital staff and managers, it covers important specialist tasks like decontaminating fluid spills. At the same time it sets out in detail how to dust, polish, mop and scrub floors ('when the mop is completely dirty, submerge into the second bucket (water) and wring'). You can see what's driving the minute attention to detail, and on one hand it's reassuring to know that every eventuality is covered. On the other hand, too much specification can be counterproductive, evening out the mundane and the extraordinary, and driving all intelligence and care out of the process. And no amount of detail is a substitute for pride, commitment or experience.

In the end, over-specification is simply dehumanizing. In Chapter 3 we saw how making roles crystal clear but leaving tasks relatively open fostered teamworking, fast responses and creativity. Clearly there are limits to how open-ended leaders can make a task, especially where public health and safety are concerned. But by transactionalizing the relationship with contract cleaners, the NHS has ensured that pride in a job well done doesn't enter into the equation.

A measuring stick to beat you with

Measurement can also be used to bludgeon partners and suppliers into submission. A multinational drinks company, for example, wanted to reduce the number of global suppliers for its bottles and at the same time radically reduce the cost of this key component. They used their knowledge of the comparative costs of different suppliers and of the glass industry to measure what they believed the cheapest cost of a bottle should be, and then set this as a target price. Because of their size, they had enough power to force suppliers to accept this deal, and for a while everyone was content. The drinks company reduced its costs, and a few global glass manufacturers had some large (if not very profitable) contracts. But as the market changed and the demand for new bottle shapes and sizes grew, the glass manufacturers couldn't afford the R&D and re-tooling costs to change their production lines. The tight measurement regime had all but bankrupted the supply base. All the drinks company's focus had been on a single goal – to secure the lowest cost of supply. They had taken their eye off the real purpose of their relationship with bottling suppliers – building the right capability to meet future needs.

In this case no one had foreseen the consequences of a tight measurement regime. But occasionally leaders have rather more Machiavellian aims. We once worked with a leader in a dysfunctional partnership who used measurement as a device to catch people out. On top of the measures already specified in the contract (and there were many of them), he invented a whole battery of his own, most involving an extra stage of approval – by him.

In this aggressive climate, someone would always be under-performing. The leader then used this evidence to beat up his suppliers. Not surprisingly, the other parties quickly stopped raising problems or highlighting awkward performance data. Issues were covered up, performance deteriorated, and finally it became impossible to address the situation collaboratively. The lawyers were called in.

Measuring with a light touch

Overloading the contract with detailed demands can wreck a relationship. So how do you measure effectively without them? The oil industry offers some interesting lessons.

Leaders in the oil industry tend to have highly honed collaboration skills. Searching for oil is a joint venture because it's hugely expensive and involves many vested interests – governments, landowners and environmentalists to name but a few. In addition it's highly uncertain. Only one in 12 wells will ever lead to commercial success. Failure is part of the process of discovery.

With all the players in the industry well used to working in partnership, contracts cover the basics in a fairly standard way. But given that oil exploration is inherently risky, there's no place for excessive caution (except on safety issues). Rather than imposing penalties for minor failures in performance, then, these contracts emphasize the mechanisms to govern, and spell out how to deal with disputes. And when a partnership fails to find oil, it learns from that for the next time.

As one very experienced CEO of an oil exploration company put it to us: 'There are only two sections I really look at in any new multi-party contract – what happens if things go incredibly well, how do we share out the unexpected profits – and what happens if things go terribly wrong, who can walk away and at what cost, and who is in it for the long term?'

Go easy on the penalties

Traditional measurement in partnerships or other collaborative relationships not only specifies multiple output measures, but attaches incentives and penalties to those measures in the contract. The problem is that the contract ossifies a particular moment. Yet circumstances change. If the contract doesn't allow for this, it can end up incentivizing or penalizing entirely the wrong things.

Penalizing a partner when they've missed a deadline has some attractions, but if it doesn't get to the cause of why the deadline was missed or how each partner contributed to the problem, it merely takes money out of the system. And throwing penalties at your partners can also start a tit-for-tat round of claim and counter-claim where no one benefits.

There are other ways to run a relationship with carrots as well as sticks to encourage improvements in performance. For example, one local authority has set up a joint investment fund for its partnership with private contractors, so that whenever the partnership overachieves a percentage of the savings are paid into the fund and then when a target is missed the fund can be used to help finance performance improvement actions to get it right next time. And in the construction phase of Terminal 5 at Heathrow, BAA set up around 20 multi-contractor project teams as 'virtual companies'. While BAA held overall responsibility for the risk of the construction programme, each team had a small joint contingency fund that they could draw on. If it wasn't spent it didn't just disappear but became available to another team. And as many of the same contractors were involved in multiple teams they had an incentive to hold back on contingency spending in one area to make it available to a project team where they knew there was a greater need.[5]

Punishing a partner for failing to deliver is not the best guarantee of future results. Instead, good measurement systems should draw clear boundaries of what is and what is not acceptable, and help all parties improve performance over time. Generosity has its own rewards.

A measurement compass – with eight directions

Recognizing that traditional output measures are easy but flawed is the first step. The next step is to understand why you want to measure in the first place. Are you doing it because you don't trust your business partner? (If so, think carefully about why you are entering into a relationship with them!) Are you trying to improve your partner's performance, or simply confirm a prejudice? Are you doing it because the contract or an external body tells you to?

Let's assume the leader's reasons for measurement are good ones: you're trying to understand how the partnership performs and to predict future needs or problems, you want to look at individual and collective performance, hard facts as well as people's feelings and perceptions. To do all that means looking in several directions at once. In fact we think there are eight directions that a leader managing a complex relationship needs to be looking in – and we've laid them out as on a compass in Figure 4.1.

The eight directions that the measurements of a collaborative relationship need to take account of are:

- **Looking forward as well as looking backwards** As well as asking whether the relationship hit its performance targets and milestones for last month, you need to ask whether you have targets agreed for next year, budgets in place and

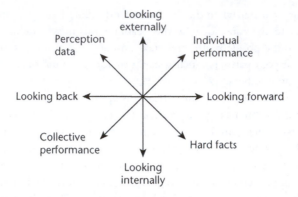

FIGURE 4.1 A measurement compass

people recruited. This could also be described as measuring contribution versus measuring results.

- **Measures of collective as well as individual performance** Measures for each partner's performance are important – for example, how long it takes one partner to close a helpdesk query. But you also need to measure collective outputs such as the overall customer satisfaction level for the whole IT service.
- **External measures as well as internal ones** Partnerships need to look externally for benchmark measures, and in many cases will have them imposed upon them – for example, government-specified best value targets. However the partnership should also jointly agree a few of its own internal KPIs – the things that the team are really motivated to achieve and will stand as symbols of success of their joint endeavour.
- **Perception data as well as hard facts** Obviously you need numerical data on key areas in order to be able to analyse how well the relationship is going. But you should also collect opinion data on the state of the relationship at frequent and regular intervals (and it can often tell a different story).

A good measurement suite covers all eight of these elements, with appropriate weight being given to each one. That way you have delivery measures *and* diagnostic measures, so you can assess how you've done so far and how you're likely to fare in the future.

Good measurement gives a relationship an early indication of problems to come. It tells all parties where to focus their attention for the future benefit of all. It discourages self-interested behaviour, and encourages collaboration. And it can be interpreted consistently by all parties – in other words, it's undeniable.

But in our experience, measures enshrined in a formal partnership contract rarely meet all the good measurement criteria listed above. They're often drawn up without reference to the people responsible for implementing the partnership, and certainly before there's any experience of operating it.

Even when leaders use the eight sides of measurement, they're not always even-handed about it. Biases creep in, because leaders have natural preferences – they're hard facts people, or benchmark enthusiasts, or sticklers for lagging KPIs. In addition, their previous experience will push them towards one type of measure or another. It's important to be aware of this possible bias and to do your utmost to give sufficient attention to each of these eight directions.

What and how to measure

The eight measures above address the *type* of measurement needed in any relationship: forwards and backwards; the whole as well as the parts; external as well as internal; and perception as well as hard facts. But *what* are we actually measuring, and *how*?

First, the output measures. A 2005 KPMG study suggests that in business alliances, financial measures tend to dominate.[6] Though important in measuring short-term results, they are clearly far too narrow. There's a lot to be said for following the classic balanced scorecard model, using indicators of customer satisfaction, financial performance, process improvement and people development.[7]

Remember, though, that output measures look backwards, and that you also need forward-looking indicators. These are harder to come by, and depend on perceptions as well as hard fact. Most of this data will need to be gathered through surveys. In fact successful collaborative leaders are often big users of surveys, regularly polling staff, customers and other stakeholders in order to drive their decision making.

Getting some regular data into the senior level discussions about the health of the relationship is vital – but often ignored. A 2012 paper by Katzenbach and Cross on the role of top teams cites the fact that 'as much as 90% of the information that most senior executives receive comes through their informal networks and not from formal reports'.[8] And of course these informal networks rarely cross organizational boundaries so the anecdotal information executives receive through these networks usually only come from one party with all the risks of bias that that brings.

The secret of a good partnership survey is to have a portion of standard data, agreed by all partners, which not only turns up incipient problems early but accumulates over time to reveal trends. The remainder of the survey then focuses on analysing a set of risks specific to its time or place. It also helps if surveys are short, easy to interpret and contain both quantitative and qualitative data.

Surveys should not be treated as a soft option. There's no point in sending out 'happy sheets' asking questions like 'how good is communication across the partnership?' and offering tick boxes from A to E. To be useful, they need to be evidence-driven, and tightly focused on measuring the effectiveness of the relationship – asking questions like 'Is it clear where and when key decisions are taken and who is involved in the process?' They also provide a useful tool for measuring diverging perspectives of the relationship – if one side thinks things are fine and the other sees a host of problems, something is clearly going badly wrong with communications at the very least.

Measure the three legs of the stool – governance, operations and behaviours

To collect good perception data, we recommend surveying each leg of the three-legged stool described in Chapter 3 – governance, operations and behaviours. Taken together the three areas of measurement under each leg of the stool give nine tests for the health of a relationship.

Governance	*Operations*	*Behaviours*
• Clarity of purpose • Quality of decision making • Clarity of accountabilities	• Aligned systems and processes • Effective communications • Capability improvement	• Role modelling • Cross-cultural awareness • Joint problem solving

Nine tests of the health of a collaborative relationship

1. Clarity of purpose. Does each party believe they are working to aligned goals and is the aim of the partnership clear to all?
2. Quality of decision making. Are the decision-making processes clear to all and are the right people involved?
3. Clarity of accountabilities. Does everyone understand who is accountable for what?
4. Alignment of systems and processes. Is the performance data transparent – available to all and supported by clear and consistent incentives?
5. Effective communications. Are meetings and communications focused on the right issues and are all parties kept informed in a timely manner?
6. Capability improvement. Are the right skills deployed in the right places and at the right time across the relationship and are all parties investing to develop future capability?
7. Role modelling. Do leaders at all levels walk the talk and are they seen to work effectively together for the good of the joint enterprise?
8. Cross-cultural awareness. Do people understand the differences in organizational culture and are they willing to adapt their ways of working to suit others?
9. Joint problem solving. Do people work together to solve performance problems and to come to the best decisions for the benefit of all?

We've used this measuring system many times over the years on different types of collaborative relationship, and the greatest value comes in being able to track changes in perception over time as the relationship develops.

In the following sections, we examine the symptoms you'll see in each area if things are going wrong, and offer a sample of specific questions or evidence statements that can be used to create a questionnaire to survey each area. Each of the areas can be expanded further, but it's valuable to keep the questions you chose constant over time so that you can determine trends. Regularly polling staff on each area of governance, operations and behaviours gives a mass of hard evidence on the health of the relationship – and reliable indicators of future performance.

In the sections that follow we have provided a set of sample questions that could be used in a survey across a partnership, joint venture, or other multi-party collaborative relationship. In reality the leader would need to tailor the language of the questions to suit their situation but for consistency throughout these examples we have used the word partnership to describe the relationship.

Governance: how clear is your purpose?

Measuring clarity of purpose starts with having an agreed document for the relationship that sets out individual and joint objectives. Everyone needs to know what success looks like – and if it changes for one party (the besetting sin of government contracts), all sides have to agree on the changes fast.

When clarity of purpose is lacking, competition heats up between the parties, especially over money or resources. If one side isn't sure what their partner is after, the natural reaction is to start protecting their own turf – with disastrous consequences for collaboration.

In addition, an unclear purpose means that decision making is likely to be confused and decisions may conflict. People lack confidence and start to dither over what to do next because priorities are not evident. If it gets too bad, it can pose a serious threat to the continuation of the relationship. Measuring clarity of purpose is especially important at the start of a new relationship when different parties may make different assumptions about what they are each working towards. It's also vital to track this measure when the purpose changes. We've noticed that in partnerships with central government departments, civil servants who work closely with government ministers tend to take changes in policy or direction in their stride, seeing it as part of the political cycle. But their partners are often shocked by these rapid changes in direction – particularly if they are from a third sector organization with an unswerving sense of mission. Measuring these tensions is only a first step in what can be a long road to resolving them – but it's a vital one.

Clarity of purpose: sample statements for a survey

- The aim of the partnership is understood and agreed by all parties.
- My own organization can achieve its objectives without bringing us into conflict with our partners.
- I believe that all the partners are heading in the same direction.
- Each partner understands how they contribute to the overall aim of the partnership.
- The collective and individual goals of partnership for the year are well documented and understood.
- There is a single set of agreed priorities for the partnership.
- The business benefits as defined in the contract are included in each partner's business plan.

Governance: how good is decision making?

Measuring the quality of decision making covers all the decision-making processes, from the mundane (do meetings have agendas?) to the extraordinary (are the right escalation procedures in place to deal with sensitive problems?). Members of the partnership need to understand the points of interdependence in the relationship in order to know what decisions they can take separately and what needs to be agreed jointly. They also need to know when to take things upwards to the Board.

If the processes aren't right, people don't feel empowered or engaged. There's likely to be frustration and confusion. And a particularly bad sign is when splinter groups or cabals begin to form.

Internal partnerships such as shared service IT or HR functions often have particularly low scores in this decision-making area. Before the shared service was set up, people across the business knew more or less how decisions were made and how to influence them – but with lots of new business partners and steering groups, no one is sure how and where key decisions are taken. Tracking scores in this area can often give useful early warning signs of an internal partnership that is heading for trouble.

Decision making: sample statements for a survey

- I know how to influence decisions taken by my partner regarding the operation of the partnership.
- It is clear where and when key decisions are taken and who is involved in the process.
- Escalation processes are clearly defined when partners cannot come to an agreement.

- The partnership has a governance process with clear terms of reference that enables effective decision making.
- The partnership has effective mechanisms to address tactical, operational and strategic decision making.
- Decisions are made in a timely fashion.
- Decisions appear never to be reversed and don't have to be revisited regularly.
- Decision-making meetings focus on the right things to meet the aims of the partnership.
- Decisions made by the partnership take into account the needs of all stakeholders.

Governance: how clear are accountabilities?

Teams work more creatively as well as more efficiently if their roles are well defined. In partnerships or other collaborative business relationships, there's an extra layer of complication: all staff also need to understand where their personal responsibility ends and where joint accountability begins.

When accountabilities aren't clear, you see duplication of effort, role conflicts and tasks falling between gaps. All too often this can turn into turf wars. People lack confidence in each other's abilities, and inefficiencies develop within the relationship as people try to do each other's jobs.

Measurement in this area can be particularly useful in industries like construction, and in 'design, build and operate' partnerships, where the many handovers from initial design to final delivery make it easy for people to duplicate some of the role of the next person in line. Tracking this area of measurement helps to involve the right people at the right time in the design and construction process.

Accountabilities: sample statements for a survey

- There is little duplication of effort between the partners.
- Partnership accountabilities are incorporated into my role specifications.
- There are no arguments about who does what across the partnership.
- Joint accountabilities are specified and documented in the partnership.
- Accountabilities for financial management and operational delivery are clear and well integrated.
- I know who to go to when I need to get things done.
- Each partner is clear about what information needs to be reported to other parties and when.
- There is little or no confusion about authority levels across the partnership.
- Individuals take responsibility for delivering their accountabilities for the benefit of the whole partnership.

Operations: are your systems and processes well aligned?

The measurement of how well a partnership's systems and processes fit together should cover not only the way data is entered but also business planning and aspects of HR such as rewards and incentives.

When there's no alignment of systems and processes, frustration builds over multiple bureaucratic tasks and arguments develop over the accuracy of data. In the end people stop making the effort and start doing their own thing. Meanwhile, when HR processes are out of sync, there's scope for frustration and resentment over differing pay scales and benefits. And if staff from one firm are incentivized to do something for the partnership, yet their opposite numbers only incur costs for doing it, the relationship can rapidly reach stalemate.

Problems at the interfaces between systems are one of the most commonly cited causes of frustration in the first few months of a new business relationship. Tracking how people see the alignment of systems and processes and whether or not this improves over time is one good measure of the success of the transition phase of a newly contracted partnership.

Aligned systems and processes: sample statements for a survey

- There is one common set of measures used by all partners to measure performance of the partnership.
- A joint planning process ensures that the business plans of each partner fit together.
- The escalation process is clearly defined if conflict occurs between partners.
- All partners have access to the same set of data on the performance of the partnership.
- The rewards and incentives for delivery are transparent to all partners.
- Staff are co-located with their partners where this is possible and desirable.
- Common standards have been defined across the partnership where consistency of operation is desirable.
- There is no duplication or re-keying of data at the interface between organizations.

Operations: how effectively do you communicate?

If communications aren't good enough within any relationship, it's not just time that's wasted – trust can be destroyed. People feel they don't belong to the joint enterprise and start thinking 'them' rather than 'us'. They invent conspiracy theories about what the other side is up to. And because of the lack of trust and openness, they make up their own stories about what's happening in the relationship as a whole.

In this climate, people don't want to help their partners out. If they know the other side is doing something wrong, they'll leave them to it and then complain after the fact. The consequences for the relationship are costly in both time and goodwill.

It's far better to over-communicate than under-communicate with your partners — but the tone matters too. We've seen far too many Partnership Newsletters with titles like 'Integrate' or 'Working Together', when the truth is anything but. That's why it's important to track people's perception of the honesty of communication as well as its timeliness.

Communications: sample statements for a survey

- The partners keep each other well informed about progress.
- The information that I receive about the performance of the partnership is believable and sufficient for my needs.
- The partnership has one communication management plan that delivers consistent messages to all parties.
- I am well informed about the many issues that face the partnership.
- I know who is responsible for what across the partnership.
- The right people are consulted and involved in decisions.
- Good and bad news is shared in a timely fashion across the partnership.
- Partnership performance meetings are effective and productive.
- I am informed about all decisions that affect me.
- Communication with the stakeholders of the partnership is proactive and effective.

Operations: are you getting the right skills in the right place and improving your overall capabilities?

Checking that a collaborative relationship has the necessary capacity and capability for the future is a complicated task. Many formal business partnerships last longer than the average management appointment, so joint succession planning and long-term capability development across all the parties involved becomes a necessity.

When it isn't working properly, there is a high turnover of staff. Because the partnership can't get the right skills in the right place internally, it ends up buying more external expertise or consultancy. The partnership doesn't grow or develop. And the same mistakes keep on happening again and again.

You know it's going badly wrong when you hear one side saying 'they don't know what's going to hit them in January'. When people stop thinking jointly, they forget that a lack of capacity or capability on one side will hurt the other. They don't concentrate on how to sort out the problem together, focusing instead on the penalties that will be incurred when one side fails to deliver. And in the long term, that helps no one.

Joint development programmes and joint skills audits are a way of seeing where the capability gaps are and what can best be done to plug them.

Capabilities: sample statements for a survey

- We have the right skills in place to manage our involvement in the partnership.
- Our partners have the right skills in place to manage their involvement in the partnership.
- There is an on-going effort by all partners to improve skills by following through on improvement actions.
- I rarely (or never) observe individuals working beyond their ability and experience.
- I believe that the partnership has access to the capability it needs to deliver.
- There is a process in place to identify and invest in the skills required by the partnership.
- The partnership has one common knowledge base of skills and experience.
- Joint development programmes exist across the partnership.
- A joint performance management process is used by all parties across the partnership.
- There are regular reviews of partnership performance and processes.

Behaviours: how good a role model are you?

Leaders of collaborative relationships need to be highly aware of how they're behaving towards their partners, because their behaviour will almost inevitably be echoed throughout their own organizations. If they have arguments with their opposite numbers, this swiftly permeates all levels, with silo behaviour being justified by the leaders' lack of collaboration. Self-interest grows rapidly, and people end up looking after their own patch. In the end, this denies the reality of the relationship.

Of course, the same applies the other way around for positive leadership role models. The UK rail industry is rarely held up as a good example of partnering behaviour – Network Rail, its private sector maintenance partners and the competing privatized train operating companies (TOCs) are often seen to be trading insults in the press. However, when Virgin Rail boss Richard Branson spoke up after the Greyrigg train derailment in 2007 in which one passenger died, he was widely praised within the industry for not seeking to blame any one party, and for setting the tone for an investigation where everyone was to work together to learn the lessons from the incident.

Role modelling: sample statements for a survey

- The leaders in my organization can share control and work for the benefit of the whole partnership.
- The leaders of the partnership speak with one voice.
- The leader of each party in the partnership encourages collaborative behaviour in their staff.
- The leaders challenge each other constructively to ensure that they come to the best outcomes for the partnership.
- The leaders balance the demands of their partnership role effectively with their internal role.
- The leaders are visible across the partnership.
- The leaders demonstrate empathy in their dealing with colleagues from other sides of the partnership.
- The leaders act as role models, meeting the behaviour standards that they set for their staff.
- Leaders put the needs of their own organization first when times get tough.
- Leaders build commitment to the partnership in their own organization.

Behaviours: how aware are you of the cross-cultural differences and how to get value from them?

Cross-cultural awareness in a complex multi-party business relationship is a complex area, and is covered more fully in Chapter 5. However the symptoms are easy to spot: embarrassing misconceptions about what a partner thinks or wants, and a resulting bad atmosphere. If people don't know what makes their partner tick, they tend to assume the worst. Certainly they hang back from communicating, and make more use of the contract to manage the interfaces.

Measuring how well each party understands the other's culture and ways of working is another good leading indicator of how close partners are becoming and when to take another step towards more joined-up working.

When one company has a particularly strong culture, it's important not to overlook the impact this could have on its partners. When Disney merged with Pixar, the leaders knew they needed to keep the cultures distinct. Pixar managers were not sent to work shifts at Walt Disney World in Florida as other Disney managers are expected to do, and Pixar switchboard operators weren't asked to end telephone calls with the words 'Have a magical day'. The key is to measure your understanding of your partners' culture, not the speed of your absorption into it.

Cross-cultural difference: sample statements for a survey

- We adapt our way of working to accommodate the needs of the other partners.
- I am aware that other partners try to accommodate how my organization operates.
- I understand the positive and negative impact of my organization's culture on other partners.
- Partnership behaviours are clearly documented and agreed by the leadership.
- Partnership behaviours are communicated regularly to all staff.
- I recognize and respect the different pressures on each of the different organizations involved in the partnership.
- The partnership invests in activities to encourage an understanding of the cultures of each of the partners.
- I observe partners trying to help each other to succeed.
- Partners are aware of the pressures on each other and try to give a hand.

Behaviours: how good is your joint problem-solving?

Do you manage to solve problems jointly or do you each take to the hills – separately – whenever a challenge surfaces? Measuring this will give you a lot of information about the health of the relationship. If parties are desperately trying to sort things out on their own, it's a sure-fire sign of impending trouble – and often on a grand scale.

When joint problem-solving isn't working, problems are left to fester and grow, and conflict is buried. A blame culture rapidly develops, and the different sides become trigger-happy – all too keen to use the contract to punish their opposite numbers.

The measures here are simple but easy to overlook. They're the sort of things that prompt unease – they provide a gut feeling that things aren't right. However, they should also prompt an intervention and the earlier the better.

Joint problem-solving: sample statements for a survey

- Staff from across the partnership regularly come together to solve problems.
- My organization has demonstrated that it has been open to new ideas proposed by other partners.
- There is evidence of effective listening in partnership meetings.
- The conflict resolution process defined by the partnership is used effectively by all partners.
- The partnership can come to consensus about the best way forward when it experiences a serious problem.

- The partnership actively looks for best practice when defining the way it achieves its objectives.
- The partnership actively encourages all partners to adopt best practice where appropriate.
- There are high levels of constructive challenge across the partnership.
- There is evidence of good 'chemistry' among partners when they are required to solve problems together.

Know when to escalate a problem

Using the measurement compass with its eight directions and the types of relationship survey described in this chapter will generate a lot of useful data – much of it leading indicators of future problems in a relationship. The task of the collaborative leader is to understand what this data is really saying and when to escalate an issue. Sometimes this is easy – the trend in the data of a growing problem in a particular area of governance, operations or behaviours can be obvious to spot – but sometimes the absence of an expected warning sign can be an important escalation signal too.

In 2010, Network Rail announced an independent review of its safety culture to be carried out by an independent safety watchdog. The trigger for this review was interesting – it came about because there appeared to be *too few* minor injuries (slips, trips and falls) being reported by Network Rail's sub-contractors. The trade union Unite (amongst others) noticed this and pressed for an escalation of the process to find out what was going on. The number of these so called RIDDOR injuries (defined by the Reporting of Injuries, Diseases and Dangerous Occurrences Regulations) is an important leading indicator of the safety performance of an organization. Low and decreasing numbers of minor injuries might have appeared a good sign of the way Network Rail was working with its sub-contractors but if these were being under-reported in some way the data could just be hiding sources of greater risk in the future.

The watchdog's report when published in January 2011 found that over five years some 500 to 600 RIDDOR incidents were not reported by Network Rail and its sub-contractors. And amongst a number of reasons, they found that this had occurred because of 'the change in both the culture of Network Rail and its relationship with its contractors since 2005. These changes are a result of the real and perceived pressure and, in some cases, fear felt by Network Rail staff and contractors if they report accidents or incidents.'[9]

Now although this negative change in culture may have been going on gradually for many years, we actually see this as a positive story of a well-designed and policed measurement. The complex multi-party system that runs the UK's railways had the right measurements and escalation processes in place, this meant that any suspicious trend in the data (in this case some unusually low accident numbers) was escalated and acted on before anything more serious occurred.

Sometimes the escalation processes don't work in such a timely manner. In 2006, a scandal erupted in the Home Office. Some foreign national prisoners were being freed at the end of their sentences without being considered for deportation. Since 1999, over 1,000 foreign prisoners had been released into the UK. Now this wasn't a secret – many people in the Prison Service, the Home Office and the National Audit Office had known about it for all that time. The issue wasn't that it had never been escalated sufficiently in order for the scale of the risk to be evaluated and dealt with. The report of the House of Commons Home Affairs select committee makes it clear that warnings were ignored.[10]

Home Secretary Charles Clarke was forced to admit that the Department had taken its 'eye off the ball'. A rapid growth in the number of foreign prisoners had led to the collapse of the monitoring process. 'The arrangements for identifying them and considering removal from the UK have not kept pace with that growth', Clarke admitted in his statement.

The National Audit Office had warned ministers nearly a year before that preparations for prisoners' removal from the UK should start much earlier, and Clarke promised that deportation procedures would now begin 12 months before a prisoner was to be released. However, his changes came too late; Clarke was eventually fired from his post and returned to the back benches.

Good measurement systems should be able to stop small problems from turning into big ones. Escalation procedures need to be specified at the start of any business relationship, but not to such an extent that they become unwieldy or unresponsive. They're about getting information to the decision makers when it matters and letting them act on it – not gathering data for a management bureaucracy. To make sure this works effectively, collaborative leaders need to be able to review the trigger points and the processes specified in their procedures in the light of practical operations.

But good escalation procedures are worth their weight in gold. Rather than over-specifying every detail in a contract, collaborative leaders would do well to rely on simple rules on escalating problems. The ability to nip impending trouble in the bud is considerably more valuable than tit-for-tat point scoring.

Chapter summary

You don't drive a car staring intently in the rear-view mirror – so why do we think we can drive a partnership like that?

Measurement systems in partnerships and other collaborative relationships are always a contentious issue. Whilst there is a great desire to keep a close eye on what a partner is doing, measurement systems that have focused solely on outputs looking back at the performance in the last period haven't stopped many high-profile collaboration failures.

Overburdened with petty details they have often been used as a stick to beat a partner with rather than as a tool to build understanding and to identify methods to improve future performance. Leaders need to learn lessons from these past mistakes and design measurement systems which contain more leading indicators of the future health of a relationship as well as key items of delivery.

By building a scorecard of measures in the areas of governance, operations and behaviours, leaders across a collaborative relationship can spot areas of difficulty and escalate them for resolution before they cause real damage. In this chapter we identify nine key indicators of future performance under these three headings and give examples of questions that can be used to construct a survey tool to periodically test the health of a relationship.

A system of measurement shouldn't be a burden on a relationship – measurement shouldn't create problems between partners, it should help you solve them.

Lessons for leaders

- Be clear about why you are setting up a measurement system for a collaborative relationship and what impact you want it to have.
- Well-designed measurement systems can build trust by giving leaders of all parties early warning signs of potential problems and enabling them to raise issues and take action. Do your measurement systems build or damage trust?
- As a collaborative leader be sure to look forwards as well as backwards, at perception data as well as hard facts, internally at causes as well as externally at outputs, and at collective as well as individual performance.
- Raise anomalies in performance data early with your partners. And remember collaboration data that looks suspiciously good can be as telling as data that appears bad.
- You are a powerful role model – the performance data that you are seen to pay most attention to and the way you react to it will have the most impact on your own people and their attitude to your partners.
- Joint problem-solving. Do people work together to solve performance problems and to come to the best decisions for the benefit of all?

5

ANALYSING DIFFERENT ORGANIZATIONAL CULTURES

They just don't understand us

When the Brazilian iron ore company Vale won the take-over battle to buy the International Nickel Company (INCO) in Canada for $19bn in 2006, it created what was then the world's second largest mining company. It seemed a great coup for the formerly state-owned Vale and evidence of the power of emerging BRIC economies. But the acquisition was only the start of many years of strikes and bitter wrangling that are a case study of the difficulties of leading and driving change across different organizational and national cultures.

Cries of 'They just don't understand us' are the commonest complaint in any business relationship. And often this is true, at the start of a relationship new partners don't understand each other. Differences, big or small, if left unaddressed can easily rub your partner up the wrong way. The challenge for a collaborative leader is to help build the understanding of different cultures over time and to generate value from the different perspectives that result.

In the case of Vale and INCO the differences were many and various and the cultural divide was deep. Management in INCO had a tradition of being 'democratic in nature and very consensus driven' and this was well aligned to a culture within Canadian industry of having consensus-based relationships between government, employers and unions.[1] Indeed, in Newfoundland where some of the new Vale Inco operations were based there was a long history of tri-partite councils of business leaders, local government and union officials. These groups met to share information, manage new infrastructure investment and to solve problems in a collaborative manner. This contrasted with the management style at Vale which was described by their new Canadian employees as a 'just do as you are told' culture – a style in which 'the concept of stakeholders does not exist in its strategic decision making. What Vale choses to do, Vale does. There is no need for discussion.'[2]

Cultural polarization

Of course it's not unusual at the start of a new relationship for each side to have rather stereotyped and polarized views of each other. The task for leaders is to build understanding and to bring parties together in ways that create value and share lessons. But at Vale Inco the situation went from bad to worse. In the years following the acquisition 3,400 workers at its Sudbury site went on strike for over 12 months at a cost to the local economy of an estimated $20m per month and this strike was followed by an even longer 18-month dispute at the Voisey Bay Nickel mine. The bitterness of the dispute was illustrated by union comments such as 'the Brazilian owners want to instil a foreign brand of subservient labour relations; run roughshod of workers' rights and cut pay…', which got a reply from Tito Martins, the Vale CEO, that the union was 'relying on a global campaign of misinformation, racism, intolerance, and xenophobia'.[3] As one local manager put it at the time 'they are both yelling at each other so loudly they are now deaf to each other's position'.

Cultural mismatches cause big problems and their impact can be felt for years if not decades. So finding ways of describing organizational culture and taking some of the stereotypes and the emotional baggage out of the debate is an important collaborative leadership activity. And it's not just perceptions of national culture at the root of these issues. The debate about public–private partnerships often starts from polarized impressions of the cultural differences between a tough, profit-driven private sector and a bureaucratic rule-bound public sector. One look at the press reporting of healthcare reform in the UK highlights the cultural difficulties the NHS faces in working with profit-making enterprises. Meanwhile in the US, a guidebook for public–private partnerships published by the Department of Transportation in 2007 warns that cultural differences between public and private agencies are one of the major impediments to successful implementation.[4]

It might be tempting to think that you can isolate yourself from all this difficulty by just finding people to work with who think and act like you – indeed later in the chapter we'll talk about how the growth in internet-based communities and special interest groups could be seen as a response to this and a way of finding like-minded individuals to work with. But in leadership terms these sorts of communities are the exception. Working across cultural difference is an inevitable reality in most leaders' lives today. If all the parties in a new relationship can start by being really clear about why they are each going into it, and what they want to gain from working with the others involved, you stand a much better chance of working positively with cultural differences and using them as a means of achieving your aims rather than just being frustrated by them.

Getting to grips with organizational culture

Our partnership survey found that understanding and accepting each other's culture was rated a critical success factor by directors of business partnerships (second only to having a common purpose).[5] In addition, 85 per cent of survey respondents said that cultural fit was a significant criterion in selecting a partner organization.

However, when respondents were asked how they analysed potential partners to see if there was a good alignment of cultures, the techniques they used appeared fairly haphazard. In fact most leaders say they assess culture mainly on 'personal chemistry'. By this they often mean a gut-feeling for something they cannot really describe or articulate to their staff. And while this is undoubtedly important, it doesn't get to the heart of understanding culture or being able to use that understanding systematically to make a new collaborative relationship work.

In fact, organizational culture is notoriously difficult to pin down. We need a way of describing in detail what makes the culture of a Brazilian formerly state-owned mining company so different from that of a Canadian Nickel company. Or just what makes Apple's culture so different from Microsoft's, and why NHS managers are so wary of working with a private healthcare provider. The range of different organizational cultures is clearly vast but in simple terms it all comes down to people and the assumptions they make about how to communicate, take decisions and get things done. And this means there are many similarities and analogies that can be drawn with the well-researched field of personality type and personal working style preferences based on psychometrics like the Myers-Briggs Type Indicator (MBTI)®.

William Bridges and the concept of the character of organizations

William Bridges pioneered the use of personality-type instruments as applied to organizations rather than individuals back in the 1990s. In his groundbreaking book, *The Character of Organisations*, he proposed that organizations differed in character and preferred ways of working in the same way that people do.[6] Basing his work on the Myers-Briggs Type Indicator®, he developed a way of analysing and articulating culture which he preferred to call 'organisational character'.[7]

For Bridges, there is no 'right' answer for organizations. He compares organizational character to the grain in a piece of wood – no grain is inherently good or bad, but each type behaves differently. Some can take great pressure, others can withstand bending, while others take a fine polish. Each is well fitted to a particular purpose. He talks about the way in which differences in organizational character will shape the way in which people experience the world and interpret the actions of their business partners: 'to an organisation of a certain character the world is a mass of detail and dealing with it successfully means having everything in its place and being error-free. But to an organisation of a different character, the world is a vast design of great forces, and dealing successfully with it means picking up early warning signs when those forces are beginning to shift.'[8]

Self-knowledge, Bridges believes, can bring great benefits for organizations. If they come to understand their character and the strengths and weaknesses that run through it, they can avoid and compensate for weaknesses and capitalize on and develop their own organizational strengths. Rather than fighting the grain of their character, they should learn to work with it.

For leaders who are used to using MBTI profiles to help them understand their own preferred working style and to work more effectively with their teams, the language of Bridges' organizational character profiles will be very familiar. But whether leaders are used to MBTI terminology or not, the concept of organizational character and the precise way in which each type is described provide a sound foundation for exploring the issues that arise when different organizations have to work together.

Analysing culture and collaboration styles: the organizational partnering indicator

When it comes to working with others – in a partnership, joint venture, or following a merger or acquisition – leaders don't just need to understand their own culture they need a tool to help describe the culture of their partner in an objective way. Whilst you can't tie down another organizational culture fully (there will always be something unexpected – just as an old friend or partner will sometimes surprise you by acting out of character – particularly when they are under stress), you *can* go a long way towards understanding the distinctions between organizational types and their preferred ways of working.

The model we use for analysing organizational cultures and subcultures owes much to the work of William Bridges described above. We should say at this point that lots of other models and tools for describing organizational culture exist – but the reason we've used Bridges' work is that it is so well established and it links so closely to the widely used MBTI personality profiles that many leaders will be familiar with from coaching or team development work.

We've built on Bridges' thinking so that not only can we describe the character of an individual organization or function, but we also identify its collaboration style and indicate how other groups might experience working with it. The resulting tool – the Organizational Partnering Indicator (OPI) – helps leaders predict the challenges when different types of organizations have to work together, and gives them the knowledge to start addressing those challenges effectively. Although Bridges favours the word character to describe the characteristics of organizational types we've stuck with the more commonly used term culture for the rest of this chapter.

The Organizational Partnering Indicator uses terminology from the Myers–Briggs Type Indicator®, which describes an individual's personality preferences on four dimensions:

- Where, primarily, do you direct your energy?
  Introvert (I) – Extrovert (E)
- How do you prefer to process information?
  Sensing (S) – iNtuition (N)
- How do you prefer to make decisions?
  Thinking (T) – Feeling (F)
- How do you prefer to organize your life?
  Judging (J) – Perceiving (P)

It applies the same concepts and language to the culture of an organization, analysing the way culture is expressed in terms of an organization's process, ways of working and habits.

The result of this analysis goes way beyond amorphous feelings of 'chemistry', giving a detailed picture of what makes an organization tick – and importantly, how it's likely to collaborate with organizations with a different culture.

The following four tables are based on the model used in *The Character of Organisations* and also on standard MBTI terminology.[9] They give an indication of the characteristics of each dimension used in the OPI.

Where does the organization direct its energy? Introvert (I)–Extrovert (E)

The first dimension of the OPI explores whether the organization looks outwards towards its customers, stakeholders and regulators (Extrovert) or inwards towards its own systems, leaders and culture (Introvert).

So for example when it comes to investing for the development of a new product an extroverted organization would naturally turn outwards and do lots of market research, talking to its customers (and its suppliers) to get ideas. Whereas an introverted organization would characteristically invest in its own R&D capacity – prizing knowledge that was generated internally and only going out to the market to test the concepts later – if at all.

What information does the organization pay attention to? Sensing (S)–iNtuition (N)

This dimension looks at whether the organization pays most attention to details and facts (Sensing) or to future trends and the 'big picture' (iNtuition).

TABLE 5.1 Characteristics of Extroverted–Introverted organizations

Extroverted organizations	*Introverted organizations*
Have open boundaries and are open to influence from external bodies	Have closed boundaries and are not often open to influence
Act quickly in response to changing situations	Respond to changing situations only after some consideration
Tend to put trust in spoken face-to-face communication	Tend to put trust in written communication
Ask others for guidance and new ideas, and seek assistance when in trouble	Believe that the best guidance comes from within the organization and close ranks when in trouble
Have an approach to new opportunities dictated by their reading of future trends in the market.	Have an approach to new opportunities dictated by their own values, capabilities and resources

TABLE 5.2 Characteristics of Sensing–Intuitive organizations

Sensing organizations	Intuitive organizations
Are at their best with specific detail	Are at their best with the big picture
Record and analyse large amounts of data	Quickly spot emerging trends and implications in data
Aim to build solid routines and prefer incremental change	Tend to be a little careless about routines and prefer transformational change
See the future as an extension of the current situation	Believe that the future can be created afresh
Like their partners to operate precisely and to keep to procedures	Like their partners to be creative and respond quickly to new demands

You can often see cultural differences between functions within a large company on this dimension. In many ways you can think of and describe the culture of a discrete function in the same way you describe the culture of an organization. For example, a typical finance or internal audit function would have a culture and working style that preferred sensing – paying attention to the details of the current situation (and the evidence from the past). Whereas a marketing function would typically be organized to look to the future and make intuitive leaps to spot new trends or create new fashions – before the competition. Often the culture of an organization as whole is determined by how these inevitable internal differences are resolved and which sub-culture dominates.

How does the organization take decisions? Thinking (T)–Feeling (F)

The third dimension looks at how the organization makes its decisions: either mainly by impersonal logic based on clear principles (Thinking), or more personally, based mainly on its values and beliefs (Feeling).

You might expect to find that the world of work is largely a Thinking one and that a T culture will dominate business life. And whilst it is true that Thinking and

TABLE 5.3 Characteristics of Thinking–Feeling organizations

Thinking organizations	Feeling organizations
Make decisions based on policies and principles	Make decisions based on values and beliefs
Think in terms of rules and exceptions	Think in terms of particular human situations
Encourage partners to live up to expectations	Encourage partners to do their best
Trust solutions that appear logical and financially sound	Trust solutions that appear to fit with the organization's beliefs
Believe that criticism leads to greater efficiency	Believe that support leads to greater effectiveness

rule-based decision making is the norm in most areas of business it is not exclusively so. Many organizations that have grown out of family run businesses or who have a charismatic Chief Executive have a preference for making decisions based on beliefs (or you could say gut-feeling). The same is true for many start-ups that grew up in the dot.com era with a culture of shared beliefs that could best be described as 'to work here you've just got to get it – or you've got to get out'.

How does the organization plan and structure its work? Judging (J)–Perceiving (P)

The last element of the OPI model focuses on whether the organization prefers to make plans and close down decisions (Judging) or to keep its options open for as long as possible (Perceiving).

The nature of the external business a company is engaged in has a big influence on this aspect of culture. If you work say for the government department that manages the courts and the administration of justice you live in an external world that is totally geared towards reaching clear decisions – a very Judging world. But does that mean you have to organize all your internal processes and the way you manage your own staff on that same basis? By contrast, the people who work in a hospital with a large Accident & Emergency department will always need to be able to keep options open and react well to sudden events. But again, managers within that hospital have to decide whether creating a Perceiving culture is the best way of improving efficiency and quality of routine patient care.

Don't forget the subcultures

Of course looking at culture in any large multi-departmental organization gets more complicated. Cultural mismatches are not just about different organizations in a partnership, but also about subcultures within a single organization.

TABLE 5.4 Characteristics of Judging–Perceiving organizations

Judging organizations	Perceiving organizations
Drive towards decisions and quickly lock into them	Keep options open and seek more information
Are often moralistic – see fairness and justice as cornerstones of their culture	Are loose and fairly tolerant – often see personal freedom as a cornerstone of their culture
Never like to sit on the fence	Never like to miss an opportunity
Value others who deliver to the plan and give no surprises	Value others who think on their feet and take the relationship in new directions
See the creation of a stable plan and clear instructions as the basis for high performance	See the gathering of good market intelligence and flexible responsive processes as the basis of high performance

Different functions within a business often have their own character. Accounts departments recruit very different people from IT or the legal team. Creatives in an advertising agency are worlds apart from account managers. Academics at a university often find themselves at odds with administrators. The subcultures have different skills, different educational requirements, and different mores. Putting them together can create unexpected behaviour and have huge impact.

Subcultures may be also based on different locations – the Manchester office and the London one, for example. When each location has a different business or customer base, the differences are even more marked. There may be significant variations in the type of people recruited, or in their length of service. The offices may even have started up as different organizations entirely – sometimes locations are the remnant of a past merger, and the old culture may well linger on. Individual leaders will also influence the culture of the parts of the organization for which they're responsible. Charismatic leaders will create micro-cultures in their own likeness. And in a small or remote business unit this can have more impact on people than the overall company culture

Notwithstanding these local variations in our experience one cultural type usually underpins an organization. And when working in partnership or entering a new collaborative relationship, having a means to describe and discuss your own culture and what you see as your partner's culture is a very valuable leadership tool.

The 16 types of organization

In practice, to get a detailed OPI cultural profile for an organization, a representative sample of staff need to complete a questionnaire, and their scores are taken for each dimension, just as a Myers-Briggs profile is obtained for an individual. Alternatively, partners can work out their preferences together, using the statements listed under each dimension above.

Either way the result is a four-letter code which serves as a shorthand to describe the cultural type, for example, ISTJ (for an Introverted, Sensing, Thinking and Judging culture) or ENFP (for an Extroverted, iNtuitive, Feeling and Perceiving one). This code is accompanied by a one or two page description of the characteristic preferences and behaviours of that type of organization.

There are 16 possible combinations of the four dimensions, and we have developed detailed profiles for each organizational type, describing the collaboration habits and pitfalls for each. These profiles provide reliable predictors of how an organization is likely to behave in collaborative situations.

Summaries of the 16 profiles are given in Table 5.5. In these generic summaries we have used the word 'partnership' throughout as shorthand to stand for whatever the collaborative relationship is that is being analysed.

TABLE 5.5 The 16 organizational collaboration profiles

ISTJ	ISFJ
Contribution to a partnership	**Contribution to a partnership**
• They are responsible partners, always fulfilling their responsibilities to other parties	• They are loyal partners who take care to keep their promises to other parties
• They are able to bring the necessary governance and formality to a collaborative situation	• They focus on implementation and want the partnership to deliver tangible results
• They ensure that a partnership is planned and avoids getting deflected into new and 'interesting' areas	• They are concerned that relationships work effectively and that conflicts do not take place
• They will ensure that all parties pay attention to the essential details required to make delivery assured	• They put a great deal of effort into delivering jointly agreed practical outcomes
Potential collaboration pitfalls	**Potential collaboration pitfalls**
When entering into a partnership, these organizations will need to:	When entering into a partnership, these organizations will need to:
• Avoid a tendency to increase the risk of introducing unhelpful bureaucracy	• Consider the long-term demands and plans of the partnership, not just the short-term challenges.
• Consider the long-term demands and plans of the partnership, not just the short-term challenges	• Take care not to avoid addressing issues when there is conflict between parties
• Take care to be patient with partners and their different ways of working	• Put effort into communicating their decisions and activities to other partners
• Put effort into communicating their decisions and activities to other parties	• Avoid becoming disorientated if the ground rules of the partnership change quickly
Typical organizations	**Typical organizations**
Most IT companies, finance and admin departments	Hospitals, insurance companies

Contribution to a partnership

- They enjoy troubleshooting and are technically competent and enthusiastic problem-solvers
- They are adept at finding the flaws and difficulties in current plans, and ingenious at finding practical solutions
- They don't spend time talking, but like contributing through practical action
- They are relaxed partners who do not make demands on others, preferring to provide the freedom that encourages experimentation

Potential collaboration pitfalls

When entering into a partnership, these organizations will need to:

- Resist the temptation to do it all on their own – they should use the skills of others
- Consider the long-term demands and plans of the relationship, not just the short-term challenges
- Put effort into communicating their decisions and activities to others – even if it means attending what might be seen as time-consuming meetings
- Be careful not to shy away from others who become unexpectedly passionate about a situation

Typical organizations

Construction and building companies

Contribution to a partnership

- They can be versatile and resourceful when circumstances demand a fresh approach
- They can be very effective in a crisis, where their calm and easy-going manner can be reassuring to others
- Their listening skills can help to discover new customer needs or to get an early warning of tensions in a relationship
- They avoid conflict and seek to understand others' points of view

Potential collaboration pitfalls

When entering into a partnership, these organizations will need to:

- Be aware that their partners may need longer-range plans than they are used to working within
- Be prepared to make their voice heard in lively or combative meetings
- Seek to develop individual relationships across the partnership to create a sense of belonging
- Make sure their own desire for independence doesn't mean they ignore the needs of others who are trying to establish rules and standards for a partnership

Typical organization

Professional practices which often work best when part of a larger group

(continued)

TABLE 5.5 (Continued)

INFJ	*INTJ*
Contribution to a partnership	**Contribution to a partnership**
• They notice when relationships start to go wrong and want to help fix them	• They act as the brains of the partnership, understanding the total situation before coming to conclusions
• They bring fresh perspectives to the partnership, challenging other organizations to think about the long term and the fundamental aims of the arrangement	• They rigorously test the ideas and strategies of other parties
	• They provide structure and process to the mechanisms of collaboration
• They tend to encourage other parties to participate and to deliver more than they thought possible	• They challenge traditional ways of working and encourage others to innovate
• They provide a degree of innovation and clear thinking to the partnership, provided that others listen to their quiet input	**Potential collaboration pitfalls**
	When entering into a partnership, these organizations will need to:
Potential collaboration pitfalls	• Avoid communicating too little and not explaining the rationale for their conclusions
When entering into a partnership, these organizations will need to:	• Avoid appearing to hold fixed and inflexible views, particularly when changes are forced on all parties
• Be more detailed about how they brief others than they would be internally	• Give particular consideration to the people impact of their style and approach
• Create whatever recording and control mechanisms work for them and meet their own needs	• Put time into building consensus with other parties where this is necessary to gain commitment
• Realize that on some occasions they will have to respond to other parties' requests immediately without time for consideration	**Typical organizations**
• Ensure that their creativity does not become too inward-focused and they are not seen as 'invisible partners'	Research organizations and academic institutions
Typical organizations	
Think tanks	

INFP

Contribution to a partnership

- Their contribution depends on the extent to which they trust others and believe in the shared values and ambitions of the partnership
- They can demonstrate inspirational leadership to all parties when times are tough
- They are willing to share knowledge and expertise in order to develop the skills that other parties need to succeed
- They are prepared to be flexible in their ways of working – but only if this flexibility contributes to meeting the shared goal

Potential collaboration pitfalls

INFP organizations are usually small, so they are likely to be partnering with organizations that are much bigger than they are, meaning that they have to adapt to a degree of process formality that is not their natural style. They will need to:

- Recognize that their expectations of the depth of the relationship are likely to be greater than most other types of business
- Communicate any issues and concerns early and formally – to avoid the development of later crises
- Be more formal about how they brief others than they would be internally

Typical organizations

Social reform and environmental advocacy groups, small fast-growing companies

INTP

Contribution to a partnership

- They act as the brains of the partnership, understanding the total situation before coming to conclusions
- They listen carefully and offer quality analysis and insight
- They encourage the partnership to be original and innovative
- They use the skills of other organizations to complete the tasks that do not interest them

Potential collaboration pitfalls

When entering into a partnership, these organizations will need to:

- Resist the temptation of only communicating when they are being critical of others
- Put time into building relationships with partners to avoid being seen as aloof by others
- Take care that other parties do not take their lack of apparent engagement as indifference or even agreement
- Pay particular attentions to facts that might be important to other organizations but can appear trivial to them

Typical organizations

Experimental, entrepreneurial new technology companies

(continued)

TABLE 5.5 (Continued)

ESTP	*ESFP*
Contribution to a partnership	**Contribution to a partnership**
• They are the fixers of the partnership, identifying ways to address urgent problems that are holding up progress	• They are adaptable partners in a crisis
• They bring great energy to bear to achieve the task, often in innovative ways	• They encourage parties to bond through their ability to focus on the social aspects of a relationship
• They work to turn strategy into practical and implementable activity – fast	• They work to turn their contribution into a service to the whole partnership
• They bring a flexible and sometimes informal approach to a partnership	• They bring a flexible and sometimes informal approach to a relationship
Potential collaboration pitfalls When entering into a partnership, these organizations will need to:	**Potential collaboration pitfalls** When entering into a partnership, these organizations will need to:
• Resist the temptation to do everything themselves	• Resist the temptation to do everything themselves
• Balance the focus on short-term tasks with time spent working with partners on defining future plans	• Be careful not to irritate others by appearing to be more interested in their organizational cultures than the task in hand
• Be careful not to alienate partners by 'taking over'	• Take care that their communication is not perceived as too informal – invest in partnership governance
• Take care that their communication is not perceived as blunt by partners – they should invest in building relationships	• Act in an expedient way when times are tough rather than worrying too much about the impact on others
Typical organizations Central government departments	**Typical organizations** Organizations involved in health and beauty treatments – such as health resorts

ESTJ

Contribution to a partnership

- They are tenacious problem-solvers for any partnership
- They bring great energy to bear to achieve the task
- They take deadlines and accountabilities seriously (both their own and those of other parties)
- They pay attention to the detail and won't leave a job until it's done

Potential collaboration pitfalls

When entering into a partnership, these organizations will need to:

- Resist the temptation to take action on their own when they see relationships becoming too complex or political
- Balance the focus on short-term tasks with time spent working with others on defining future plans
- Give their partners room to operate – and avoid giving too much detail when specifying requirements
- Invest time in understanding other parties' needs to agree some of the less immediately tangible aspects of the relationship such as shared vision and values

Typical organizations

Traditional military-style big corporations

ESFJ

Contribution to a partnership

- They are solid and dependable partners and are good at delivering regular tasks to a high standard
- They will encourage a co-operative approach to tackling problems and will listen to everyone's opinions
- They will work to define clear roles and structures
- They will take care of people throughout a partnership

Potential collaboration pitfalls

When entering into a partnership, these organizations will need to:

- Make sure their great loyalty to their own staff doesn't create barriers to working with people from their partner organizations
- Adapt their normal slow-moving and stable style in novel or rapidly changing situations
- Take care not to be too accommodating of the needs of other organizations
- Be careful to avoid promoting unsatisfactory compromises which try to keep everyone happy

Typical organizations

Outgoing people companies, for example, small communications companies

(continued)

TABLE 5.5 (Continued)

ENFP	ENTP

Contribution to a partnership

- They support the process of developing vision, values and shared objectives for a partnership
- They can function well as change agents – which draws on their characteristic positive outlook, and their ability to engage others in the vision
- They enjoy taking the role of coach or facilitator in any cross-organizational situation
- They are good at picking up external trends

Potential collaboration pitfalls

When entering into a partnership, these organizations will need to:

- Balance their enthusiasm for starting new lines of work with the necessary persistence and follow through
- Take the necessary time and effort to make realistic plans and to be specific about roles and responsibilities
- Be wary of going off on too many tangents and getting distracted by new opportunities
- Be aware of their discomfort with conflict and make sure that difficult relationship issues aren't avoided

Typical organizations

PR, training and marketing departments

Contribution to a partnership

- They tend to engage others in new ideas and lateral problem-solving
- They are willing to experiment with new untried courses of action
- When and if they respect the other organizations' competence and contribution, they are very able to collaborate and to partner
- They enjoy the complexity of making a multi-party structure work

Potential collaboration pitfalls

When entering into a partnership, these organizations will need to:

- Recognize that collaborative relationships need good governance and process to hold them together
- Take care not to over-delegate the detail to others
- Avoid giving up when results take time to deliver – as they often do in multi-party relationships
- Be careful not to overwhelm or distract other parties with too many novel or lateral ideas

Typical organizations

Technical engineering consultants

Contribution to a partnership

- They tend to articulate the mission or vision for what a partnership is trying to achieve
- They identify and try to resolve conflicts and problems between all parties
- They will be sensitive to the needs of other parties and the individuals who work for them
- They ensure that plans support the joint mission

Potential collaboration pitfalls

When entering into a partnership, these organizations will need to:

- Be concise, and avoid taking too long to express their requirements to other parties
- Avoid investing too much time trying to involve all parties and keep them all happy
- Avoid taking on all the tasks of the partnership and overloading their own people
- Take care that their high principles and aspirations can realistically be implemented by other parties

Typical organizations

Creative values-driven organizations – some in the third sector

Contribution to a partnership

- They take the lead in establishing strategy and direction for a partnership
- They can quickly bring structure and organization to the chaotic early days of a new relationship
- They bring clarity to decision making
- When they see there is a problem, they can deal directly with conflict

Potential collaboration pitfalls

When entering into a partnership, these organizations will need to:

- Resist the temptation to take over too much of the running of the partnership
- Take time to listen to the views of others and check that their own communication has been understood
- Be aware of small dissatisfactions or potential conflict that may be bubbling under the surface
- Be prepared to flex their plans to meet new demands or changes to stakeholders

Typical organizations

Most common types of large American organizations

The 16 types

How to use the profiles: get under each other's skin

Understanding your own organizational profile and those of others sheds remarkable light on the frustrations within a business relationship. It also allows you to use cultural difference effectively by tailoring your approach towards partners of a different type and taking their preferences into account.

To illustrate the profiles in action, we'll look at an example of three different organizational types in partnership together. A large engineering and project management consultancy is in a long-term contract with a government department to deliver a major infrastructure project. In addition a small hi-tech start-up company is supplying some innovative touch-screen technology as a key part of the overall contract.

However, things are beginning to go wrong. Decisions get reversed and ideas blocked, the right people aren't consulted at the right time, and there's no evidence yet that the pilot system is going to work. A team-building day has had no effect. Something needs to be done.

Finally, the partnership assesses each partner's organizational type using the Organizational Partnering Indicator. This throws up some interesting results.

The engineering consultancy has the profile ISTJ – introvert, sensing, thinking, judging. Its people are focused on implementation and want the partnership to deliver tangible results. They're also good at rules and procedures, and at putting the right governance in place. As partners, they need to be given time to digest ideas and come back with an analysis of the challenges. But they're pretty demanding. They want evidence and precision. And if someone makes a commitment, they expect it to be delivered in full.

The government department is ESTP – extrovert, sensing, thinking, perceiving. They're single-minded and task-oriented. They like to take charge when time is critical, and they're good at unblocking bottlenecks. They'll get involved in the detail of their partners' work, but want partners to communicate concisely and stick to the point. However, long-term planning doesn't come naturally to them and they're likely to spring some surprises on their partners.

Finally, the hi-tech start-up is INFP – introvert, intuitive, feeling, perceiving. They're passionate about what they do, though not always articulate about it. They hate bureaucracy, and sometimes rebel against it. But they're happy to be flexible and to share knowledge and expertise in the pursuit of shared goals. As partners, they need to be given the freedom to get on with what they do best, and to question the beliefs and values of their partners. Tying them down to processes too early is a big mistake – they'll react against it. Probably the best way to get to know them is to spend some social time with them – they don't believe life is all about work.

Understanding each other's culture is a vital first step to tackling some of the clashes that characterize this sort of three-way relationship. Once each partner understands a bit more about the others, they can start accommodating their preferences far more than they have in the past. So, for example, they could choose to start holding forward looking 'pathfinder meetings' where the government department can talk about a range of possible future requirements without having to commit anything to paper. The hi-tech start-up can respond to these with creative ideas of its own, just flying a few kites at this stage but starting to explore what this could mean. Meanwhile the consultancy can take note of possible implications for their core infrastructure and take away the ideas with the biggest potential to do some behind the scenes work on the practical issues that would have to be overcome if they were to be taken forward.

As the three partners get used to each other and are able to work with the different cultures rather than fight against them, they can start to use some of the other collaboration tools we've discussed elsewhere in this book to help them jointly analyse where the priorities may lie. The collaboration spectrum (described in Chapter 2) will help to identify the key points of interdependence in their relationship, and the three-legged stool of governance, operations and behaviours will help the leaders to focus their efforts in the most critical areas. There's a long way to go, but having these conversations and noticing when and where different cultural preferences make things uncomfortable for some of the partners, or just get in the way of an open discussion, is a stronger basis for effective collaboration.

Shifting the culture

Although organizational type tends to be deeply ingrained, it is not immutable. Organizations change over time. A start-up will gradually settle down into a more process-driven organization, and, over time, a process-driven organization can ossify into a slow-moving bureaucracy. Even a change of CEO can herald a new culture, since many CEOs build a culture in their own image, whether consciously or unconsciously.

One organization that has successfully shifted its culture is Royal Parks, the body in charge of Hyde Park and other historic London green spaces. When Mark Camley took over as CEO, the prevailing culture was inwardly focused, concentrating on preserving the landscape and heritage. The parks' many stakeholders came low down the list of priories – as did balancing the budget. And while marketing staff had ideas for using the spaces in new ways to generate income, the horticultural staff were vetoing every initiative.

'We were often on the back foot, governed by the seasons rather than a business plan', says Camley in an interview in *HR Director*.[10] 'We needed a new culture of decisive planning and implementation – a more proactive and extrovert approach based on information gathered from the outside world, not just horticultural issues.'

Using the Organizational Partnering Indicator, we helped Mark Camley analyse Royal Parks' culture at the outset of the process. This score gave him a baseline measure for his process of change, and was followed by training in collaborative leadership for senior managers.

One of the insights from the training was that different functions were working on radically different timescales. When one horticulturalist was asked for his view of the long term, his response was: 'See those trees we're planting right now? We'll see whether we planted them in the right place in 100 years. Governments come and go, but trees remain.'

Twelve months later the different functions were able to understand each other far better, and to look externally as well as internally. The Royal Parks successfully hosted the London stage of the Tour de France and seven events for the London 2012 Olympics, as well as winning Green Flag Awards for all eight parks under its management.

A second OPI measurement confirmed that the culture had shifted significantly towards planning and implementation. According to Camley, the detailed analysis helped 'unstick' the organization. 'Understanding your organisational type helps you convince even the most sceptical people that you're making progress.'

Avoiding the lure of community

Of course, any relationship is likely to run more smoothly if you share similar values and interests with those you are working with. The temptation can therefore be to avoid the leadership challenges of cultural difference by seeking out others who are like you in some way or other. Nowhere is this more obvious than in the growth of on-line communities. In the vast expanse of the internet it's quite easy to find people with similar interests and to work on joint projects together. Sociologist Richard Sennett describes these as 'islands of similarity in a sea of diversity'.[11] Much has been written about various forms of on-line collaboration, with volunteers working together to: create software (such as LINUX), write all sorts of expert reference works and encyclopaedias (like Wikipedia), or even search for extra-terrestrial intelligence (SETI@Home).

The leadership effort involved in creating these on-line communities of interest, whilst important, isn't the same as the collaborative leadership challenges discussed in the rest of this book. On-line communities are defined by their very similarity and there is little need for interaction with other communities to achieve their purpose. The real work of collaborative leadership is about bringing together different organizations with distinct and different cultures – and getting results and generating value across that divide.

The same holds when faced with selecting organizations to work with in a long-term partnership contract. It can be tempting to be drawn to the comfort of working with 'people like us' but is that where the real benefit will come from? In situations that require innovation or the transformation of a business, similarity of organizational culture may actually be a barrier to progress. But for collaborative leaders this means facing up to those three challenges of sharing control with others who hold different views, handling the conflict that will arise in a positive and healthy manner and, through all this, building long-term relationships.

Getting value from difference

Some successful business partnerships are nevertheless formed because there's a natural fit between the players. And as Rosabeth Moss Kanter has shown, some leaders use highly romantic language about their partners −'love at first sight' or 'the company of our dreams'.

'Business pairings aren't entirely cold-blooded', writes Kanter. 'Indeed successful company relationships nearly always depend on the creation and maintenance of a comfortable personal relationship between the senior executives.'[12]

However, love at first sight is far from a universal experience in business partnerships. In fact, some are forced marriages, where partners have to learn to make the best of it. Most of these are formed precisely because the partners have different things to offer and hope that by pooling skills and expertise they will create new value that neither could produce on their own.

In recent years the success of the iPhone has led to the emergence of a vast and lucrative market for new smartphones. Responding to this technological challenge requires a combination of diverse software and hardware capabilities that rarely sit within the ranks of any one organization. We've seen several different 'forced marriages' in this arena as traditional mobile-phone manufactures have looked for access to the new design skills they need. Ericsson, Nokia and Motorola have all been forced down this path in recent years, in seeking out their different relationships with Sony, Microsoft and Google respectively − with perhaps different degrees of willingness from each party. In each case the differences in outlook, and the access to new capabilities that exist between the partners, have the potential to drive innovation and new product development that would have been impossible without the other's involvement. But exploiting that potential means overcoming a range of cultural as well as technical challenges.

The truth is that organizational difference can be fruitful in all sorts of ways if you can harness it. It's well worth getting over the initial difficulties that cultural diversity causes in order to understand each other's working style and point of view. Difference in culture can be the grit in the oyster of a collaborative relationship − leaders who can work with that sort of difference properly can use it to generate a pearl of great creative value.

Three common reactions to difference: deny, ignore, obliterate

Few leaders know how to value and nurture cultural difference. In fact we see many leaders of multi-party relationships in denial busily pretending the differences aren't there at all. Partners forge on, bravely ignoring the festering resentments springing up at every level and blind to the need to adapt and change.

Another reaction is to recognize the differences in cultures, but do nothing to tackle them. Partners shrug their shoulders, shake their heads and get on with things as separately as possible. In some cases they just walk away. In others, where a contract forces them to stay, the partnership may become completely dysfunctional at enormous cost to all concerned.

Finally, many leaders seek to stamp out difference altogether in the belief that conformity will make things easier to manage. One way is to make everything as transactional as possible to squeeze out any room for frustration. But reducing everything to process and contract, as we saw in Chapter 2, saps morale and certainly destroys initiative and innovation. However, try to make your partner part of the team and you create a different set of problems.

When a UK county council entered into partnership with an engineering design firm to build local transport infrastructure (roundabouts, bridges and so on), a clash arose between the designers on each side. The leaders' response was to put the designers in the same office and manage them under the county council structure. The result: three of the best designers promptly left. In the end the remaining designers settled down, but tensions still reigned and standards dropped to the lowest common denominator. Squashing out the difference had destroyed the potential value of the partnership.

And therein lies the problem. Culture clashes can be extremely damaging to a partnership. But if you try to deny, ignore, or obliterate differences, you risk ruining what brought you together in the first place. Instead you have to face them – and learn to use them effectively.

When cultures collide

For many business relationships, the differences between cultures are not immediately visible, and the effort to understand is correspondingly low but the consequences can be business critical. It's interesting to see the lessons about culture that car makers Daimler Benz, Nissan and Renault each learned over the years leading up to their strategic alliance in 2010. In 1998, Daimler Benz launched what it called 'a merger of equals' with Chrysler – it was hailed as creating a transatlantic automotive powerhouse but it proved to be anything but. The merger cost Daimler $37 bn but ten years later it sold what remained of Chrysler to a venture capital company for $7 bn and, in 2009, Chrysler filed for bankruptcy. The reasons for this failure are complex but with hindsight managers point to a failure of Daimler to bridge the cultural divide. Daimler Benz attempted to run Chrysler operations in the same way as it would run its German operations. This approach was doomed to failure. In September 2001, *Business Week* wrote, 'The merger has so far fallen disastrously short of the goal. Distrust between Auburn Hills and Stuttgart has made cooperation on even the simplest of matters difficult.'[13]

Contrast this with the approach Renault and Nissan took to get to know each other in the run up to their alliance in 1999. The portents were not good – the deal was described as 'a marriage of desperation for both parties' but both sides took the issue of culture seriously.[14] In late 1998, Renault and Nissan executives went through a six month experiment of working together with the objective of understanding each other's culture as the basis of forming a lasting alliance. They focused on the glue that would help link the two cultures: job rotations, cross-company leadership teams and communication rituals (including a company-wide definition of essential English words that could be misunderstood by either party such as authority, objectives, transparency).[15] The Renault President was quoted as saying 'We did not try to forge a common culture … we never talked about an alliance of equals.'[16]

Some commentators took this to mean that Renault wasn't interested in organizational culture, in fact it was the opposite. They understood the importance of culture and working with difference to create value.

If you then spool forward to 2010 it must have been with some irony that Renault Nissan signed a long-term alliance with Daimler Benz for the development of a common platform for smaller cars and electric vehicles. Daimler seems to have learned their lessons. Deiter Zetsche their CEO said the two groups 'had found the right cultural fit for the partnership' – and two years later Mercedes were able to launch the first of their new front-wheel drive A class models based on the fruits of the Renault–Nissan relationship.[17]

Tools like the OPI discussed earlier help leaders to make judgements about culture when choosing partners and to think through how to bridge some of the gaps, but sooner or later problems can still surface. Based on the examples of Daimler Chrysler, Renault–Nissan and other cross-organizational partnerships we have worked with we've outlined some typical flashpoints.

A clash of values

Differences in values can be hidden under the surface and be difficult to spot in a new relationship when all parties are being polite to each other. Often it's the seemingly small things that grow to become major stumbling blocks. For each side they can acquire symbolic status and get talked about again and again as proof that the other partner is 'not like us'.

One example we witnessed was a partnership between an engineering consultancy and a building firm. At the building company, the culture was about solving problems, dealing with the unexpected and doing whatever was necessary to get the job done. The consultancy company, however, believed in the mantra 'time is money'. New recruits were drilled into accounting for every hour of their day, and if they couldn't charge time to clients, they needed to allocate it to some internal project code on their weekly timesheets.

In the early days of the partnership there were considerable problems.

Finally, in a spirit of collaboration, the building firm set up working groups and joint problem-solving sessions to find innovative ways round the difficulties. These worked well and everyone felt the partnership was making progress. Then at the end of the quarter the consultancy company presented their bill – including several thousand pounds of fees for participating in these working sessions. They added a note to say that they had discounted the fee rate by 50 per cent in recognition of the partnership.

The building firm was outraged. For them it wasn't just the money, but the principle. Common reactions were: 'How dare they charge for something like that?

Whose side did they think they were on?' Meanwhile the leaders of the consultancy company were thoroughly confused. They thought they had been generous in discounting their fee rate.

Working at different speeds

Making decisions at different rates can also cause serious misunderstandings. One example we witnessed was a large high-street bank and a small software house in a long-term partnership to develop internet banking systems. The relationship was going well and producing some award-winning results. Then one day the joint steering group decided that in response to customer concerns they wanted to put a whole new layer of security into the system.

The software house quickly went into action. They put forward an innovative idea to solve the issue, but pointed out that this would mean moving the software to a different (and more secure) development platform. The bank agreed in principle to the plan, so the software house immediately started retraining their developers and went out to the market to recruit some new and highly expensive staff.

Imagine their frustration at the next steering group a month later, when the bank's head of technology announced a delay. Before going ahead, he wanted a review of possible software development platforms, to see what was available that answered both the new security requirements and the bank's technical standards. Suddenly everything was on hold pending the review.

For the bank it made perfect sense. Although they'd agreed in principle to the software house's recommendations, they hadn't yet gone through a lengthy process of approvals. The software house, however, felt they had been put in a difficult position, and resented it. It wasn't just the cost of the delay that frustrated them – they felt the bank just 'didn't get it' and wasn't operating in the same world as them.

Mismatched communication styles

Often a difference in culture can show up as a difference in communication style. An organization that is used to working by informal channels and expecting important messages to cross the company on the grapevine, for example, may have real difficulties in working with a partner that is used to minuting all its meetings formally and keeping an audit trail of all communication. This difference in communication style is often raised as one of the classic symbols of a culture clash between traditional public and private sector organizations and so often surfaces as an issue in public–private partnership deals.

In this situation a leader needs to first recognize the difference in style and then make it explicit so that staff in both organizations can see that their communication needs and traditions have been recognized. You then have a choice – if the situation demands closer integration between the two organizations, you could set up and sponsor a cross-organizational working group to design a new communication process and guidelines which take the best of both but are not branded to look like either heritage. Or if there is value in keeping the organizations feeling distinct from each other then acknowledge that, but be sure to define what communications must happen at their points of interdependence – for example, which meetings must they both attend and how will these be run and documented?

Mismatched leadership style

Leadership style is generally a strong indicator of organizational culture, so when leaders approach things from very different perspectives, cultural clashes are likely to follow further down their organizations.

We once worked with a partnership between a private sector technical consultancy company and a government agency to help them out of one such clash. The leadership style of the consultancy was to expect leaders to delegate to the maximum possible degree. The people below were then used to stepping up to the mark and thriving on seizing extra responsibility – or leaving the organization if they couldn't take that pressure.

The government agency, meanwhile, had a much more paternalistic model of leadership, which was all about protecting junior staff and placing great value on fairness and equitable opportunity. The result was that what was seen as model leadership behaviours on one side were seen as either threatening or stifling by the other. Leaders on both sides lost the respect of their partners and, over time, relationships at every level suffered.

Again the first step is to recognize the difference and to acknowledge it. From there the leaders can decide whether there is greater value to be gained from maintaining the difference and therefore putting effort into helping people to understand different leadership styles and getting used to working with them (this was rather the approach that Renault and Nissan took in the early days of their alliance), or whether a common leadership style consistently applied will deliver the joint objectives more quickly. In which case there is value in jointly creating a new set of leadership behaviours as one of the early defining symbols of the partnership or alliance and then managing people and promoting in line with those behaviours.

Chapter summary

In making a collaboration work, understanding culture trumps everything

Effective collaboration doesn't mean being blind to your partner's differences nor does it mean trying to change your partner into a clone of yourself. But it does demand a great deal of time and effort to understand an organizational culture different from your own and to learn where the opportunities and risks may lie when you put two or more different cultures together.

If you are really clear about why you are going into a new relationship and what you want to gain from working with the other party from the outset you stand a much better chance of working with the cultural differences to achieve your aims rather than just being frustrated by them.

The Organizational Partnering Indicator (OPI) is a tool we have developed for describing organizational culture – based on the work of William Bridges and the language of Myers Briggs (MBTI). Using an analysis tool like this can help people to discuss cultural differences in precise and non-emotive language. And cultural analysis tools provide a way of easing some of the uncomfortable surprises of working with a new organization by being able to predict how each party is likely to respond in a given situation.

Cultural difference can be the grit in the oyster of a collaborative relationship – understand it and use it properly and it can turn into a pearl.

Lessons for leaders

- Culture clashes are the most commonly cited cause of the breakdown of a partnership or other collaboration – so as a collaborative leader go into a new relationship with your eyes wide open. Don't be surprised by the impact of cultural difference.
- Start by looking hard at the culture of your own organization: What do your partners need to understand to get the best out of you? What contribution can you make to the relationship? What might some of your organizational blind-spots or pitfalls be when you work with others?
- Be open with your partners about your own organizational culture and get them to be open about theirs – using a cultural analysis tool like the OPI can help.
- Challenge assumptions and stereotypes wherever you see them.
- Cultural difference can be at the core of much innovation. Look for where the value might be created at the rough edges between the different cultures in the relationship – and what might put this value at risk.

6

THE PARTNERSHIP ROADMAP

A beginning, a middle and an end

This book is about the challenges leaders face in making collaborative business relationships work, and just like human relationships, collaborative business relationships are multi-faceted and vary greatly in their form and duration. Most of this book is a guide to the tools that leaders can select from to help them plan for or react to any particular collaboration challenge at any moment. But some types of relationship follow a more predictable path, with distinct stages and likely risks. Prominent amongst these are formally contracted fixed-term partnerships. This form of organizational collaboration has grown enormously with the move towards business process outsourcing and the transfer of the delivery of many public services to private sector contractors.

Much of the emphasis in managing these partnerships has been on getting the terms of the contract right and much good work has been done by standards bodies and others to create model framework contracts that support collaborative partnership working (see for example the NEC3 family of contracts produced in the UK by the Institution of Civil Engineers which are now very widely used).[1] But a good contract is not enough to make a partnership work throughout its lifecycle.

Know where you are

A partnership is not a static relationship, but a journey, made up of distinct stages covering different terrains. The beginning of a new business relationship is often difficult, with lots of deep dips, hazards and hairpin bends, and many ventures run into serious trouble. Get through these obstacles, however, and with some careful navigation you can end up getting to your destination in good shape.

As the landscape changes, the behaviour of people within a partnership changes with it. In fact you can predict with reasonable accuracy how people are likely to behave at different stages of any partnership lifecycle. This means that leaders in charge of many partnerships at one time can't afford to standardize their approach – they have to be sensitive to the stage each individual partnership has reached. Driving flat out when you are in the mountains and the rain is starting to fall is courting disaster.

This chapter is a roadmap for leaders of all types of partnership to follow. If you've been through plenty of joint ventures, public–private partnerships or alliances already, the four stages we describe – selection, transition, maintenance and ending – should be familiar to you, and you'll probably want to skim through and only look in depth at the stages you habitually find hard. If you're starting out in leading a partnership, however, we recommend you read through this chapter in full. It shows you how to plan and deploy your resources, and which activities to prioritize at each stage – some need considerably more of your leadership time than others.

At each stage we give you two sets of road signs – first, the indicators that you're on the right track, and second, the danger signs that you're straying off the road. Pay attention to these and you should have a considerably easier ride.

Stage 1: selection – fit for the future

Selecting a partner and cementing the relationship can seem like an end in itself. Adrenaline-fuelled teams work around the clock to seal the deal, hordes of advisers descend to fight it out, the contract is scrutinized in minute detail, and the whole process accelerates faster and faster up to the moment of signing.

But a partnership is considerably more than the deal. The early selection process should look not just at current fit but whether the relationship can go the distance. After the champagne and balloons comes the hard reality of getting on with

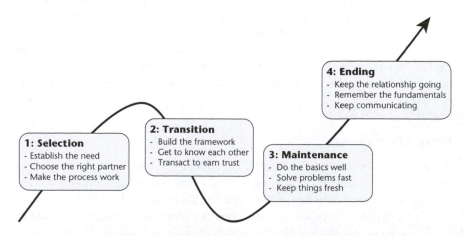

FIGURE 6.1   The partnership roadmap

the job. And while partnerships aren't for life, they tend to last many years and sometimes decades.

Establish the mutual need

The first step in selection is to understand the exact nature of the mutual need. All parties should know what they stand to gain from a partnership and what each party can contribute towards it. Even more importantly, they need to understand what the real value is in the relationship and how it is created in ways that no one party could achieve on their own.

From there they can decide on the right model – which may not be a partnership at all. There might be a case for another kind of relationship altogether – a purely transactional one, or even a merger or acquisition. A 2004 study in *Harvard Business Review*, suggests that many acquisitions should be alliances and vice versa – resulting in high levels of failure for both. All too often firms adopt the wrong strategy for their particular circumstances, destroy the value, and watch the talent walk out of the door. The authors argue that acquisitions work best when you are combining hard resources like manufacturing plants, or when you generate synergies by sharing knowledge iteratively and customizing resources to a high degree – that is, by working more as a team. However if you're combining human resources rather than buildings or machinery, if you aim to generate synergies by one company completing a task and passing it on to the next, or if the outcome is very uncertain, you are best off choosing an alliance.[2]

Once you're set on a partnership route, it's important to unpick the meanings of terms like 'alliance' or 'partnership' and make sure all parties are using them in the same way. The collaboration spectrum discussed in Chapter 2 can help would-be partners work out the most appropriate model of joint working to deliver their business case. Mapping out each party's resource contributions and drafting joint success criteria will also help clarify the model.

Far more difficult is working out whether a potential partner has the right capability for your needs – not only now but later on in the relationship's lifecycle. John Yard, leader of the Inland Revenue's massive IT outsourcing project in the 1990s, believes it is crucial to see beyond short-term suitability. 'I look for partners with the capability to give me what I asked for in the first year or two, then look for evidence of a capability to understand what my challenges might be in years three and four', he says. 'I want to have confidence they can deliver today, and that I'll be able to have profitable conversations about the future, when the time comes.'

However that assessment can be tricky. 'It's difficult to get people into the room before a contract is in place, to talk about what is really possible', says Julie Baddeley, adviser and board member on several major partnerships. 'It's hard because until the partnership is established, people don't want to enter into those conversations.' Without them, however, you have no idea of what you're letting yourself in for.

Choose a partner you can work with

Even when partners can demonstrate both current and future capability, it may not be enough. It's not just what you do, but how you do it – as a conservative-minded north of England building society found to its cost. Seeking to launch a new credit card, the building society eventually found a partner that seemed ideally suited to its needs. The credit card company was well known, respected and efficient. The problem was that its marketing methods were way too aggressive for the building society's taste.

While the credit card company tried to seek out new customers, the building society worried about its members getting into debt. The consequence for each side was profoundly unsatisfactory – the building society felt it was putting its relationship with members at risk and the credit card company couldn't generate the volume it expected. The partnership soon foundered.

This doesn't mean that organizations should only seek out like-minded partners – collaboration is not about cloning. Characters and approaches can be radically different, yet still complementary. Difference matters – it's often the reason for the partnership in the first place.

However, you do need to know yourself thoroughly before being able to partner effectively. If you trade on your reputation as a local bank, you can't outsource to a call centre on another continent, however attractive it might seem. If paternalism is paramount to your business, you shouldn't choose to collaborate with people who thrive on opportunism. And if you want to change the world, there's little point in entering a partnership with people who only want to change their bottom line.

Don't let the process ruin the relationship

Unfortunately the process of selecting a partner often seems designed to cause maximum damage to a fledgling partnership. At the point when you most need to get below the surface with potential partners, you're least likely to be able to do so. 'You end up with two principals surrounded by a sycophantic entourage of advisers, all focusing on doing the deal within the timeframe and pulling the leaders away from each other', says Julie Baddeley. 'It makes it very difficult to focus on what's happening post-deal.'

In public–private partnerships in particular, the need to demonstrate fairness and value for money to a sceptical public has led to complicated, costly and highly formal tendering processes. Creating an enormous machine to run an apparently fair process puts heavy pressure on leaders to close the deal at all costs. Yet such tenders can become deeply adversarial: instead of assessing each other's cultures, would-be partners end up trying to extract the last pound of flesh from each other.

Defining the contract can be especially hostile – and this may well set the tone for the partnership in later stages. For some relationships it can prove a death knell.

When London Underground's partnership with Metronet to refurbish the tube system ended with Metronet going into administration, Christian Wolmar wrote: 'Flawed at the outset, the contracts proved to be unworkable. Their sheer detail and complexity ensured that. They were full of enormously complex formulae and ridiculous notions like rewarding contractors for moving toilets nearer the drivers' cabs at the end of the lines so they would take less time going to the loo between journeys.'[3]

While advisers insist on caution, it is leaders who have to deliver the partnership later down the line. 'It takes self-confidence to put your foot down', says John Yard. 'I'm straight with procurement – I say "you're advising me, but I will decide what to do, and I will decide the level of risk".'

For some would-be partnerships, the burden of the selection process is simply too heavy. The £12.4 billion NHS National Programme for IT is a good case in point. In May 2003, potential bidders for what was to be the world's largest non-military IT project were given a 500-page 'output based specification' document which was described as 'work in progress' and told they had to submit proposals in a little over a month. Little wonder that some of the most prominent bidders pulled out at the proposal stage. Contracts were awarded in October 2003, when only 190 days had elapsed between advertising the contract and awarding it. This was described as a 'ground breaking schedule' – but its enormous intensity had disturbing consequences. Not only did several potentially useful partners pull out in the selection phase, but Sir Christopher Bland, chairman of BT, which was one of the successful bidders, described the process as 'slightly like a dog chasing a car. What do we do if we catch it? Well now we've caught it'.[4]

Learning from the lessons of failed partnerships, the government is now approaching selection with greater sophistication. Local authorities, for example, are being advised that price is not the be-all and end-all in choosing a partner. Potential partners need to be clear about their own goals, vision and values and those of their partner, the objectives of each, the different partnership models available and the economic case for each model. They must also pay attention to 'softer' issues, such as 'a clear understanding of each others' organizational imperatives, and how those imperatives are likely to feed through into day-to-day working arrangements'.

There are encouraging signs of these less adversarial methods coming into use in the most high-profile of projects. When the government was looking for a key partner to manage the construction of the London 2012 Olympics site, it ran an assessment centre for bidders to rate them on a wide range of criteria, not merely on price. The purpose of this approach, according to the ODA draft procurement policy document, was to 'dispel the misconception that bids will be won on lowest price alone'. The success of this strategy has been proven by the fact that all the major construction work has been completed on time and to budget which is quite remarkable given the history of Olympic building projects.

Selection road signs

You know you're on the right track if:

- There is a business requirement for two or more organizations to form an alliance or partnership.
- All parties are involved in drawing up contractual arrangements.
- There is clear understanding of the risks involved, and of who is best able and best placed to manage them.
- Lessons from previous partnerships/contracts have been recognized and taken into account.
- The evaluation process includes mechanisms for learning from previous experiences of working with these potential partners.
- The selection process allows you to get to know your potential partners, you feel that you understand each other's strengths and weaknesses and are confident that you will be able to work together.
- As a result of the selection process and the relationships formed through it, there is a good understanding of what needs to be done in the transition phase to get partners up to speed and to bridge cultural gaps.

You know you're going off track if:

- There is no clear understanding or agreement about the terms of the relationship needed to meet the business requirement.
- There is disagreement and conflict about where risks should be allocated between parties.
- Parties are talking about partnership and alliance but meaning different things by the terms.
- Key players (stakeholders) aren't engaged in planning discussions – conflict is being avoided.
- No allowance is made for relationship measures in the evaluation process.
- The mechanics of the selection process are throwing up a prime candidate that people feel will be difficult to work with in some way.
- Key business representatives who will implement the contract are not involved in the selection process.

Stage 2: transition – suspend judgement

In the transition stage – the vital first 100 days – partners have to learn to work together instead of merely building a contract together. It's easy to erode the value of a partnership for good here, and getting this stage wrong is a prime reason for the failure of many contracts.

None the less, you can't expect the partnership to work from day one – the transition phase is characterized by things going wrong – or what one of our clients calls 'the expected unexpected!' The key to managing here is not relying on perfection from your partners, but being able to put problems right fast. Leaders need to suspend judgement, and persuade key people throughout the partnership to do the same, making a transition successful means managing expectations on all sides. There are many good guidebooks to managing transitions – (our favourite is by William Bridges)[5] and all emphasize the fact that there is likely to a be a performance dip in the first few days as people get used to new ways of working or reporting relationships. Of course it is possible to avoid this initial blip by adding extra staff or other resources and many experienced partnership contractors plan to do this and build it into their budgets. But of course that can just delay the real performance issues and leadership challenges to later down the track when the contract has to start delivering costs savings or other value improvements.

Getting all parties to understand and buy into the overall transition plan and the implications it will have for performance at different times is an important collaborative leadership task in the early days of a new partnership.

Build the framework

Early actions have long-lasting impacts. So it's important to avoid rushing the bonding process on a partnership. Don't take a bunch of managers out white-water rafting in the Lake District during the transition phase and think that is the relationship job done – it will be a disaster. This is absolutely not the moment for formal team-building, and at this stage you don't know that taking a one-team approach will be the right answer anyway. Instead, get the structure right. Leaders should use this time to set up the relationship properly and jointly define governance processes, the measurements of performance to be used throughout the partnership, escalation procedures, communication plans and so on.

The three legs of governance, operations and behaviours (discussed in Chapter 3) are the foundations of any partnership framework. Remember, however, that the first 100 days are a special case and need to be treated separately. Set up dedicated and experienced transition governance and project management – research suggests that under-investment here can jeopardize the long-term health of the project.[6] In addition, our poll showed that 86 per cent of respondents agreed that 'more planning at the set-up stage would have helped to avoid most operational problems later on'.[7]

So create a joint 100-day partnership plan. Identify champions within each business to support the partnership. Work out the ground rules for compensating each parent organization for contributing specific services to the partnership. Go through the contract with a fine toothcomb and pick out the incentives and disincentives to what you're trying to achieve – and start ironing out the disincentives.

Above all, don't try to be too close. The first 100 days should stay relatively transactional. Each party needs to get on with their own side of the project and keep out of each other's hair. That way they can begin to build trust by delivering what they've promised. You can use the collaboration spectrum (described in Chapter 2) to track how each party sees the level of collaboration within the relationship developing over time. Our advice would be to start by delivering reliable transactions to each other and build up from there. In the early days, you shouldn't attempt to operate with the level of closeness you may aspire to once you know each other well. So be clear about the direction of travel, but don't be surprised if things slip back at times.

The need to track the progress of a relationship in the early days means that measurement also needs special consideration during transition. Over-expectation breeds failure and a partnership can't start using the contractual productivity measures from day one. There is no point in hauling new suppliers over the coals in the first few weeks for missing their targets – that merely causes bad feeling and sets up a relationship to fail. By the same token, if you've changed a supplier, you shouldn't expect the new one to achieve the levels of your previous one straightaway. Instead, leaders need to set transitional measures with joint 100-day targets – and include relationship measures as well as financial ones.

Get to know each other

This is also the time for all parties to get to know each other better. That doesn't mean pretending you're a team – you're not, and nor should you be. In fact we'd go as far as to say that if a newsletter emerges during transition proclaiming 'One team – one vision', you're asking for serious trouble.

In Chapter 11 we talk about three stages of group formation to describe the psychological states that people go through when joining a newly formed group. Trying to short-circuit this process and leap straight to a state of assumed closeness will always appear false and simply doesn't work.

However, informal ways of learning about each other are very useful at this stage. Leaders should arrange a set of dinners for key people to meet each other out of their business context. Teams on one side should meet their opposite numbers (without having to perform tasks or play games). Inductions should be arranged for anyone joining the partnership who hasn't been involved earlier. And as far as possible down the hierarchy, individuals should get a chance to meet their counterparts within the partnership.

It's also worth incorporating more formal methods of understanding each other's culture. Transition is a useful opportunity to take a baseline reading of each party's organizational character in order to understand strengths and weaknesses on either side and to work out how best to collaborate in the future.

Show what success looks like

After the adrenaline charge of making the deal, the transition stage can be an abrupt return to reality. You may find that staff are cynical about the partnership and that disagreements flourish. New people come on board who weren't part of the selection process and who want to make their reputation by doing things differently. And inevitably a whole lot of things will go wrong.

The first 100 days are testing times. Mistakes get blown out of all proportion. People revert to their original prejudices or happily embrace new ones. They may even start questioning whether they made the right decision in choosing a particular partner. The honeymoon is definitely over.

When this happens, it's time to go back to transacting. Each party has to earn trust – and the best way to do that is to deliver. In addition leaders need to demonstrate what success for all parties might look like. One way is to develop a partnership charter in which the leaders of each of the parties involved can set out some of the principles of how they will work together and what benefits they will generate as a result. For a charter to be valuable, it must be practical and help people at all levels to make decisions about how they deal with their partners.

For example, the partnership charter between the London Borough of Kensington and Chelsea and their waste disposal and recycling partner states that 'to foster a successful working partnership at every level, the partners will ensure that:

- The contractor's staff will work immediately alongside the Council's staff, and not occupy separate rooms.
- Staff secondments between the partners will be encouraged.
- Joint training and induction of staff will be encouraged.
- The partners will share the same information and communication systems.'[8]

Another useful activity in these early days is to find a number of pilot projects in non-critical areas where you can get teams working across boundaries to learn lessons in collaboration in a relatively low-risk environment. Pilot projects allow you to notch up some quick wins, not only in terms of delivering results, but also in understanding each other's processes and culture and in building interpersonal relationships that will be invaluable as you move into a steady state.

Finally, leaders should make sure everyone understands when transition is over. Transition is a countdown. It shouldn't drag on – people need a definite end point to work towards. They need to gear up to full-scale measures. And everyone has to understand that after this point, the real business of partnership begins.

Transition road signs

You know you're on the right track if:

- All parties have put the necessary time and resources into the induction and set-up process.
- There is a single transition timetable and resource plan that all parties refer to on a regular basis.
- There are early opportunities to observe the capabilities and culture of all parties on pilot projects and other real-life tasks.
- Special transition governance arrangements are in place to facilitate rapid decision making in this phase.
- Partnership project meetings focus on short-term joint problem-solving and risk management.
- There is evidence that partners are delivering on their short-term promises (in other words, transact before you can partner).
- There is a communication plan that has credibility with stakeholders, and consistent messages are being communicated across the partnership.
- A set of measures has been defined for the partnership, including a good balance of relationship measures as well as delivery measures.
- A clear end to the transition phase has been defined, which people are jointly working towards.

You know you're going off track if:

- Leaders are talking cynically about their new partners from day one and the general feeling is 'I don't know why we chose this bunch!'
- Partnership project meetings are taken up with lengthy discussion about the contract.
- The main decision-making body (or steering group) isn't due to meet until the transition phase is nearly complete.
- Partners are working to their own plans, which are not shared.
- The first version of the partnership performance scorecard is mostly red, because delivery of performance isn't up to the target specified in the contract, rather than specific targets for transition.
- Stakeholders complain that they don't know who to contact anymore to get things done.
- New people have come in to manage the delivery (on all sides) and don't seem to know about the overall intention, let alone the details of the contract that was signed only a few months ago.

- One hundred days in, many people haven't met their opposite number in the partnership outside of a formal meeting.
- The phase seems to be dragging on and on, and no one knows when the partnership will enter a steady state.

Stage 3: maintenance – keeping the machine running and improving

When you reach the third (and usually by far the longest) stage of a partnership, you take the brakes off and start motoring. This is where you drive out the real value of the relationship – fulfilling financial and productivity measures, rising to new challenges and taking advantage of the opportunities that come your way. But amid the rush to realize the objectives of your collaboration, you also need to remember to maintain and nurture the relationship. Success in this stage is all about building a culture of learning and continuous improvement across all parties.

There are some standards and models that can help leaders assess their own organization's capability to drive out process improvements and also to assess the capability of their partners. Two of the best to look at are the Capability Maturity Model (CMM) created by software engineers at the Carnegie Melon University and the new UK standard for collaborative business partnerships BS11000.[9] Both take a systematic approach to diagnosing and managing incremental improvements across the whole lifecycle of a partnership. But at the start of this maintenance stage, leaders needs to focus on getting the fundamentals right.

Do the basics well

After the first 100 days or so partners should have settled down into their roles, recognized each other's competencies (and deficiencies), and begun to get used to each other's different ways of working. Now you need to get the fundamentals absolutely right, honing governance, systems and behaviours to make them work as well as they possibly can. Look at things like the joint risk register – does it sit in a drawer for three months, or does it reflect the reality of the partnership and give early warning of the things that matter? Are the escalation procedures being used? And are partners sticking rigidly to their own information gathering or using one set of data?

It will gradually become clear how well individuals are able to collaborate when necessary – and leaders need to support and coach subordinates in acquiring the requisite skills.Even more crucially, the partnership needs to keep developing talent so that staff don't see it as a dead end. Put in place joint programmes to build leadership capability and develop skills that will be needed in the future.

Leaders should also continue to monitor how cultural differences are affecting performance, and how they can use differences to best advantage. If a baseline reading in the transition phase was taken, then it should be followed up. If not, do it now, and keep on building the understanding of each other throughout the maintenance phase. Now is the time to invest in building joint teams in specific areas of the partnership that require close co-operation or integrated working. All the traditional tools of individual and team development – personality profiling, 360° feedback, away days and the like – can come into play here. The point is not to apply them uniformly, but to focus team-building effort where it is most required, in areas of high interdependence between the partners.

As the relationship deepens, each party should get more comfortable about sharing more information and activities. Meanwhile, leaders need to continue to keep up the communication – involving people in both the short-term and long-term objectives, and highlighting both successes and failures, without resorting to propaganda. As things settle into a more established routine, it's easy to get blasé about these basics, but without good communication, a partnership will get bumpy surprisingly fast.

Tackle problems fast

Problems will of course continue throughout the maintenance stage – and they may get considerably bigger. 'The start of a partnership is like a honeymoon – and then you go skiing', says John Yard. 'Round about year one or two you find you're going right down a slope, and you realise you can't go on like this. Either you crash or you start slogging back up the hill.'

The obvious issues are productivity failures – one or more parties may miss a milestone, raising the spectre of penalties and all the resentments they can cause. Other problems may be less overt but more invidious. For example, poor decision making, mismatches in how you measure progress or define success, a general lack of trust or faith in the future, or even a relationship breakdown between individuals. All of these need to be addressed – and it takes confidence, tact and firmness to deal with them effectively.

It's the job of leaders to spot the risks, prepare for them and tackle problems before they spiral out of control. No one can iron them out completely – problems are part of the process. But when they happen, leaders should go back to the fundamental framework of the partnership and check that it is all sound. Is the governance sufficiently robust? Are escalation procedures well defined and used when necessary? Have all parties aligned their systems and processes? Are measurement processes well-defined, understood by all and forward-looking as well as retrospective? (For a detailed look at measurement, see Chapter 4.) And is behaviour – either individual or organizational – getting in the way of your goals?

It's important to read the warning signals early and to act swiftly when things go wrong. A classic example is the story of Nokia and Ericsson's different reactions to a failure in supply.[10] In March 2000, a fire in a Philips semiconductor plant in New Mexico destroyed or contaminated millions of mobile phone chips. Nokia and Ericsson accounted for 40 per cent of the supplier's business and were duly prioritized by Philips. However, the difference of speed in the way each firm reacted had a radical effect on the outcome.

Three days after the fire, Nokia realized orders were not coming through as expected, so phoned the supplier and were told deliveries would be disrupted for about a week. They sent engineers to New Mexico to investigate, but when this was discouraged, they started daily checks on incoming supplies. As the depth of the problem emerged, Nokia exerted pressure to ensure all other Philips plants would deploy spare capacity to meet the order, and worked with other suppliers to escalate their production. At the same time it reconfigured its products to accept slightly different chips from other sources.

Meanwhile Ericsson accepted the suppliers' assurance that the problem was a small one. By the time Ericsson finally acted, Nokia had secured all sources of supply. Ericsson lost an estimated $400 m in new product sales and Nokia consolidated its pole position in the market.

Sometimes the problem is closer to home and you need to grasp the nettle within your own organization. John Yard tells a story of a personality clash between two otherwise extremely able managers that was causing problems in a partnership. Realizing the problem was continuing, Yard gave the managers a deadline – either they dealt with their relationship within a month or one of them would have to go. A month later he had to follow through with his threat. 'It wasn't about their capability, and I helped the guy who left to find another job – it was just one of those things that you can't have in a partnership', he says. 'But dealing with the problem definitely raised my credibility within the partnership.'

Finally if things are seriously breaking down, the best thing to do is to step back from collaborating and go back to transacting. When each party is delivering their side of the bargain effectively, you can start rebuilding trust in the relationship.

Keep things fresh

The maintenance stage is very different from the heady early days of a partnership. It's about getting on with the job – and some people will inevitably feel that the job has already been done. As things settle down, people become complacent and leadership gets delegated down the hierarchy, deputies appearing at meetings and constant changes of face.

Collaborative leaders need to work hard throughout this stage to keep improving day-to-day performance and to keep renewing relationships within the partnership. Running regular health checks on the quality of the relationship – including detailed perception data – is essential. As the partnership matures, the potential problems are less obvious and you risk being taken by surprise, perhaps by something that didn't even feature on the risk register. Forward measurement (covered in Chapter 4) will help you predict the pitfalls and scenario planning helps you prepare for them. Even more important is keeping your ear to the ground and regularly asking your subordinates about what worries them.

You also need to respond to changing circumstances, and be alive to both risk and opportunity. Key people will change and new people need to be inducted into the partnership. Political, legal or regulatory changes may force a rethink of strategy. The business environment may alter dramatically. In every case the partnership needs to be prepared and poised to act. Whatever happens, it's important that the whole partnership understands the new climate and the possibilities it offers. Run one-off events to involve all parties in re-setting the strategy to take account of the changes, and make sure you communicate the new direction to all stakeholders.

When change happens, you need to rely on the relationships you've built. Close personal relationships, with your opposite numbers within the partnership and with other stakeholders, will come into their own and increase your flexibility in responding to change. For former oil company CEO Charles Jamieson, they're the cornerstone of running a successful partnership – especially in an industry like oil where there are major highs and lows. 'You need to make friends with people', he says. 'And when something happens, you need to have a good enough relationship with your opposite number to ring them up and jump on a plane.'

Maintenance road signs

You know you're on the right track if:

- All partners are using the same set of data to view performance of the partnership and leaders in all areas are committed to improving that performance.
- There is evidence of regular review of the quality of the relationship.
- There are practical and efficient escalation processes – used by all parties to identify and progress problems quickly.
- There are mechanisms in place to engage staff in the objectives and the progress of the partnership and to encourage them to feed in ideas to improve the way that the partnership functions.
- Joint programmes exist to develop leadership capability across the partnership.
- There is a single joint risk register with agreed plans for mitigation for common risks.
- Senior leaders take personal responsibility to undertake the difficult conversations they need to solve partnership problems actively with their opposite numbers.
- The partnership looks ahead for significant changes, and picks them up and responds to them.

You know you're going off track if:

- Delays occur in addressing problems in the partnership – people are kept waiting for formal meetings, or communication is very poor.
- There is always a last-minute scramble to get the right skills in the right place – and therefore a sense of chaotic resourcing.
- There is an unwillingness to share resources, information or even space between parties.
- Leaders don't have a personal relationship with their opposite number.
- Deputies appear regularly at partnership meetings, or meetings are cancelled.
- There is no clear communication of successes or of progress in the relationship to staff or stakeholders.
- Leaders are not bringing in ideas and best practice to the partnership from outside.

Stage 4: ending – don't burn your bridges

Breaking up is hard to do. Yet collaborative leaders need to get good at it, because partnerships rarely last for ever and most have an inbuilt obsolescence. Skill in handling endings may often not be seen as being as crucial as getting the launch right, but it's none the less important. Sometimes a partnership drags on without a managed ending long after it's ceased to create value. Sometimes you need to re-tender to inject new life into the project or re-set its direction. And if a partnership truly isn't working, you have to walk away from it. Whatever the ending, remember that it's a small world – and you may end up working with the same partner again.

Nowhere is this clearer than in political partnerships or coalition government. Since 2010 the UK political system has had to come to terms with the demands of managing a coalition government with a declared fixed five year term, and this timetable produces many of the same dynamics that we have looked at in commercial contracted partnerships. Political leaders need to learn how to negotiate coalition agreements with individuals or parties that may have been long-term political adversaries. They have to find ways of making the relationship work for the duration of a parliament and then as they come towards an ending disentangle and distance themselves sufficiently so they can compete against each other through an election campaign with the knowledge that after the vote they may be working with the same partner – or a radically different one the following day.

Re-tendering a contract: keep the relationship going

When a contract approaches its end, but there's still the need for a future partnership, it's time to re-evaluate existing relationships and learn the lessons. Leaders need to assess what has worked in the partnership and what hasn't, and determine what they would like to change in the new contract, whether they intend to switch partners or not. This assessment should cover not just productivity and performance, but how the process worked, which skills were needed and which were in short supply, how leaders performed, and how cultural difference and communication was managed between partners.

The problem of course is that this is a difficult time for the incumbent. It's important for the lead side to maintain a strong relationship with their partner throughout this time – if the relationship is suspended because of procurement obligations, it will be hard to rebuild it later. Don't destroy the open communication you've developed over the course of the partnership by suddenly closing down and refusing to share information in deference to unwritten rules. Above all, don't bad-mouth your partner to other organizations tendering for the contract.

It's also important not to get distracted by the new contract. Create specific governance for the tender in parallel to the partnership governance, so that leaders keep focused – they need to be highly involved in concluding the old relationship, particularly during a handover period. Be clear about accountabilities, and don't leave it to chance that the outgoing partner and the new one will work collaboratively. You need to incentivize collaboration to make it happen – not only through financial incentives, but by building pride in a job well done.

You also need to communicate to everyone within the partnership exactly what will be happening and how. Whenever one of the construction companies we work with succeeds another contractor in a roads maintenance project, managers are aware of the risk that essential hand tools and road-digging equipment could disappear overnight in the changeover. So as part of their plan, they go round the road workers in advance explaining that if there are any scrap or waste materials as part of the handover, they are welcome to keep them, but that all tools will be logged in an inventory and needed from that day on.

Job done – remember the fundamentals

Many partnerships have very specific and time-limited deliverables and so come to a natural end. A new hospital gets completed. An aircraft is finally built. A contract runs out. Even if a new contract is to begin immediately afterwards, all alliances need well-managed conclusions. The last thing you want is for performance to fall away as people take their eye off the ball.

In the final months and weeks, everyone needs to understand exactly what needs to be delivered before the close of the project and what they are accountable for. The relationship should become more transactional again, with each side getting on with their list of deliverables.

Even though the end is visible, you can't afford to neglect the basics. You need fast decision making, and specific, detailed communications throughout. You're likely to have to spend more time on governance, not less. And you should avoid disengaging from your partners too soon – keep the relationship open and direct.

Finally, as the end of the project approaches, you also need to build in time to identify the learning before everyone goes their separate ways. This should embrace not just technical issues, but what you've learned about behaviour in the partnership.

Forced endings: keep communicating

Unfortunately some partnerships will end in tears. Disasters happen – businesses go into administration, stock markets crash, companies merge or get taken over – and all can have fatal consequences for partnerships. And sometimes the problem may be in the choice of partner: if there's no way of reconciling opposing objectives or conflicting values, you need to part company.

When disaster strikes, don't panic. This is the time for sober assessment before taking action – fast decisions are usually ill-advised. And the reality is that partnerships usually take a long time to disentangle. When Charles Jamieson was head of Premier Oil, he entered a partnership with Shell in Pakistan, when each side's strategies began to diverge so much that collaboration was proving impossible. Realizing the joint venture had become unworkable, Jamieson began the elaborate process of dismantling it. 'They were very sensitive about why we would want to do this', he says. 'I had to explain it was for corporate reasons and nothing to do with them personally. It took us 18 months to get into the partnership with Shell – and 18 months to get out of it.'

Charles Jamieson believes it's crucial for leaders to hammer out a preliminary solution before resorting to legal niceties. 'You need to go to your opposite number and get them to agree in principle before you let the lawyers work it out', says Jamieson. 'It's important to have agreed it at a high enough level before you throw it to the wolves.'

You're also likely to need changes of governance to address the demands of the new situation. Level-headedness is important: rather than rushing around to little purpose, exert control by re-setting the relationship, for example by getting leaders from all sides together on a weekly basis with a new remit.

Finally, communicate more rather than less throughout the break-up. You need to get stakeholders on your side to support you through the difficulties, and if you've built up a network of strong relationships within and outside the partnership, this investment will pay off in a crisis.

Endings road signs

You know you're on the right track if:

- Leaders keep communicating with their opposite numbers, no matter how difficult the circumstances.
- Everyone is willing to learn and share the lessons from the partnership experience.

- Partners are willing to write references or testimonials for each other.
- Partners are jointly aware of the end point of the contract and are clear about their own accountabilities right up to that point.
- There are clear and agreed handover plans and a process to involve the successors in what happens next.

You know you're going off track if:

- Leaders are distracted by negotiating the next contract rather than paying attention to managing the current situation.
- Performance falls away over time and this is not effectively addressed by the existing performance management/incentives process.
- Key people leave because they don't see future career opportunities in this contract.
- Vacancies are left unfilled without agreement.
- Leaders bad-mouth existing partners as they start the selection process for a new contract.
- Response times increase for any query or request for change.

Chapter summary

Partnership is a cross country marathon not a sprint – you need plenty of practice and a good map

Whilst every collaborative relationship is different, one group of relationships, that of contracted fixed-term partnerships, does tend to follow a fairly similar pattern. Their lifecycles go through a number of distinct stages each with its own specific risks and warning signs.

In this chapter we identify four stages for a typical partnership lifecycle:

- Selection
- Transition
- Maintenance/improvement
- Ending

and we highlight signs to look for to tell whether a partnership is on-track or approaching a danger zone at each stage.

The way a leader needs to work and the amount of time that they need to devote to a particular partnership will have to change as the relationship moves from one stage to another. These changes of leadership focus and style can take an organization by surprise and feel uncomfortable for a leader who has to be ready to get more involved at key transitions. But the warning signs described in this chapter will help leaders to prepare for the different leadership challenges in the stages yet to come.

Lessons for leaders

In the selection stage:

- Make formalities of the selection process work for you so that you come out of it with the right long-term partner and the right form of contract that really suits your business need.

In the transition stage:

- Get to know your partners and start to earn trust by delivering reliable transactions. And from the evidence gained from these early encounters review and refine the operational processes and behaviour that you will need to set in place for the long term.

In the maintenance and improvement stage:

- Bring people from all parties together to solve problems fast – and publicize the lessons learned. Keep an eye on succession and focus on system-wide communication and capability development processes.

And in the ending stage:

- Keep the relationship going and remember the fundamentals of delivery right up to the end of the contract – but also help people to leave a positive legacy of their time working together by celebrating their joint achievements.

And finally:

- It's always worth trying to stand in your partner's shoes. How would they rate your organization as a partner? And what would they say about your organizational capability? (Not just the capability to manage at the current stage of the road map but also your state of readiness for the challenges of what is likely to come next.) If you don't know – ask them.

PART 2

The collaborative leader in action

This section of the book focuses on the experience of being a collaborative leader and some of the challenges that have to be faced in today's business environment.

We have distilled the lessons from ten years' experience working with many collaborative leaders (successful and unsuccessful) to help you accelerate your own development and to avoid some of the pitfalls. We have also focused on some key areas that leaders tell us they find particularly challenging in collaborative situations: managing risk across organizational boundaries, dealing with the inevitable conflict that occurs and dealing with the particular demands of working with Boards.

Lastly we look to the future. There is no doubt that as the world becomes ever more interconnected, the need for collaborative leaders will grow. But what will they look like and what are the new challenges that they will face?

The attributes of the collaborative leader

Collaborative leadership is one of the most sophisticated and mature styles of leadership as it demands that individuals have the skills, attitudes and self-awareness necessary to build relationships, handle conflict and share control in highly complex situations.

Based on our research, there are three critical skills:

- Mediation – the ability to address conflict situations as they arise, building the confidence of others in the process.
- Influencing – the ability to match the most effective method of influence to the needs of the situation and the parties involved.
- Engaging others – building relationships, communicating with clarity and involving others in decision making.

In support of these skills, there are three essential attitudes for every collaborative leader:

- Agility – to quickly assimilate facts, ask incisive questions and handle complexity with ease.
- Patience – to take a calm and measured approach, reflecting on new information and giving confidence to others.
- Empathy – to truly listen, understanding personal impact and taking an open-minded attitude to the views of others.

These specific skills and attitudes build on the traditional attributes of conventional leadership. However, without competence in these areas, an aspiring leader will fail to meet the changes of being an effective collaborative leader.

In this section

Chapter 7: Secrets of success – conversations with collaborative leaders

There is no substitute to learning from those who have risen to the challenges of collaborative leadership and have the track record to prove it. In this chapter some successful collaborative leaders reflect on their own experience and share what they have learned about building relationships, sharing control and handling conflict.

Chapter 8: Why some collaborative leaders fail

Collaboration does not come easily to many leaders and, often for understandable reasons, many fail to meet the challenges of leading across organizational boundaries. This chapter focuses on the story of four fictionalized leaders – all typical of their types – who didn't understand the nature of collaborative working, with disastrous results for all involved.

Chapter 9: Collaborative leaders in the boardroom

Perhaps one of the most complex but important places for leaders to practise the skills of collaboration is in the boardroom. This chapter looks at the particular challenges of getting effective working between all the parties involved in an effective Board and the role of collaborative leadership. We do not focus exclusively on formally constituted Boards but on all groups who might be described in this way.

Chapter 10: Relationship risk

Risk management and mitigation are core parts of any leader's role. But for the collaborative leader the identification and management of risk are even more complex. This chapter explores the challenges highlighted by relationship risks, risks that originate in complex interconnected systems where several parties are working closely together.

Chapter 11: Conflict and the collaborative leader

Interconnected collaborative situations will cause conflict – this is inevitable. The collaborative leader has no option to avoid such situations, they have to handle and manage these conflicts creatively and constructively. This chapter explores the skills, attitudes and self-awareness essential to create positive outcomes.

Chapter 12: The future collaborative leader

Collaborative leadership is a fast evolving discipline, driven by an increasingly interconnected world. In this chapter we summarize the collaborative leadership tools and attributes and we identify the trends that will make this style of leadership increasingly essential in the years ahead.

7

SECRETS OF SUCCESS –
CONVERSATIONS WITH
COLLABORATIVE LEADERS

A personal leadership journey

It was over 60 years ago that Mahatma Ghandi said 'I suppose leadership at one time meant muscles, but today it means getting along with people'; he was right then and his words are still pertinent advice for leaders in the twenty-first century.[1] Achieving results in today's world means leaders 'getting on with people' in lots of different circumstances. Carlos Ghosn the CEO of the Renault Nissan alliance put it well when he said that leaders of the future will need 'global empathy' – 'not just empathy and sensitivity for people from their own culture but for people from completely different countries and cultures'.[2] To achieve this, collaborative leaders need to be part politician and part psychologist and that can be quite a personal challenge.

So far we've looked at the building blocks of collaboration in terms of the processes and tools you can use to analyse and guide you through the difficult task of leading collaboratively. But there's no simple formula to applying these tools – making any partnership or other collaborative relationship work is a learning process. And it's not just about instilling the principles of collaboration into your organization – it's also a journey of personal learning for you as a leader.

This chapter is based on interviews with a number of successful leaders from very different fields that we have worked with over many years. Their individual approaches to collaborative leadership bring out some important lessons which we have then distilled into a set of six attributes that we believe underpin their success and define the collaborative leader. Their careers span both public and private sectors, they're experts in joint ventures, alliances, public–private partnerships and internal collaborations, and all have made collaborative working a way of life. We asked them what qualities it takes to lead effective collaborations, what they've learned along the road and what advice they would give to others.

All of these leaders have achieved extraordinary things through collaboration.

David Sterry, former Chairman and chief executive of May Gurney, established long-term relationships with public sector partners in an industry famed for its confrontational tactics.

Sir Don Curry ran a diverse farming business in the north east of England for many years before joining the Board of NFUM (the mutual insurance company started by members of the National Farmers Union). In 2003, he became its Chairman and he was also responsible for chairing the UK Prime Minister's commission on the future of food and farming, set up following the BSE crisis.

When John Yard took on the leadership of the Inland Revenue's outsourcing project with EDS – at that time the biggest in Europe – his move was widely seen, he says, as a 'hospital pass'. Yet the project ended up being a model for governmental collaborations.

The oil exploration and production industry is a sector that understands about collaboration. Most new projects rely on several global partners sharing the financing risk or to supply specific technical capability. And as the number of global players is relatively small you will run into the same partners again and again in different situations. After a career in this industry heading up Premier Oil for 13 years Charles Jamieson is now chairman of Salamander Energy which operates in Indonesia and Thailand. Charles was succeeded at Premier Oil by Simon Lockett who has been CEO since 2005, leading a phase of significant growth for the business.

While they're very different in character, these leaders share a common philosophy: in today's world, collaboration is not just desirable but essential to delivering their business.

The draw of collaboration

What attracted these leaders to the collaborative style of leading? For David Sterry, an engineer by training, it's a practical solution to a problem: partnership is quite simply the most efficient way to get things done. The construction industry was – and to a large extent still is – traditional, relying on unforeseen extras to inflate low-margin initial prices, and generating huge confrontation along the way. Opting for long-term partnerships changes all that. 'In reality I don't like confrontation', says Sterry. 'It just got in the way of solving problems and I got very frustrated. It's a waste of effort bringing in the consultants and the lawyers. I'm looking for any way I can to avoid that.'

For Sir Don Curry it's because you get better results. 'You are more likely to get a decision implemented if you've got all the people with a stake in the result around the table when the decision is made', he says 'It's simple really – working and taking decisions collaboratively means you get to results that have been tested by people with different backgrounds and perspectives.'

In the capital-intensive and highly risky oil industry, collaboration is nothing new – it has long been a necessity. Oil companies enter joint ventures with each other, work alongside governments, and employ a vast array of skilled contractors. 'For every exploration well you drill, only one in twelve has a chance of leading to commercial success', says Charles Jamieson. 'You can spend tens of millions of dollars. Even big companies will need to offload some of the risk by being in partnership.' Simon Lockett agrees – for him collaboration is simply a necessity, 'the oil and gas industry just couldn't function without effective collaboration', he says, 'although the style that works is different in every case'. Beyond the inevitability of working in partnership within the industry, Jamieson is also naturally drawn to the personal relationships on which collaboration depends. 'I'm not particularly gregarious but I enjoy meeting people from different cultures', he says. 'Business school is all about strategy, but when you get down to it, it's personal. You get people to help by helping them.'

For John Yard, the attraction is – in part at least – the novelty of swimming against the tide. When he took on the Inland Revenue outsourcing project, he found himself in his natural element. Instead of changing jobs at the end of a four-year stint (the norm in public sector management) he chose to keep on heading partnerships. 'Successful organizations are ones that can find ways to work across corporate boundaries', he says. But for him, partnership is more than a route to being successful. The real excitement lies in having to approach problems in completely new ways. 'I like coming at things where the solution is counter-intuitive', says Yard. 'If you're going to make partnerships work, you have to do things a bit differently.'

Make it matter – for everyone

One of the most important attributes of a leader in any partnership is being able to engage people in what you're trying to achieve. 'Communication is the most important thing', says Charles Jamieson. 'Any leader needs a simple, clear vision. When I first started giving presentations to the City, the strategy was a bit complex, and fund managers tended to nod off before it had been fully explained. You have to go in there and within one minute be able to say, "this is my strategy, this is what I'm going to do". Being simple is just amazing.'

Simon Lockett says 'you've got to get buy-in from all concerned. It starts with your own Executive team but goes right through the organization. You must understand the pressures that working in partnership puts on your own people and make sure they can deal with that – and that their own frustrations or intolerances are not communicated to your partners.'

Of course, getting buy-in is necessary in many areas of leadership. But in collaborative ventures, you don't have captive audiences of staff whose salaries you pay. You've gone beyond your own power block and now have to win people over for a living. And there are many more stakeholders to deal with. Not only do you need clarity, but also the ability to flex the message according to your audience.

The great communicators are ones who can relate the overarching vision to the needs of different partners and different groups. John Yard tells the story of going to a partner's organization and giving a rousing talk to the staff there, taking a good look at things from their side of the fence, and being candid about what the Inland Revenue was getting wrong. It won a standing ovation. 'There was some concern about whether I should have been so open and said all that', says Yard, 'But it was important in order to win trust.'

Sir Don Curry says 'collaborative leaders also need to be great motivators. They need to be able to motivate people to achieve shared goals – goals that people might not have named themselves in the first instance but goals they come to feel they have shared ownership of over time.'

Don't blame when things go wrong

'If you think collaborative partnerships are going to go swimmingly, you're wrong', says Charles Jamieson. It's a sentiment that strikes a chord with all the leaders we've spoken to. Not that they are pessimists – far from it. They simply know from experience that partnerships are complex and fraught with difficulty. It's far better to acknowledge this up front and prepare for the worst, than to come to blows further down the line.

'I sit down with customers right at the beginning and say "let's look at how to deal with something that goes wrong"', says May Gurney chief executive David Sterry. 'You have to build a relationship that allows you to deal with difficult things.' In the past, he believes, people were trained to trip each other up and catch each other out. Collaboration requires a very different approach, where you can admit to weakness in your own organization without becoming defensive. 'If you're always trying to score points, it doesn't help. It just makes people behave as if they're under attack', says Sterry.

Of course, this doesn't always work: sometimes the customer doesn't want to drop the defences – or won't ease off on the attacks. 'Sometimes you can only conclude that their whole life is like that', says Sterry. 'And if they're not going to recognize the benefits of change, it's best not to work with them.'

'We need a greater recognition that things do go wrong on complex projects', says former Inland Revenue boss John Yard. 'We need to get people off the blame culture. The natural reaction of both sides when something goes wrong is to get the contract out, argue about how the terms haven't been met, and seek penalties wherever possible, instead of working out how to solve the problem in order to achieve the outcome both sides need. It's all very well winning an acrimonious contractual debate, but how do you get both sides focused on the real issue afterwards? And there are always problems on both sides!'

When John Yard headed the Inland Revenue's IT outsourcing project in the mid-1990s, the IT provider, EDS, hit a performance problem early on in the deal and failed to deliver all of the targets specified in the contract. The natural reaction of the Inland Revenue Board was to seek penalties from EDS, particularly given the difficult financial position at the time, but Yard argued that this approach on its own would not solve the underlying problem. He persuaded the Board to allow him to work with EDS to ensure that the real causes of the problem were understood, before looking for a solution that was acceptable to both parties.

This revealed that the structure of the contract was causing problems, and the terms needed to be adjusted to make the deal more commercially viable, in return for delivery improvements and clarification of the way the contract would work in the future. Despite the difficulties of getting this accepted by the Board, John Yard secured their agreement to what was in effect a counter-intuitive decision. 'The easy thing is to agree with all your peers', he says, 'but to make partnerships work across corporate boundaries, you have to recognize that there are times when you need to stand up and be counted.' The decision put the partnership back on an even keel, and it became a model for government collaborative projects.

'Too often people focus on the wrong thing', says Yard. 'The focus shouldn't be on winning the short-term penalty battle but on winning the long-term delivery war.'

Put yourself in other people's shoes

Building trust starts with service delivery. In the early days of building a relationship, doing exactly what you've promised is the way to convince partners they've made the right choice. May Gurney's David Sterry recalls a partnership where trust was decidedly lacking because the original architects of the deal had moved on. 'We just concentrated on delivering what was required', he says. 'As soon as you fail to deliver, you lose the relationship. Then progressively we managed to break those barriers down. Trying to maximize the contract always comes undone. So we take a long-term view.'

Keeping your promises is the first step. But to build truly collaborative relationships you need to go further and put yourself in other people's shoes. Our five leaders have become remarkably good at thinking through what motivates other people.

'We spend a lot of time trying to understand what the customer's drivers are – how they're encouraged to succeed and how they're incentivized', says David Sterry. 'Sometimes incentivization can drive the wrong behaviours, and you need to get the issues out on the table.'

John Yard is equally diligent. 'I need to understand why x gets his bonus and how I help him get it. What you're looking for is a mutuality of objectives – they're not the same.'

Sir Don Curry agrees. He says, 'the most important thing is that people respect each other and listen to each other so they can understand where everyone is coming from. This takes time, they might not even understand each other at first – but they have to want to. And it's the leader's job to set that tone of mutual respect and to help people build that understanding of others over time.'

It's something that Charles Jamieson excels in. The opposite of a typical Texan oil supremo, he quietly goes about forging real and lasting relationships all over the world. At the beginning of his career in the oil industry, when he was evaluating investment projects for different businesses owned by Gulf Oil, he had to convince people that he was on their side. 'People hate accountants and people from head office. I tried to make them see I was someone who could help them', he says. 'It was the first time that I saw that personal relationships are the most important thing.'

Later, he had to work with government officials all round South East Asia. 'They're often poorly paid civil servants, and you're not going to bribe them. How do you get work done? The only way I know is by being human and decent – understanding and appreciating their position. You need to be interested in people as people.'

'Glad-handing skills' are of course part of it, but there's far more to it than that. Charles Jamieson is a great believer in 'just pitching up and talking to people on a regular basis' to maintain a true personal connection. 'There was one senior bureaucrat in a country in South East Asia I used to visit seven or eight times a year', he recalls. 'Whatever time I got in the previous night, I would meet him on the golf course at six o' clock in the morning and we'd play nine holes and have breakfast and talk through business before we had formal meetings in the rest of the day. It meant that he was aware of everything I was going to say beforehand, and he would say, "I can't do it that way, but we can do it this way". So we built up a strong degree of trust – and frankly I don't think we'd have been able to do all that we achieved if we didn't have that relationship.'

This isn't just negotiation, although finding something for each stakeholder is important. It's genuinely getting on with other people and putting the effort in to maintain relationships, however time-consuming and difficult it may be. And when things go wrong – as they always do in partnerships – leaders like Charles can call upon many others for help.

Patience is a virtue

Collaborative leaders need patience. While aspects of the original deal may force leaders to make decisions at breakneck speed, getting to the contract can take ages and the actual partnership is likely to last many years. It can take a long time to yield results. So it's important to be flexible enough to have both a fast and a slow mode.

Sir Don Curry is keen to emphasize that you mustn't force decisions too early. 'If things get stuck I ask people to go away and find out what information they need to enable them to make a joint decision. Often that can mean sending people with opposing views away in twos and threes and asking them to come back to the meeting next time with a joint proposal for a way forward. Everyone needs to be able to go back to their different constituencies with some progress to report. You need to keep talking until everyone can find that.'

In addition, when you work outside the bounds of your own authority, every-thing takes longer. You can't simply tell people what to do, as you could if you led your own organization – you have to bring them round. And sometimes you have to bite your tongue and let things happen in their own sweet time. 'Early on you need to listen a lot, and not form opinions too quickly', says David Sterry. 'You need to understand why the other party is how they are. Then you need to test it to make sure you understand. Try to ensure that they own the solution. People are willing to move if they can contribute to change.'

For Simon Lockett the challenge is balancing patience and pace. 'You need to walk a tightrope to ensure that you can keep the pace up but without you or your partners getting overstretched and making mistakes.'

Share the credit, share the load

As we have said many times collaborative leadership means sharing control – but it can also mean being prepared to share the credit and to share the work in ways that are not always immediately apparent.

When Sir Don Curry was asked to chair the Prime Minister's commission on the future of food and farming, he knew he had to bring together a group of people with very strongly held and diverse views. People from the big food retailers, farm-ers and special interest groups like The Soil Association and the RSPB. He started by encouraging people to get to know each other – and to value their colleagues as individuals. He says 'I knew that they all had lots to contribute – I wanted everyone else to know that too. We all knew that there was a very important job to do and one that would take a lot of effort – but at the first meeting I didn't aim to conduct any real business at all – just to get people to listen to each other. People need to feel comfortable with each other as individuals before they can really listen to other's opinions.'

But listening to each other is not enough, a collaborative leader needs to create the governance and group spirit that will ensure joint action. 'I told them there was only one ground rule', says Curry, 'that there would be no minority reports from this commission. And if it ever looked like we were heading towards that I'd go to the PM as Chair to say that we had all failed and that he should disband the com-mission. And of course no one wants to be associated with failure.' It was perhaps a high-risk strategy but in the end it created an immense sense of togetherness in the group. And evidence of that was that they all continued to meet, to monitor pro-gress, and to hold the government to account long after their report was published and the formal work of the commission completed.

Simon Lockett has some similar lessons from a very different industry. Oil explo-ration is essentially a risky business and leaders need to feel that they are sufficiently in control of the financial and technical risks. As he puts it, 'you need to feel in control even when you are sharing control and that comes down to trust in your partners. The win–win is when both parties have a feeling of confidence about what the other is doing and so a sense of control over the process.'

Exercise your inner steel

'Working collaboratively in a partnership is not about taking a soft and fluffy approach', says John Yard. 'It's hard and difficult. You need to have a backbone of steel.' Although collaborative leaders have to form strong personal relationships, they also need to be direct when necessary. Developing both the skill and stomach for difficult conversations is a key skill.

'It's about getting the emotions on the table – telling a supplier that you think they're being greedy, for example – and not getting people's backs up', says John. 'You need to defuse the emotion and start looking at the real issues. Both sides need to state the problem and be prepared to listen and understand problems from the other party's perspective.'

It's important to get this right from the outset. 'You need to establish early on in a relationship that it's OK to do that', says Charles Jamieson, 'so you can put your hand up and say "I think you're talking rubbish" without destroying everything.'

'You've got to remember why you started working together in the first place – and that was to get a financial return', says Simon Lockett, 'you must never lose sight of that. And don't get too close to your partner – you need to be able to observe what they are doing and be able to check out whether any worries you may have about them are legitimate.'

Leading a collaboration may need a gentle touch but it needs some inner steel. Working together with people from different organizations and different cultures and getting performance from them is a tough job. Some people may think making collaborative relationships work is all about being nice to people and paying attention to 'the soft stuff'. But talking to these leaders we see that they are tough-minded individuals who are unafraid of tackling difficult situations and challenging long held beliefs with powerful partners if that is what is required to deliver joint results. Collaborative leadership requires courage.

The six skills and attitudes of a collaborative leader

Working with collaborative leaders over the years and based on all the interviews we've carried out researching both editions of this book, we've been able to distil a number of common characteristics that leaders regularly describe as underpinning their success. We've taken these broad characteristics and created a developmental model with six components – three of which could be described as critical leadership skills with the other three described as essential attitudes of a collaborative leader.

This doesn't mean that all successful leaders have to score highly in all six areas before they can take on a role that requires a high degree of collaboration – rather that leaders facing collaboration challenges should focus on these skills and attitudes in order to assess their own abilities and to plan appropriate development actions.

Three critical skills and three essential attitudes

The performance of the collaborative leader is dependent on them having all the basic experience and skills of any leader, but it is also this set of skills and attitudes that is necessary to address complex interdependent situations. The three essential skills are:

- **Mediation** – this enables the leader to address conflict as soon as it arises. It is based on an ability to help people understand each other's motives and perspectives. This knowledge can then be used by all parties to find ways of working together which are constructive, sustainable and which achieve the objectives of their joint enterprise. After running many collaborative leadership 360° feedback programmes, it is clear that the demands of handling conflict and the associated mediation skills that leaders need to respond to those demands, are often the number one leadership development priority.
- **Influencing** – this enables the leader to match their method of influence to the needs of the situation and of the organizations involved in the collaborative situation. This is different to the conventional interpersonal influencing that is taught on many personal development programmes. In a collaborative context leaders need to share control across complex systems of different organizations and external stakeholders. This ability to influence often requires an understanding of organizational culture and personality type as well as an objective analysis of the business situation to hand.
- **Engaging others** – this includes the skills of networking and relationship building required to support the delivery of objectives in an interdependent system. But it also includes communicating with clarity, often in high stress situations, and involving others in decision making at the right time. One thing is certain about collaborative leadership – you cannot do it on your own so the ability to engage others is critical.

As well as these three skills, collaborative leaders can only be successful if they develop three essential attitudes in order to meet the challenges of the role:

- **Agility** – an inquisitive attitude with an ability to quickly assimilate facts, ask incisive questions and handle complexity with ease. In these complex situations, collaborative leaders need to be quick thinking and to be able to respond to developing issues in a timely manner.
- **Patience** – managing relationships takes time and collaborative leaders need to be able to take a calm and measured approach, reflecting on new information and giving confidence to others. We've sometimes described this attitude as 'stickability', leaders building relationships for the long run. They know that in a true collaboration you can't always dictate the speed of progress on your own. This may seem at odds with 'agility' but all the most successful collaborative leaders we've seen combine both. They can think on their feet and jointly

develop innovative ways forward – but they are also invested for the long term and have a patient attitude towards their partners.

- **Empathy** – perhaps the underpinning attitude of a collaborative leader is a willingness to truly listen, to be open-minded to the views of others, however different they may be, and to have a high degree of self-awareness of the impact their leadership behaviour has on others. An empathetic attitude is last on this list but it's often the first thing you notice about a really experienced and successful collaborative leader.

The chance to make your mark

Just because the leaders in this chapter are confident about giving away control, it doesn't mean they're driven by altruism. For each the gains are considerable – it's just that they achieve more by giving power away than by holding tightly on to it.

'In my early career I could be as commercial as anyone else', says David Sterry. 'It was great fun and a bit of a game – how could you outwit the next guy? But it's not very constructive. This isn't how I want my approach to the built environment to work. I want to be more innovative, and I want to achieve more.'

When Sir Don Curry was asked to Chair a highly contentious government commission with members from very different interests groups some people told him it was a poisoned chalice – 'Well at my age that's the only kind of chalice I do' – he goes on, bringing diverse groups of people together to tackle difficult problems – 'because all the problems worth solving are like that – no one can solve them on their own so you are wise not to try'. This may also contribute to his view that, 'You more often find good collaborative leaders in the chairman's role than the CEO – they are necessarily different beasts.'

For John Yard, the real kudos lies in making organizations work better in a complex world. 'How do we move away from an environment where giving of my best stops you giving of your best?', he asks. 'Most organizations have hierarchical models – people have to compete against each other to get the best jobs. These people are competitive, rarely collaborative – they're mostly about personal gain and sometimes at the expense of their colleagues. But delivering success for an organization with complex services or products depends on a whole set of skills in the team, not just the skills of one person.'

Charles Jamieson believes a spirit of collaboration allowed Premier Oil to do things the bigger players could not. 'You can't just walk into a foreign country and say, "if it's good enough for Houston, it's good enough for Outer Mongolia"', he says. 'We were offering a package of treating people the way they wanted to be treated, building relationships and managing projects the way they should be managed.'

And for Simon Lockett working in collaboration with different partners across the globe is the only way to grow the business. 'Success in one area feeds future success in another. You build your reputation as a good partner and people want to work with you. It's as simple as that.'

They're impressive legacies. And in a world where everything is interconnected, it's increasingly hard to make a lasting mark unless you learn to collaborate.

Chapter summary

Collaborative leadership is not for the faint hearted

Whilst picking up tools and methodologies for collaboration can be a very useful way to build leadership skills, you can't beat learning from the experience of someone who has been there ahead of you. You can find many examples of great collaborative leadership to learn from in many different walks of life.

The leaders we talk about in this chapter are all very different individuals, but some common characteristics shine through and similar themes emerge. First, they all start from a deep conviction that getting people to work together and be guided by shared values isn't just desirable, it's essential to delivering sustainable results. And you can't leave any of your partners or colleagues out of that delivery equation. The leaders in this chapter may all use different language to describe it and different techniques to achieve it but getting buy-in and emotional engagement from everyone involved is a prerequisite to a successful collaborative enterprise.

But that doesn't mean that once you've got buy-in everything else is easy. All the leaders here have faced very real adversity – and often a deal of conflict along the way, but they have responded with patience and with empathy for the pain that their partners are enduring at the same time.

They have not been afraid to ask their business partners for help when troubles arise. Support works both ways. Whilst these leaders will always look to support their colleagues to achieve their joint long-term goals, they will also be prepared to lean on others and let them carry the leadership load when they need to.

It has been a privilege working with them.

Lessons for leaders

- Find the personal motive for collaborating. It's not just about the hard business case – you also need to work out what's in it for you at a personal level.
- Find ways of simplifying complex situations for your people – the implementation will often be difficult and messy but the principles or the policies you follow need to be elegant and simple to communicate.
- Prepare for how you are going to handle conflict well in advance. Start with the assumption that some conflict will occur and look hard at your own habits and the typical reactions of your organization to conflict situations.

- Have the courage to act for the long term. Good collaborative leaders look at success over the whole lifetime of the relationship.
- Invest in strong personal relationships all the way through the partnership, and externally with stakeholders. Nothing can beat real human connections when things go wrong.
- Have the confidence to share the credit generously.
- Continually develop your personal leadership capabilities, in particular the six key attributes of collaborative leaders: mediation, influencing, engaging others; agility, patience and empathy.

8

WHY SOME COLLABORATIVE LEADERS FAIL

Don't depend on old skills to meet a new challenge

Although most commentators now agree that many forms of business collaboration, whether partnerships or strategic alliances, are now essential, there is also consensus that making these arrangements work effectively is difficult. In fact around half of all of alliances break down prematurely, resulting in financial damage for both partners. Research on alliances between American firms found that 48 per cent ended in failure in less than two years.[1] An Audit Commission report comments that the failure rate of strategic alliances may be even higher at up to 70 per cent.[2] The same report points the finger at the contribution of the leader, suggesting that these business collaborations demand 'a different set of skills and capabilities that are in short supply and different to the traditional business skill set'.

So where are leaders getting it wrong? The simple answer is that they just don't understand the nature and complexity of collaborative working. While they might have a great track record in leading a single functional area, department or organization, the distinctly different challenges of running a highly collaborative venture leave them incompetent – literally. Habits that leaders have developed over years of success in situations where they could exercise positional control become major barriers to working effectively in a partnership or strategic alliance. Like the warnings about choosing high-profile fund managers to manage your nest egg, past performance is no indicator of future performance – or not unless recruitment panels start looking for the proven collaborative skills of building relationships, sharing control and handling conflict!

For leaders who find themselves in charge of a partnership or other collaborative relationship without being prepared to change their leadership style, it can be a stressful experience and a painful one for those who have to work with them. Suddenly the approaches these leaders have used for years don't work anymore.

Some leaders learn rapidly from the experience but others stick to their guns and either try to bluster their way through, or gradually lose their self-confidence. Either way, it's the quality of their decision making that ultimately suffers, with colleagues and business partners picking up the pieces.

In this chapter we'll look at four types of leader – the control freak, the idealist, the incrementalist, and the selfish high achiever. In each case their actions (or inactions) manage to ruin a variety of different business collaborations – failing to achieve the hoped-for value, leaving acrimony and chaos in their wake, or, at the extreme end, forcing the contract to be abandoned and started afresh. This is not a random sample. These four portraits illustrate typical leadership styles, which in the right circumstances can take someone a long way in their career, but which prove disastrous in collaborative ventures.

The portraits are fictional, they are caricatures, but we hope you will find lessons to learn in each of them. In our many years of working with leaders, we've seen aspects of all of these behaviours and the risks they pose to building effective organizational relationships.

The control freak

The context: from consulting to corporate leadership

Kevin was the new IT director of the largest division of a major manufacturing company. With a long and successful track record as a technologist and a middle manager, he now wanted to cement his reputation for fast delivery of complex IT systems in a very different environment. He was approaching retirement and this was his most senior perhaps last corporate role, providing him an opportunity to work at Board level in an established company, and in the manufacturing sector where he had started his career.

In taking up the IT director post, he quickly became aware of two factors that were to define his tenure in the company. The corporate centre of the parent company was becoming more powerful and its demands were increasingly in conflict with those of the largest division for which Kevin worked. At the same time there was a move towards company-wide single source contracts for corporate services. Procurement planning on one such IT outsourcing contract had already started before he arrived in his new post. The work was being led by the corporate shared service function, supported by members of IT staff from each division, and already Kevin was finding faults with it.

The leadership challenge: turning round the reputation of IT

Kevin was a man with a lot to prove. He was fiercely keen to ensure that his IT function improved its reputation within his division. The history of IT throughout the company was one of poor investment and user disappointment, and the current supplier was widely considered to be providing a terrible service. Kevin realized that the new contract – for company-wide IT desktop services – was critical to his achieving his own objectives.

He also knew that his fellow directors on the Board of his division were concerned about the move to concentrate services at the corporate centre. They had little faith that this approach would improve service. This view was reinforced when HR was moved to a corporate shared service model and service levels deteriorated significantly.

Kevin was expected to deliver significant improvements in service and knew that he could only do this if the new contract and new supplier delivered for him. In addition, he had to manage at the centre of a complex web of relationships (the current IT suppliers, the bidders for the new contract, his new department, his director colleagues, and the corporate IT function). And finally, he had something personal to prove – could he cut it as a 'proper' IT director?

Kevin's character: the expert loner

Kevin was a technical expert. He really knew how to implement IT systems, and the more complex the better. He understood how to set up IT service centres and make an outsourced IT contract work. After all, he had implemented outsourced arrangements in the past, although not in a corporate leadership role.

However, for all his technical knowledge and experience, he was a bit of a one-man band. He tended to work on his own, and when in the lead he would select the most competent people to work with him and then direct them closely in the detail. He had no time for what he saw as incompetence and found it quite acceptable to criticize others in public using very direct language. He liked people that he had worked with in the past – they were predictable and they understood and tolerated his style.

Kevin was highly committed to his work. He had little private life, living on his own without forming strong personal relationships. As a consequence he had lots of time to give to work issues. It was not unusual for him to send emails or make calls in the middle of the night if there were IT problems. No issue was too small to avoid his comment or involvement.

This energy and commitment was welcomed by his colleagues in the senior team in his own division. After his predecessor, who was considered lightweight and indecisive, Kevin was a breath of fresh air. If another director called with an IT problem, he was on to it immediately. Soon his reputation for 'driving IT forward' attracted the positive attention of his peers, although his impact was somewhat different with his own staff and his stakeholders in other parts of the manufacturing group.

The consequences: obstruction, bullying and conflict

Unhappy with the outsourcing contract, Kevin spent several weeks delaying its completion. At each stage he wanted more and more changes to the details.

These delays caused frustrations to his staff, who were increasingly unsure of their authority to define the contract. The goalposts constantly moved. The frustration also extended to the heads of the IT functions in other divisions of the company. They saw Kevin's behaviour as obstructive and selfish. Concern grew among all parties (including bidders) that the delays in letting the contract were eating into the planned transition period.

The contract was eventually placed, but immediately Kevin wanted to deal with the new suppliers on his own, outside the collective governance arrangements. The demands of his division were paramount and he intended to get rid of the incumbent supplier as quickly as possible. However, he also had wholly unrealistic expectations of the service improvements he could achieve with the new one. He expected significant improvements from day one – and when these did not happen, he demanded ever more detailed involvement in the supplier's business.

Things went from bad to worse. Service levels did not improve in the short term. In fact, with a reduced transition period, work on defining new roles and training users was inadequate and some high-profile failures of service occurred. With every new problem, big or small, Kevin's behaviour became more aggressive. He felt he knew the answers to the deteriorating situation, but no one was listening. His IT colleagues in other divisions were publicly criticizing him, and the new suppliers began to get different messages from different people.

As the commercial impact of Kevin's behaviour became apparent, disputes arose between the heads of IT across the company, and the problems were escalated to CEO level. At first the directors at Kevin's division supported him – after all, he was looking after their needs. But this support did not last. Service levels failed to improve and costs escalated at a frightening rate, as claim and counter-claim were made against the contract. Communication between the various parties broke down, with Kevin holding his own crisis meetings with suppliers in conflict with the corporate governance meetings.

Finally there was a formal complaint from a supplier regarding Kevin's behaviour towards one of their members of staff. At the same time a grievance was taken out by one of the corporate directors on the same issue. Kevin's approach could no longer be supported, even by his divisional colleagues. He was paid off and an interim IT director was quickly brought in to stabilize the situation.

However, Kevin's impact lasted much longer than his relatively short tenure in post. The relationship with the suppliers was in tatters and costs were out of control. In the end the decision was made to break the contract, bring in an interim supplier, redefine the outsourcing requirement and start the whole contracting process again – from the start.

This was a disruptive and enormously costly exercise for the company, resulting in a dramatic change in the structure of IT across the divisions, with the corporate centre now taking a strong lead. Relationships between the centre and the divisions were significantly damaged and the impact of this situation could still be felt in the organization some three years later. There were no winners – except the lawyers!

Messages for aspiring collaborative leaders

- The successful operation of any collaboration is ultimately dependent on productive relationships between the leaders involved. Leaders are role models for the behaviour of the rest of their organization and the way they act is particularly important at the start of any collaboration – early experience forges the behaviours and habits that others will adopt.
- The risks – both perceived and real – for an organization entering any collaboration are high. Failure has a huge financial impact and, perhaps just as importantly, an impact on reputation. The personal stakes for the collaborative leader in any partnership are also high. This pressure is real and corrosive for those who find the complexity of collaborative relationship-building a challenge.
- You can't do it all on your own. Not only do you have to share control with partners, you need the special skills of others in your own organizations (perhaps from other functions like procurement, commercial, legal or HR) to help you build the partnership constructively.
- You can't always pick the personalities of your partners, and bullying behaviour unfortunately does take place. You need a strategy to manage such situations:
  - Agree the ground rules on how to treat each other from the start.
  - Build strong relationship governance to deal with inappropriate behaviours.
  - Avoid colluding with a bully just to have a quiet life – it never works in the long term.
  - Address the first signs of bullying behaviour – don't let a problem become a crisis.
- Be aware of your own need for control – when things are going well most people behave reasonably, but when the pressure is on, it's easy to lose flexibility and the need to control everything and everyone can become destructive.

The idealist

The context: delivering complex public initiatives

Tony had spent his whole career in public service, working up through the ranks of the civil service. At last he achieved a long-held ambition to win a director-level post in a central government department, where he led an initiative to reduce the cost and improve the care of several chronic conditions. These were all complex challenges with high political priority, and each initiative involved many different stakeholders. In most cases these included several central government departments

(Health, Education and Pensions) along with organizations from the voluntary sector and some private sector drug companies.

This was the challenge that Tony had been waiting for. At interview he had impressed the panel with his commitment to the issues and the energy and zeal he had demonstrated in driving his previous team to deliver. References from his colleagues and stakeholders had also been impressive. Many mentioned his inspirational leadership style and how he created and motivated a very close, committed team.

The leadership challenge: making a difference in well-trod territory

Tony had no time to lose. He now had the remit and authority to drive this forward and he intended to make every minute count. Making a difference was his mission, and he was sure everyone else would be equally committed.

However, Tony was not the first person to try to address the cost and management of these chronic complaints. Many had tried before him and failed to get the various parties involved to collaborate. Although aware of past failures, Tony felt that sufficient passion and commitment had been missing. All you needed, in his view, was one team with a single-minded focus on a clear objective.

Tony's character: a driving passion

Tony passionately believed in the public service ethos and, in particular, in the values of the NHS. This was not surprising given his background – long-term chronic illness had afflicted several members of his family, and his own childhood had involved many trips to the hospital, visiting his mother who had died when he was a teenager.

His new role took him into unfamiliar cross-functional health policy issues and away from the simpler functional leadership he had exercised in the past. Tony was not a technical expert in the specific chronic complaints that he was now to address, but he knew how to get a team to deliver and he had boundless energy.

His style was to lead his team from the front. Membership of the team was rather like a club where only fully paid-up members were trusted completely. All others were outsiders. Tony took time to trust individuals – but when he did trust them, his loyalty to them was absolute. When things went wrong, he could see no fault with members of his team – the fault was always with other people or organizations. His loyalty to his team was returned by his own staff, who gave him their complete devotion. When Tony was successful, everyone knew about it and his team loved it.

Behind the scenes, however, the impact of this charismatic, driving style was more evident. Tony's family life suffered as he worked long hours, often away from home. And there was an illness a few years ago that was put down to stress and over-work. But these problems were not discussed openly by Tony in the office.

The consequences: dwindling trust and commitment

Within a few weeks of taking on the new role, Tony had gathered his team around him, selecting several members from his previous job. They spent considerable time together understanding the challenges they faced and the objectives that they had to achieve. They drew up a detailed plan describing how they were going to deliver the healthcare outcomes and cost savings, with such ambitious timescales that even members of Tony's own team were sceptical. However, their belief in Tony's ability and leadership meant that these doubts were never aired in public.

The next step was to launch the project. This was done with some fanfare. All potential partners were invited to a conference where Tony took centre stage. The challenge was laid out and the gauntlet thrown down. Either you were with him in his mission to improve chronic illness, or it was quite clear that you were making a choice to work against the project. In fact, this was no choice for most of the parties present. It was inconceivable for the other government departments not to sign up to the plan – any other approach would have been political suicide. The drug companies saw the potential damage to their reputation if they did not join in, and charities believed the initiative might help them deliver their own long-term aims.

The project started well but quickly hit problems. Relationships between the leaders of the various organizations involved in the partnership quickly became strained. Tony either dominated discussions at partnership meetings, or decisions were made in private with partners being told about them afterwards. As time passed, Tony's passion was undiminished, but the rumblings of discontent from other parties grew louder.

Tony's response was to initiate a team-building event over two days in a country house. All the leaders from all the parties were invited and – under some pressure – they attended. Conversation was polite until the director of another government department criticized Tony's decision-making style and 'autocratic approach'. The department's officials explained that they felt excluded from direction setting and planning and did not see how the current project could be successful. Several other parties then supported this argument.

Tony was shocked and hurt by their response. Did they not see the importance of the mission they were on together? Had he not made this absolutely clear at the launch meeting? Wasn't it obvious that the project needed one overall leader to drive it forward? The discussion became a quiet stand-off. It was evident that Tony did not have the support of his partners but also that he was not about to change his approach to any great extent. Although he regrouped his team after this event and altered the governance of the project to try to involve other parties more, his style remained much the same. Levels of trust slowly dissipated.

The voluntary sector organizations were first to walk away from the project – they didn't have to be involved and the effort of getting their voice heard was too great. The drug companies sent more junior members of staff to meetings, watching developments but becoming less active. Their promises of funds and support did not materialize. The other government departments did not change their involvement on the surface, but meetings were less well attended and deadlines were missed.

Tony and his team worked harder and harder to compensate. They pulled the drawbridge up and focused their efforts on forcing through change – but to little impact. In the end the funding was reduced, then quietly removed for the project, and the team disbanded. Tony had a recurrence of the stress-induced illness and was off work for three months.

Lessons for collaborative leaders

- For any collaboration to operate effectively there has to be common agreement among partners about the objectives and the operation of the relationship. However, the alignment of the leaders is most important, and without this agreement from the start, the arrangement is under threat.
- Not all parties enter a business collaboration with the same level of enthusiasm. Some may see it as something of a forced marriage – and leaders of all parties need to recognize this at the outset.
- When things begin to go wrong, it is important that leaders have an open relationship where difficult issues can be discussed and resolved. Most difficulties in a collaborative relationship are evident to the leaders if they listen to their people and ask the right questions. Leaders who are overly enthusiastic can discourage difficult feedback from others.
- Charismatic leadership might be engaging and motivating in some circumstances, but in a collaborative relationship, there is more than one person in a leadership role. A single leader cannot influence all the parties and stakeholders equally.
- Ambition and drive are important, but so are realism and planning. Things will inevitably change and problems emerge, and mature collaborative leaders should be able to recognize when other parties are losing engagement with the objectives of the partnership, stop and listen to difficult messages, and change their approach to deal with the concerns of others.
- Collaboration is about sharing control. Driving all parties forward without thinking about the consequences demonstrates unhelpful control of others. This will create conflict.
- As a leader, you should listen to your own motives – what do you personally want out of the collaboration and why. This is important information, as it will drive your behaviours. Share this information where possible with your partners – it is an important enabler to building trust.

The incrementalist

The context: the leader in waiting

John was a lifelong engineer and had recently been appointed Director of Works in a local authority in the north of England. Several years before he took up post, people had talked about him as 'director in waiting' – doing most of the work in the role of deputy, and waiting for Jim, the old director, to retire.

Jim's swansong had been to negotiate a 12-year contract to outsource much of the local authority's building and property maintenance to a private sector contractor in a public–private partnership deal. This involved transferring 150 members of his department's direct labour force over to the contractor, as well as bundling up a number of existing sub-contracts and managing them through the PPP. It was widely seen as a groundbreaking contract, with terms ensuring that any savings made were shared between the public and the private sector.

In taking up the director post, John was faced with the task of making the contract work and delivering value for money, as well as hitting all the authority's maintenance targets. The problem was that the contract was failing to live up to the expectations of the architects of the original deal. They had believed that on top of achieving efficiency savings, importing best practice ways of working from the private sector to the council would generate internal cost savings. They also assumed that as both partners got used to working together, the number of inspections and the amount of paperwork needed to manage the contract would also reduce, in a virtuous spiral of increasing joint efficiency. But none of this was coming to pass.

The leadership challenge: taking decisive action

John wanted the same goals as his predecessors, but the means of achieving them posed big challenges for him. The internal cost savings would necessitate staff cuts, but the people he wanted to lose were those least keen to take early retirement, and the unions were out to protect them at every step. Meanwhile he was getting conflicting messages from his senior stakeholders – one group of councillors were forever pressing him to deliver the savings, but another group (including some councillors from more marginal wards) was anxious that he should do nothing to cause unrest among the staff or more bad news stories in the papers.

In addition, the managing director of the private sector contractor had been supportive at first, but was now saying openly in the steering group that the council was failing to live up to their side of the contract and needed to press ahead with internal changes if the partnership was going to hit its first year targets.

Finally, John's own management team was behaving defensively, with each member of the team withdrawing into their own area of technical specialism and leaving John to make all the decisions about cross-departmental issues.

John's character: a safe pair of hands

John was an incrementalist – his character and his career as an engineer and a civil servant had taught him to check his ground at every step. He was uncomfortable with uncertainty and with plans that hadn't been fully worked through and documented from every angle. Most of all, he wanted to be sure of the details before he started.

John was a popular and respected leader, but the foundation of his leadership was his grasp and control of the details of the task. His staff trusted him because they knew he wouldn't act until he was sure of all the consequences of those actions.

He genuinely respected the private sector contractor, and believed they had most of the technical capability to do the job, but deep down he was convinced that they didn't understand the realities and constraints of the public sector – and that could make them a risk. He needed to hedge his bets.

The consequences: lacklustre performance and lost potential

Time passed and very little changed within John's department. The old control structures remained. However, the cost of administering the contract and managing orders and payments was going up, not down, and John's managers complained that the private firm was reverting to type and becoming 'old style contractors' rather than the profit-sharing partners they had hoped for.

On the other side of the partnership, the contractors were increasingly frustrated at the lack of progress. Their best managers started asking for transfers on to other projects where they could have more responsibility and impact. They had put forward some radical ideas, but these had all been squashed or 'bludgeoned to death by bureaucracy'. The cautious approach of the authority was holding back innovation, which in turn meant that the managing director was less prepared to invest more senior management time and money in the relationship.

For a while none of this was particularly visible outside of the management team of the partnership, but then project milestones started to slip and some early delivery dates were missed. This started to raise wider concerns. However, when John was challenged on these points, he asked colleagues to consider the risks in any alternative approach – possible industrial action, political risk in giving a contractor more responsibility when they were perceived to be delivering poor quality work, and financial risk in removing some of the control and inspection structures without totally understanding how the contractor would respond

Most of his colleagues agreed that these points were valid and that on balance John should stick to his guns. Eventually, some two years after taking up the post, John was able to complete the long-promised reorganization – which on the whole was greeted with a sigh of relief. However three months later there was a local election and a change of the political complexion of the council. New councillors were appointed to chair the major committees, it was clear they had very different priorities to their predecessors and they wanted to see change. John had to tell his management team that a further, costly, reorganization might be on the cards.

The contract rolled on. The private contractors did a reasonable job but not a great one – and they didn't make as much money from the contract as they had been expecting. John's reputation as a 'safe pair of hands' within the authority was, if anything, strengthened by the experience. The contract had failed to deliver the savings that had been predicted, but it hadn't been a disaster either and all sides could point to lots of politically inspired changes in priorities as the reasons for the overspend. But when John and his old boss Jim met up for their annual lunch, as was their habit, John was the first to confess that the last couple of years hadn't added up to half as much as he had intended.

Lessons for collaborative leaders

- The successful operation of any collaboration usually means that both sides have to change to get the best from the new relationship. In public–private partnerships, this often means significant organizational and managerial change for the public sector side of the partnership.
- Making these changes for the benefit of the collaboration will often be seen as risky and unpopular. The constant complaint leaders hear is 'Why should we change just to fit in with the private sector?'
- Driving through this sort of change takes personal leadership courage – daring to be unpopular in your own organization because you can see the long-term benefits for the whole collaboration. But self-confident, driven leaders are not often found in these public sector roles.
- A two-speed approach to change, with one partner wanting to go much faster than the other, will create tensions and can often lead to one of the partners disengaging from the process.
- Control means different things to different people. A leader who is used to incremental change and being sure of every step will struggle with partners who are used to making a leap of faith in the confidence that they will thrive in any situation.
- Incremental leaders can get caught in the vicious circle of their own lack of confidence with radical change:
  - team members who expect them to be on top of all the detail;
  - colleagues who would rather collude with risk-averse behaviour than have a radical role model in their midst;
  - external stakeholders who are risk-averse by nature and demand an audit trail of all decisions and actions.
- Frustrated partners who offer increasingly radical suggestions to try to break the log jam will only reinforce the belief that they need to have strong controls on them to prevent them from doing something that seems stupidly risky.

The selfish high achiever

The context: bringing private sector drive to the public sector

Rachel had recently been appointed as the finance director of a large central government agency. She was ambitious and saw herself as on a fast track career within the civil service as a whole. Her background was in the private sector – she had worked her way up through a number of finance director positions in smaller privately owned companies. Her recruitment into the civil service was part of a Whitehall initiative to improve the financial capability of agencies and to bring private sector commercial awareness to the role.

As finance director, she had responsibility for procurement and commercial contract management as well as for the conventional central finance function. When she arrived, one of the highest-profile items in her in-tray was the imminent procurement of a complex facilities management and building maintenance deal. The scale of it was enormous – much bigger than the organization had ever attempted before. Progress to date had been led by a project manager from inside the property function and was painfully slow. There was a project Board that was supposed to be chaired by the agency CEO to indicate the significance of the deal – but so far it had only met once.

Within weeks of Rachel's joining she had volunteered to take over the chairing of the project Board until the end of the procurement phase. In addition she promised the CEO that under her guidance the deal would be done and the contract ready for signature on the original timescale – even though the project was running several months behind schedule.

Rachel threw herself into her new task with a passion, recruiting a 'heavy hitter' finance project manager who had led the procurement of a similar outsourcing deal for a pharmaceutical company in the previous year. She also made personal contacts with the managing directors of the three or four most likely bidders in order to demonstrate the agency's strategic commitment to driving through this deal.

The leadership challenge: building alliances

Getting this job was a big step up in responsibility for Rachel. Her salary wasn't much higher than the one she had been earning in the private sector, but the scale and breadth of her role were much bigger than anything she had experienced before. The reputation of the finance department across the agency was poor, and some of that was justified – capabilities within the team were not very high – but the department had also made enemies over the years among the heads of other parts of the business. Rachel needed to make a positive impact fast.

She also needed to build alliances with the existing head of facilities management and the heads of the biggest divisions, whose budgets would be funding the on-going costs of the contract. They saw the whole thing as a major risk and a bit of a distraction from their day job. They were rather pleased when this new high flyer came along and offered to take the difficult decisions out of their hands.

Meanwhile the major facilities management suppliers were delighted – on paper this looked like a long-term profitable deal, with someone driving it who was prepared to take decisions swiftly.

Rachel's character: ambition without flexibility

The first impression Rachel gave was of a confident, ambitious leader, with a high need for status and recognition. Her career trajectory was one of rapid promotion and moving on – she had rarely stayed in any job for more than two years. Now she wanted a job close to the heart of government and this role looked like a good stepping-stone along that path.

Underneath this confident exterior she was scared, scared that she had made a mistake in taking this job, and fearful that she could get stuck in a morass of public sector bureaucracy that would slow down her career. She was used to working in businesses small enough for her to have her fingers in most of the pies and a high degree of control. She was also used to working with dynamic and highly capable businesspeople who understood the commercial implications of business decisions as a matter of course.

Rachel found it very difficult to cede control of the details, and especially difficult to cede control to people she did not rate as particularly competent.

The consequences: apparent success, actual disaster

The deal went through on schedule, and was feted in the trade press as highly successful, with a groundbreaking procurement process. Rachel herself was featured in much of the press coverage and she was quick to point out the benefits of bringing her commercial expertise to the aid of a public sector procurement process in all her interviews.

Under the surface, however, the few months leading up to the signing of the deal had been very stressful for all involved. As the contract paperwork was finalized, the heads of the main operating divisions finally engaged in the detail and didn't like what they saw. One declared that he wouldn't sign up for his share of the budget, and two others formed a hasty alliance with the head of facilities management to try to delay the procurement process by six months in order to give all parties time to reconsider. It took all Rachel's belligerence to force the deal through, and she had to persuade the CEO to lean on his other directors so that the procurement timetable to which they had both publicly committed wasn't totally compromised.

Rachel was triumphant when the deal was signed, and made sure most of the limelight fell on her. After all, it seemed a personal vindication of her hard-driving and commercially savvy approach. But signing the deal was only the start. As soon as the new suppliers came on board, it was clear that the transition and implementation timetables were completely unrealistic. In one area, the original plan had been for a three-month transition, but after twelve weeks' hard work, there weren't even any transition plans on paper that everyone would sign up to, never mind an end date in sight. All the internal and external relationships that needed to work with a degree of give and take in order to make a complex transition operate properly had been strained to breaking point by the antagonistic atmosphere created throughout the procurement. And although few would say it openly, most people put Rachel's leadership style at the heart of the problem.

By refusing to share any of the decision making during the procurement, and taking all the credit for the deal being done on time, she had also personalized the whole situation to a high degree. When the situation became difficult, her colleagues weren't going to put themselves out to help her succeed. Six months later, Rachel applied for and, somewhat to her own surprise, got a high-profile job as global finance director for a major charity, which was about to embark on procuring a major IT outsourcing deal and needed a successful director with private and public sector experience to guide them through. But in the press, stories were already emerging about her 'abrasive' management style, and amongst her peers her reputation was beginning to tarnish.

Lessons for collaborative leaders

- Ambitious leaders move roles and organizations frequently as they further their career. The developing collaborative leader should use these moves to learn from the experience of others and build new relationships quickly. This is challenging because it means being open about your lack of knowledge and willing to accept advice and ideas from people you don't know well and who may work in a different way to you.
- Building an effective coalition at the start is crucial. If it is not built early, leaders will have to spend time attempting to salvage it at the later stage – with inevitable delays in the timetable.
- Many collaboration projects have distinct phases of procurement, transition, operation and close down and although these may be led by different people from different functions, the tone and style of the relationship will be carried over from one phase to the next. You can't have an antagonistic procurement and then expect a co-operative transition.
- With large collaborative projects, organizations need to build governance and processes that avoid placing all the power with one person, who may then choose to move on when the going gets tough.
- Leaders need to share the plaudits as well as the pain. If a leader is seen to be drawing all the praise to themselves and acting as a personal figurehead for the programme, then don't be surprised if others are less than willing to throw their own weight behind the wheel.

Recognizing the need for new skills

Sadly, these four stories of floundering leaders are not that unusual. Anyone who has been around a collaborative relationship for a time will have their own story of isolationism taken to extremes, over-cautiousness that stifles innovation, passion unchecked by realism, or ego unchecked by humility and patience. And these experiences are unlikely to end happily.

However, as the fictitious accounts in this chapter illustrate, leaders in these situations are not often viewed as failures. Even when others in the collaboration are well aware of their shortcomings, the outside world is not. The selfish high achiever can be celebrated for the success of 'doing the deal' and move on to her next high-profile post, quite possibly to wreak havoc once again, before the consequences of her previous actions are all played out. Yet all four destroy both the goodwill and the value of the collaborations that they lead, costing huge amounts of money and setting the tone of the relationship in years to come.

If organizations are to avoid failures like these, they need to put the right governance in place to ensure that decision making is transparent and designed to meet the needs of all parties involved. If the leader is failing to collaborate effectively, this should be noticed early by others in authority and action taken to change the situation or to change the leader! In addition, partnerships need the right operational processes and measurement to ensure leaders get the data to do their job effectively, to capture lessons learned along the way and feed them out to the whole organization. Finally and most important, the right leadership behaviours need to be encouraged and incentivized to ensure that positive relationships can be built and sustained between all the parties involved.

If we are to get past the 50 per cent failure rate to the point where a respectable majority of collaborative ventures can create real value, then the quality of leadership needs to improve. Leadership development and training needs to address collaboration skills throughout the leader's career. We also need to get much better at selecting the leaders with the right skills and attitudes. Leading a business collaboration is complex and challenging. Traditionally in any major venture, we analyse the risks and create appropriate mitigation plans. We might have to invest in the right infrastructure; we now also need to invest in our leaders. Beating the 50 per cent failure rate is not yet in sight.

But we'd like to believe it's somewhere just over the horizon.

Chapter summary

Not all leaders are natural collaborators

Leading a collaborative venture is difficult and challenging with a failure rate of over 50 per cent. The leader's role is critical, but many are unprepared and unskilled for the challenges that they will face as they progress through their career. Traditional leaders have gained their experience leading their own team, owning the resources required to deliver and seeing themselves as the ultimate authority. In a collaborative arrangement this is not the case anymore.

The examples in this chapter are fictionalized examples of leaders who have struggled to adapt their leadership style to meet the demands of roles that require higher degrees of collaboration than they have been used to before. These four stereotypical leaders, a control freak, an idealist, a cautious incrementalist and a selfish high achiever, have found their careers stalled by their failure to respond to the challenges of collaborative leadership. These leadership stories are fictional but you may well recognize some aspects in your own leadership style or that of your colleagues. The bullet point checklist at the end of each section highlights lessons for leaders who are facing similar challenges to each of these stereotypes.

One lesson is clear from all the accounts – just keeping on doing what you have done before and expecting partners or colleagues to fit in around you just won't work in many modern leadership situations. Collaborative leadership is a skill that can be developed, but the starting point is being prepared to leave behind a leadership style that may have worked well in the past but isn't suited to today's challenges and start sharing control with others who do things differently.

Lessons for leaders

- You will need to share control with your partners.
- Value the contribution from your partners – you can't do it all on your own.
- Agree with your partners about how to run the collaboration and how to manage the relationships between the leaders.
- Be courageous and take the difficult decisions, balancing the needs of the whole collaboration with the needs of your own organization.
- Share the plaudits as well as the pain across the collaboration.
- Accept advice and ideas from others in order to build relationships and learn from others' experience.
- Accept that you may need to learn new skills to lead a collaboration – this is not business as usual.

9

COLLABORATIVE LEADERS IN THE BOARDROOM

Leaders need to work with Boards

Even within their own organizations, leaders rarely have complete autonomy over all the decisions that they make. In every organization there are stakeholders to manage, staff to engage and colleagues to get aligned to the leader's agenda. Most organizations have designed their governance structures to provide the right checks and balances, ensuring that individual leaders' decision making does not go unchallenged – sometimes with varying degrees of success! In PLCs the Board is the ultimate controlling element of the governance structure and no senior leader can avoid having to influence and interact with the members of this group in order to get their business strategy agreed. But even outside the formal world of the PLC, organizations from across the private and public sectors have implemented a variety of governance structures which emulate at least some of the roles of the more formal PLC Board.

In this chapter we explore the Board as a group of leaders with a particular governance requirement to collaborate to meet their individual and collective accountabilities. We look at how the attributes of the collaborative leader can really assist the effective operation of Boards. For most of this chapter we focus on the principles that guide how PLC Boards in the UK operate where their role and constitution are clearly defined. These principles vary for Boards in different countries but we believe that the same messages around collaborative leadership apply. At the end of this chapter we describe some other governance groups, often called Boards, although with different purposes, and show how the skills of collaborative leadership can also apply in these situations as well.

The role of the Board

According to the New York Stock Exchange Commission on Corporate Governance, the fundamental purpose of a Board is to 'build long-term sustainable growth in shareholder value for the corporation, and the Board is accountable to shareholders for its performance in achieving this objective'.[1] This seems clear as it is described here, but perhaps this understates the complexity of the role of the Board in practice. Another description from Nikos Mourkogiannis who authored the book *Purpose: The Starting Point of Great Companies*, highlights this complexity in more detail 'Great leaders are driven by a purpose that goes beyond the profit motive; shareholders are primarily interested in profit. It's up to the board of directors to bring them together'.[2]

This second description of the Board's purpose gets to the heart of the tensions that can occur in any PLC Board. These tensions can be driven by the unique constitution of the Board. The roles on a PLC Board are clearly defined and fall into two groups – the executive directors who are the full-time leaders of the business and a number of non-executive directors who are part-time experienced individuals expected to influence the executives to ensure that the business achieves its core purpose. To simplify the situation somewhat, the executives want to implement the strategies that they have developed themselves for the business as they see it, but they still need to get them agreed with the Board. On the other hand, the non-executives want to scrutinize and sometimes challenge the decisions of the executives in order to get the best strategy for the business and its shareholders.

To achieve agreement between these groups, it is clearly important that the whole Board operates effectively as a collective decision-making body and this is the responsibility of the Chairman. In order to achieve this, it is generally agreed that the mix of directors is critically important, but even with the right blend of experience and expertise, if the dynamics of the Board don't work then the outputs and decisions of the Board will be sub-optimal. The Chairman has the accountability to ensure that appointments to the Board create the right blend of capability for the business and, in turn, Board discussions use this capability effectively to deliver constructive challenges and to avoid ending up as 'group think'.

In support of the operation of the Board are two additional roles, the SID (Senior Independent Director) and the company secretary. They each hold very different accountabilities. The SID provides a counterpoint to the chairman. He or she can act as an alternative point of contact for executives, lead the evaluation of the performance of the chairman and they can also act as a sounding board for the chairman when required. The company secretary basically ensures that the Board is aware of its legal and corporate governance responsibilities.

The whole Board could not fulfil all its responsibilities as a single group when it meets only a few times each year. So a set of Board committees (audit, finance, nominations and remuneration) focus on particular aspects of the Board agenda in detail. These committees are chaired by non-executive directors appointed from the main Board.

Together, the Board and its committees have a complex constitution and it is, therefore, no surprise that bringing all the parties together to create an effectively operating Board is a significant collaboration task. Because of the potential tensions that can occur in such a structure, there is a need for Boards to pay attention to all aspects of our three-legged stool, namely:

- The right governance to ensure that roles and accountabilities are clear. This means meeting the requirements of any relevant governance code, in the UK it is the Combined Code produced by the Financial Reporting Council which is described later in this chapter.[3]
- The best Board operation to ensure that the right information is available and shared appropriately. This includes ensuring that the Board committees (audit, finance, nominations and remuneration) operate seamlessly as part of the overall Board governance process.
- The most constructive behaviours to ensure that the Board can manage any tensions but also encourage constructive challenges and deliver the best decisions for the future of the business.

Like most top teams, if the Board is operating well then the shareholders will have confidence in its decisions. In addition, good co-operative and collaborative Board operation can set the tone for effective and appropriate leadership behaviour throughout the business. Naturally, if the Board becomes dysfunctional, then this can become visible to stakeholders inside and outside the business. In these circumstances, Board members individually as well as collectively can see their reputations damaged – so demonstrable collaborative behaviour matters.

Lessons on Board collaboration

Let's look at some of the classic tensions that have to be addressed (often by the chairman) to make the Board able to deliver full value and to ensure that it can carry out its statutory accountabilities.

- *Board challenge and scrutiny is perceived as limiting the freedom of the executive directors.* Naturally most executives want as much freedom as possible from Board scrutiny – they don't want the Board to slow down or change their decision making. This tension between the executive and non-executive directors is designed into the Board process for good reasons. Better decisions will be the output of robust debate where all parties constructively communicate and influence each other. If relationships are not strong then this debate can become destructive or it will be avoided altogether. In extreme cases, executives will limit the information brought to the Board for discussion. This is an area where executives need to realize that they are required to share some control with their non-executive colleagues.
- *Non-executive directors (NEDs) perceiving that their scrutiny and input is being over-looked in Board decision making.* Sometimes, seen as outsiders, the non-executive directors can occasionally feel overlooked or marginalized by the Board process. This might be shown by Board papers arriving too late to allow effective preparation before Board meetings or allowing insufficient time for debate and curtailing scrutiny of the big issues that face the business. The result can be that NEDs don't have sufficient opportunity to contribute. In these

situations, the Board cannot get full value from the experience that non-executive directors can and should bring to Board decisions.

*   *Tensions between the CEO and the chairman.* This is a critical one-to-one relationship and one on which much of the conflict resolution and smooth operation of the Board hangs. This relationship demands time so that both parties really understand how the other operates and a degree of trust is built up. Fortunately, if problems arise between these individuals, the SID is available to intervene in order to mediate a resolution.
*   *Poor communication between the Board committees and the whole Board.* The network of committees carries out a range of important roles on behalf of the whole Board, however in some situations, they can be perceived as operating too independently of the whole Board. This perception can be created by poor communication from the committee back to the core Board meeting. Here ensuring that there is attention given to the governance rules and effective Board operation is the priority. This again is driven by effective leadership from the Chairman.

But even in Boards where they perceive that all members of the Board are working well together and Board operation appears sound, things can go wrong. Let's look at two high-profile cases where Boards have been criticized but the business context is very different.

At Royal Bank of Scotland, the demise of the business has been well-documented. In December 2011, the Financial Services Authority in the UK published a report into the failure of RBS.[4] Amongst many criticisms, the FSA commented that 'with hindsight it is clear that poor decisions by RBS management and Board during 2006 and 2007 were crucial to RBS's failure'. The FSA team highlight the following questions with regard to Board decision making: 'Whether the Board's mode of operation, including challenge to the executive, was as effective as its composition and formal processes would suggest. Whether the CEO's management style discouraged robust and effective challenge and whether the RBS Board received adequate information to consider the risks associated with strategy proposals, and whether it (the Board) was sufficiently disciplined in questioning and challenging what was presented to it.' Even the large size of the Board (17 Board members) was a problem, it 'made it (the Board) less manageable and more difficult for individual directors to contribute, hence reducing overall effectiveness'.

These criticisms go the heart of Board operation and point to failures in all elements of the three-legged stool, namely clear governance, the right information to enable Board operation and behaviours that encourage appropriate challenge and avoid group-think. It is worth considering the role being played by the Board chairman at this time when these weaknesses were becoming evident at RBS. This example demonstrates that Board operational effectiveness demands the highest levels of leadership behaviour to make this collaborative structure work.

At Apple the criticism of the Board is different, the response was different and the performance of the business compared with RBS could not be more extreme.

Back in March 2003 Apple enhanced its corporate governance by adding two additional independent directors – one of those was former US vice president Al Gore.[5] At the same time Apple expanded the role of its Audit and Nominations Committees. Along with changes to stock options, Apple aimed to meet the needs of the Sarbanes-Oxley Act and proposed SEC and NASDAC regulations – these pieces of legislation are discussed later.

However, as the years passed and following the death of Steve Jobs, the Apple Board faced more scrutiny, often criticized for being too cosy, and that the message from the Executive to the Board was just 'trust Steve'.[6] Al Gore who had remained as a director since 2003 responded in 2011 saying, 'I have the deepest respect for my fellow board members, we're all good friends … but I wouldn't change a thing about the way the Apple board operated.'[7] Any Board needs to ensure the confidence of its stakeholders and regulators and in an article for Reuters, corporate governance expert Nell Minow suggested some changes for the Apple Board – a bigger Board to bring in more experience and greater diversity and a new independent chairman to retain investor support.[8] In the same article, Jeffery Sonnenfeld, professor at Yale School of Management suggested that the Apple Board needed 'someone who was going to stir the pot'.

In November 2011, Apple announced the appointment of a new non-executive chairman Arthur D. Levinson (an existing Apple Board member since 2005) and a new Board member Robert A. Igor who was President and CEO of the Walt Disney Company.[9] Time will tell if these changes will provide sufficient challenge for the Apple Board in the 'post-Steve' era.

In both cases – RBS and Apple – the Boards may have lacked sufficient challenge. With RBS the collapse of the business has led to radical change in its governance structures, corporate behaviour and its shareholding. With Apple, in time we will all know if the changes made to the Board since Steve Jobs' death can replace his contribution and create a more diverse group and more robust challenge.

But for all businesses, regardless of their own preferred ways of working, external regulation of Board operation will continue to develop as shareholders become more demanding. The section that follows provides a summary of how the current system of corporate governance rules has evolved in recent years.

A brief history of corporate governance codes

The history of developments in corporate governance in the UK over recent years is a roller-coaster of high-profile scandals, attempts at self-regulation in the City of London and government sponsored reviews and subsequent legislation. This multiplicity of initiatives – combined with similar regulatory change in the EU and the USA has led to a potentially confusing environment of legal rules and best practice guidance that executive and non-executive Board members need to navigate.

Much of this work can be traced back to the Cadbury report of 1992 – which was itself a response to a series of company scandals such as the collapse of BCCI and Polly Peck and Robert Maxwell's misuse of pension funds.[10] This report was produced by a committee set up by the London Stock Exchange, the Financial Reporting Council (FRC) and the accountancy profession, with the aim of agreeing some self-regulation before the government of the day stepped in with legislation. The key aspects of Sir Adrian Cadbury's recommendations concerned the separation of powers between chairman and CEO, the transparency of financial reporting and the need for auditable internal controls.

This was soon followed by the Greenbury report which recommended the establishment of remuneration committees and the disclosure of directors pay packages in a company's annual report.[11] In 1998, another committee of the FRC looked at implementation of the Cadbury and Greenbury recommendations and enshrined their principles and detailed provisions in what was called a combined code of good practice. This became adopted by the London Stock Exchange and so all companies that wanted to be listed on the LSE had to state how they had applied the principles of the combined code and that they complied with the detailed provisions or explained to their shareholders why not. This concept of comply or explain became a key foundation of all future UK corporate governance codes.

In 2001, the government commissioned Lord Myners to review the relationships between institutional investors and the companies they invested in – and included recommendations for how investors should take a responsibility as owners. This in turn led to the Treasury sponsored Higgs review in 2002 which looked at 'The Role and Effectiveness of Non-Executive Directors'.[12] Recommendations from this review included a new definition of the role of the Senior Independent Director (SID) with responsibilities for the evaluation of the performance of the Chairman – and a role in providing another means of communication between the shareholders and the Board. Higgs also emphasized the importance of the independence of NEDs and the role of the nominations committee in running a rigorous process for selecting and appointing Board members.

In parallel to all this, in the US, the Sarbanes-Oxley Act (SOX) was going through Congress. This much amended Act was seeking to respond to the fall-out from the Enron and WorldCom collapses which had shown unhealthy relationships between companies and their auditors. As well as aiming to ensure that accounting firms were objective in their work and independent of their clients, the Sarbanes-Oxley Act required a company's executive directors to certify that they had undertaken an evaluation of their internal controls and to disclose any weaknesses that they had identified.

The global financial crisis of 2008 gave governments and regulators further cause to review corporate governance guidelines. In the UK, the Walker Review looked at corporate governance failures in the financial sector and particularly the effectiveness of risk management at Board level.[13] And, in May 2010, after much consultation the FRC published a major update to its 'combined code' which aimed to incorporate all the best practice from these reviews into a new guidance document for executive and non-executive directors. This new UK Corporate Governance Code again used the concept of comply or explain to let Boards define their own detailed procedures that would enable them to abide by the principles of the code but in a way which met the needs of their own operations.[14]

Throughout all these attempts to codify the complex relationships between executives and non-executives, shareholders and Boards of directors, two things stand out:

- the need to set clear expectations of how a Board should operate with well-defined principles and consistent structures for sub-committees and annual reports;
- the need to give Boards some flexibility as to how they apply these principles in accordance with the circumstances of their business – as long as they can explain to shareholders and other stakeholders what they are doing and why.

How Boards are expected to behave

Principles not rules are the chosen methods to encourage the best Board behaviour and operation. In the US, the Commission on Corporate Governance set up by the New York Stock Exchange in 2010, in the wake of the financial crisis, laid out a set of principles which aim to influence the behaviour of directors, management and shareholders. But critically the Commission 'recognises the interdependence and inter-relatedness of the Board, the management and shareholders' and it is making these principles work in such an interdependent system that is the work of the collaborative leader.[15]

The UK Corporate Governance Code produced by the Financial Reporting Council (FRC) sets out the principles of good corporate governance and a 'comply or explain' approach. The FRC make it plain that their code 'cannot guarantee effective Board behaviour because of the range of situations in which it is applicable is much too great for it to attempt to mandate behaviour more specifically than it does'. This means that once again, these principles are used as guidelines, where non-compliance is acceptable if it is rationally and acceptably explained. Again this focus on principles enhances the flexibility of the code but puts pressure on the members of the Board to justify their behaviour to others.

The act of making a Board operate effectively can be influenced by codes of good governance, but the focus on principles over tight rules recognizes that the effectiveness of any Board is linked to how the parties involved treat each other and work together.

The principles of the UK code

The principles of the 2010 UK combined code are summarized here to provide an example of the demands made on leaders who have to operate at Board level. It is clear that these demands fall into the same areas that are essential to create any effective collaboration, namely: governance – operations – behaviour. The groupings chosen by the code are leadership, effectiveness and accountability with the additional specific topics of remuneration and relations with shareholders, but the focus is on getting the roles and decision making right, supported by good communication and behaviours. The principles of the UK code are listed below, so that you can evaluate whether your own Board measures up!

Leadership

- **The role of the Board.** Every company should be headed by an effective Board which is collectively responsible for the long-term success of the company.
- **Division of responsibilities.** There should be a clear division of responsibilities at the head of the company between the running of the Board and the executive responsibility for the running of the company's business. No one individual should have unfettered powers of decision.
- **The chairman.** The chairman is responsible for leadership of the Board and ensuring its effectiveness on all aspects of its role.
- **Non-executive directors.** As part of their role as members of a unitary Board, non-executive directors should constructively challenge and help develop proposals on strategy.

Effectiveness

- **The composition of the Board.** The Board and its committees should have the appropriate balance of skills, experience, independence and knowledge of the company to enable them to discharge their respective duties and responsibilities effectively.
- **Appointments to the Board.** There should be a formal, rigorous and transparent procedure for the appointment of new directors to the Board.
- **Commitment.** All directors should be able to allocate sufficient time to the company to discharge their responsibilities effectively.
- **Development.** All directors should receive induction on joining the Board and should regularly update and refresh their skills and knowledge.
- **Information and support.** The Board should be supplied in a timely manner with information in a form and of a quality appropriate to enable it to discharge its duties.
- **Evaluation.** The Board should undertake a formal and rigorous annual evaluation of its own performance and that of its committees and individual directors.
- **Re-election.** All directors should be submitted for re-election at regular intervals, subject to continued satisfactory performance.

Accountability

- **Financial and business reporting.** The Board should present a balanced and understandable assessment of the company's position and prospects.
- **Risk management and internal control.** The Board is responsible for determining the nature and extent of the significant risks it is willing to take

in achieving its strategic objectives. The Board should maintain sound risk management and internal control systems.
*   **Audit committee and auditors.** The Board should establish formal and transparent arrangements for considering how they should apply the corporate reporting and risk management and internal control principles and for maintaining an appropriate relationship with the company's auditor.

Remuneration

*   **The level and components of remuneration.** Levels of remuneration should be sufficient to attract, retain and motivate directors of the quality required to run the company successfully, but a company should avoid paying more than is necessary for this purpose.
*   **Procedure.** There should be a formal and transparent procedure for developing policy on executive remuneration and for fixing the remuneration packages of individual directors.

Relations with shareholders

*   **Dialogue with shareholders**. There should be a dialogue with shareholders based on the mutual understanding of objectives. The Board as a whole has responsibility for ensuring that a satisfactory dialogue with shareholders takes place.
*   **Constructive use of AGM**. The Board should use the AGM to communicate with investors and to encourage their participation.

The behaviours that encourage Board performance

Adherence to any governance codes is simply not enough to ensure effective Board operation. Recent research into 'The Behavioural Drivers of Board Effectiveness', which canvassed the experience of 70 Board directors, identified seven areas of critical importance.[16]

1.   The level of emotional intelligence of the chairman in order to set the right tone for discussions and lead the composition of the Board.
2.   The willingness of the CEO to constructively engage with the Board and ensure that there are constructive relationships between executives and non-executives.
3.   The best Boards have good balance of relationships; between the CEO and the chairman, between the CEO and their team and amongst the non-executive directors.
4.   The 'character' of the non-executive directors is as important as competence and experience by which is meant the commitment, motivation, independent mind-set and a collaborative style. These individuals put the needs of the business above personal reputation.

5. The Board is designed and managed by the chairman as a high-performing unit dealing with the constitution, size and the attitudes of all Board members.
6. The best Boards make the best use of the senior independent director, the formal Board effectiveness reviews and the support of the company secretary to surface and address issues that are affecting how well the Board is behaving.
7. Identifying and managing the critical issues that can derail even successful Boards. This means the chairman and the best directors having the courage to manage conflicts and intervene in these issues before they become critical.

Taken together, these drivers of Board effectiveness do not constitute close teamwork and they actively aim to avoid the 'cosy club' that is not uncommon on some Boards. Instead a Board that demonstrates these attributes is an effective collaboration with clear roles and respectful relationships all focused on the single aim to work together for the long-term benefit of the business and its shareholders.

Analysing Board dynamics

In the UK the chairmen of PLC Boards are 'encouraged to report personally in their annual statements how the principles related to the code have been applied'. This personal reporting is seen as a way to improve communication with investors and to avoid what the FSA describes as the 'fungus of boiler plate which is so often the preferred and easy option in sensitive areas but which is dead communication'![17] Making this self-evaluation process really useful is important. In the past leaders have reported a self-evaluation process based on endless questionnaires where the nature of the numeric scoring meant that conflicts, difficulties with individual performance and communication issues could often be avoided.

As collaborative leaders, building relationships and handling conflict are core attributes, so Board evaluation processes (whether conducted internally or by external partners) need to address these issues. The chairman is in the best position to drive the evaluation process which assesses whether the Board adheres to the governance code and demonstrates effective collaboration.

This means that any Board evaluation process should be designed with two aims in mind, to enable company Boards to improve their effectiveness and so deliver their full contribution to the success of the organization, while at the same time ensuring that the evaluation process addresses the requirements of any relevant corporate governance code – or can explain why it is non-compliant.

Our experience suggests that *Board collaboration* is the product of three aspects of how the Board works:

Board operations – the processes and mechanics that ensure that the Board is an efficient structure with internal good communication; the effectiveness and communication with the Board committees and the appropriateness of Board appointments.
Board governance – how the Board directs its efforts for the benefit of the business; its contribution to the business strategy and its attention to the management of risk and internal controls.

Board behaviours – the quality of relations between Board members, the contribution from each of the Board roles, the dialogue with shareholders and the effectiveness of Board collective decision making.

The Board evaluation process can address these aspects of Board collaboration by focusing interviews with Board members in the following areas of Board dynamics.

Board meetings – reviewing the efficiency and effectiveness of the meetings where most of the Board's decisions are taken.
Board contribution – examining individual and collective impact along with critical Board relationships.
Board composition – exploring how the balance of Board skills and experience meets the business need now and into the future.

This activity is complemented by reviewing Board documentation and reports to ensure that they comply with the more procedural elements of the governance code.

This assessment process, sponsored by the chairman, focuses on roles, relationships, group dynamics and is ultimately on the quality of decision making which is the core activity of any Board. Driving forward the assessment process demands the skills and attributes of a collaborative leader – one who will not avoid raising the difficult issues and potential conflicts which inhibit effective collective decision making.

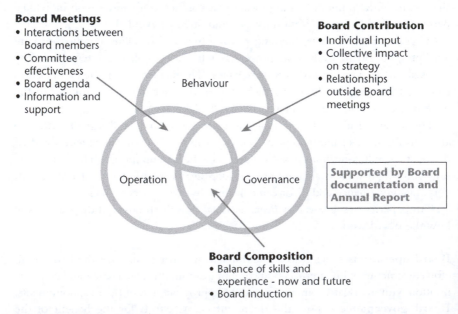

FIGURE 9.1 Analysing Board dynamics

How collaborative leaders contribute to Board performance

Sometimes Boards are referred to as 'teams'. This can be short hand for an effective decision-making group where the participants get on well together. The danger with this definition as we have already seen is that it does not adequately describe how Board members need to work together to be collectively effective as the ultimate decision-making body for the business. If 'getting on well together' really means a 'cosy club' we have missed the point of the true collaborative structure of the Board.

Each of the members of the Board has a contribution to make to the effective collective operation of the whole based on the role the individual holds. Executives, non-executives, chairman, SID, CEO and company secretary all hold personal accountabilities based on their individual role and the collective accountabilities as a member of the Board. As such, these roles have a significant amount of interdependence but also a need to be separate from each other so that each person can demonstrate their own independence and personal accountability when this is necessary. We could use the collaboration spectrum to assess levels of interdependence because Board operation needs to be much more than transactional but a lot less collaborative than a team.

In fact the independence of non-executive directors is an essential component of effective Board operation. The tension that often occurs between the executive and non-executive roles can be a necessary part of the Board decision-making process. This can be similar to the leaders from different businesses trying to collaborate on a joint project, so it is our contention that all members of Boards need the attributes of the collaborative leader as described in more detail in Chapter 7.

All of these skills and attitudes are applicable to each member of the Board but some skills are especially important to particular Board roles.

Mediation – the ability to address conflict situations as they arise is critical to all Board members but especially the chairman and sometimes the SID, who have the responsibility to resolve issues between members and ensure that the Board process is effective.
Influencing – the ability of the individual to match their method of influence to the needs of the situation is particularly important for executive directors who know that they need the support of their non-executive colleagues when Board approval is being sought for their proposals.
Engaging others – building relationships and communicating with clarity is essential for any senior Board roles when dealing with shareholders and other stakeholders who need to support Board decisions.
Agility – quickly assimilating facts and asking incisive questions is necessary for all non-executive, part-time roles where the individual needs to be able to quickly get to the heart of the issue being discussed without necessarily being part of all the preparatory discussions.
Patience – taking a calm and measured approach is often cited as an essential attribute of a good chairman, however, the SID, and CEO also need to be able to lead their

constituencies within the Board in a measured fashion, often taking the long view on what is best for the business.

Empathy – truly listening, understanding their personal impact and taking an open-minded attitude to the views of others applies to all Board members. In such a complex group, all participants have to be able to listen if they are to fulfil their responsibility to contribute positively to effective collaboration.

The skills and attitudes of collaborative leadership, as much as any rules and procedures, are the essential elements of effective Board operation. Hence the need to evaluate Board operation from the perspective of group dynamics, robust relationships and decision making, without this focus there is a danger of the 'cosy club' or the 'dysfunctional group' emerging. Demonstrable collaborative behaviours are necessary from all parties who aspire to make an effective contribution to Board operation.

Other Boards

Although some readers will not be directors on a FTSE 250 Board, many of you will be closely involved with 'Boards' in one form or another. In fact Boards now appear everywhere. Programme Boards, Departmental Boards, Partnership Boards and many others besides. The drive for this proliferation of Boards comes from a desire to bring more formal governance into organizations to replace external control structures that have disappeared, for example, in the UK, schools are moving away from Local Education Authority control and hospitals are being set up as Foundation Trusts with autonomy from the regional Health Authority.

On the whole it seems a good idea to apply the lessons learned and codes of practice from the world of corporate governance to these new Board structures. But there are also risks in simply lifting the language and processes of the PLC and applying them to such a diverse range of decision-making groups. You cannot assume that this will lead directly to effective strategy development, oversight of performance, transparent decision making and all the other good things that the creation of a Board structure aims to achieve in the corporate environment.

Programme Boards, Charity Boards, Partnership Boards and the like, may all use the same language but they have different stakeholders, different members and different terms of reference to a PLC Board. So it's worth looking a bit more closely at some of the differences before exploring where and how aspiring collaborative leaders can apply the thinking described earlier in this chapter to these 'Board-like' groups.

Programme Boards

In formal project and programme methodologies the Board is the one place where the customers and users meet with all the parties who are supplying resources to deliver the programme and with the project/programme manager who is responsible for planning and co-ordinating the work. The PRINCE (Projects in a Controlled Environment) methodology specifies the Board role and constitution as follows:

> The Project Board is made up of the customer, someone who can represent the user side and someone to represent the supplier or specialist input … The Project Board is responsible for providing the Project Manager with the necessary decisions for the project to proceed and to overcome any problems.[18]

Project and Programme Boards therefore have some of the characteristics of a PLC Board with plans being presented to the Board for scrutiny and challenge – but the relationships between the parties can be very different, for example, the supplier will come from an external organization and will have a commercial/contractual relationship to manage. So when, as a collaborative leader, you try to introduce best practice principles into a programme Board you need to be aware of these particular interdependencies.

Partnership Boards

The term Partnership Board is a broad one – it can cover the body that runs a contracted joint venture, a public–private partnership or consortium such as those common in the oil and construction sector. In all cases the thing they have in common and that sets them apart from PLC Boards is that their members are employed by or represent different organizations with different (although hopefully well-aligned) objectives.

The need for good governance, efficient operational processes, and collaborative behaviours is never more essential than in a Partnership Board. But the balance of these three is critical. Our own research has shown that most partnership members say that they spend most of their time focused on governance but that they need more effort into developing the right behaviours across all Board members.[19]

Boards in the public sector

The government desire for more local control of public services coupled with a public demand for greater transparency of decision making when it comes to spending public money has led to an enormous growth in the number of public sector Boards. Public sector Boards have often adopted many of the governance codes and processes of PLC Boards but they have a number of distinct differences that a collaborative leader has to take into account.

In many cases their meetings are open to the public and all their formal Board papers are public documents. This public transparency can have an impact on Boardroom collaboration. After all, few Board members want to be seen to be behaving unreasonably in front of members of the public. But this can also make it difficult for Board members to be honest with each other in the open meeting. Of course these disagreements and discussions can take place behind closed doors, and often do, but the collaborative leader still has to manage the formal Board process in the public arena.

Charity Boards

Charity Boards are covered by different legislation and regulated by the Charity Commission in England and by similar bodies in other parts of the UK. The Charity Commission have produced some excellent guidance on Board effectiveness which outlines six principles of good governance covering role, purpose, integrity, accountability and ways of working.[20]

Of course the key responsibility for the Trustees or members of a charity Board is to ensure the charity abides by charity law and operates within the definition of its charitable purpose as defined by its registration with the Charity Commission. But the layer of external regulation, coupled with Board members who are likely to have joined the organization because they were very committed to its original mission, can make it very challenging for a collaborative leader who is trying to gain consensus to a programme of change in the organization.

Different challenges

Looking across these examples of 'other' Boards we can draw out a number of different challenges to those faced by the collaborative leader on a PLC Board.

• **Lack of clear accountabilities** – this is often a complaint we've heard from members of these other types of 'Board'. Indeed the question should be: 'What makes this Board a Board and not just another committee?' Defining clear accountabilities for the chair, the people who supply information and reports to the Board and the other members who scrutinize that information is a key foundation of effective Board collaboration. This is particularly true for any non-executive directors who often feel rather confused and sometimes frustrated with the definition of their role.

• **Board members acting as representatives of different interests** – in a PLC Board the members are united in a joint responsibility to safeguard shareholders' interests. In other Boards, members may not have such a clear common interest. In partnership Boards there is an inevitable tension for individuals between the interests of their own employers and the joint interest of the partnership. And in many public-sector Boards there are members, like school governors, who are specifically elected to represent the interests of staff or parents.

• **Many non-financial targets** – this is one of the biggest differences in the decision-making priorities of these other Boards compared to a PLC. Of course PLCs have to hit many competing targets but they can trade-off under-performance in one area with over-performance in another and as long as the sum comes out with a good profit the shareholders and the Board are probably going to be happy. Collaborative leaders on other Boards have to juggle resources and strategy to satisfy a range of stakeholders, each with different objectives and desires. It's a struggle to trade one target off against another without a common currency to compute the relative benefits.

- **Shortages of skills and resources** – the UK corporate governance code talks at length about the importance of getting the right skills on the Board and right resources to support it. And indeed many of the Board evaluation processes that we've participated in are focused on just this point. But for other Boards outside the PLC arena getting the necessary skills and resources can be a major barrier to effective functioning. In the public and third sector many of the NED roles are not paid posts and so rely on finding individuals who can afford to contribute their time for free. Programme and partnership Boards don't have this constraint but often their membership is made up of people who are on the Board because of the job title rather than because they have the skills required to contribute to the group.

Regardless of the challenge and the nature of the 'Board', the collaborative leader can still apply the three core elements of a good collaboration (governance, operation and behaviour) and these can form the basis of effective codes of conduct and terms of reference no matter the type of Board environment.

Chapter summary

Comply or explain

Collaborative leaders in senior roles may be part of the corporate Board or at least have to work closely with this group. The Board is the place where executive and non-executive directors, each with different accountabilities, are required to work together for the benefit of the business. But the constitution of the corporate Board has tensions (creative or otherwise) designed in, so effective Boards require our three-legged stool – clear governance and authority for who makes decisions on what, the right information to enable efficient Board operation and behaviours which encourage appropriate challenge and that avoid group think.

Good Boards operate by following clear principles not detailed rules – and best practice for these is enshrined in codes such as the UK Corporate Governance Code covering leadership, accountability, remunerations and relationships with shareholders. It's important to regularly evaluate individual and collective Board performance to avoid becoming a cosy club – this is a criticism made of Boards where the internal challenge between members of the Board has been replaced with a friendly compliance. So Board evaluation should review behaviour, operations and governance to assess if the Board is meeting the standards of the governance code and if not compliant then to explain why not. But also, by examining Board dynamics, this also gives the Board the opportunity to raise and deal with any difficulties that are inhibiting good collaboration between those involved.

As an executive director you may get frustrated by the scrutiny provided by the Board – but you can't avoid it. In a non-executive role, you may get frustrated that your experience is not being fully put to use. Whatever your role, there will be tensions, and the attributes of the collaborative leader will be essential if the Board is to build relationships with stakeholders, handle internal conflict and share control between executives and non-executives.

And if you are not involved on a PLC Board you may well be involved on other Boards (programme Boards, partnership Boards etc.) where similar issues arise and many of the same lessons apply.

Lessons for leaders

- Recognize that the corporate Board is designed to create tensions and this, in turn, will deliver better outcomes from the business. So a Board is not a classic team but a genuine collaborative group.
- The focus on governance, operations and behaviour can, once again, help focus the Board on the right priorities to make the group work.
- Use the governance codes as best practice to encourage better performance. The 'comply or explain' approach provides the vehicle to evaluate Board operation and address weaknesses in a variety of situations.
- Use Board evaluations as a means to address simmering conflicts and to avoid the danger of the 'cosy club'.
- Many organizations who are not PLCs are adopting the Board structure. However, it is important that clear terms of reference are built to ensure that a 'Board-like' group can operate in a very different non-corporate environment.

10

RELATIONSHIP RISK

The challenges of managing risk in collaborative relationships

'Mind the gap' – it's a phrase every visitor to London has heard a thousand times. Originally recorded in the 1960s as a short automated announcement to passengers to watch out for the gap that opens up between the platform edge and the tube train door at curved station platforms, it has become an English language cliché. But as a safety announcement it contains a simple truth. People have always known that the greatest risks in any system are at the boundaries between one element and another – and that's never been more true than in today's interconnected business environment.

There are many cases of safety risks opening up at the boundary between organizations working in partnership. We've mentioned the BP Gulf of Mexico oil disaster in earlier chapters. In April 2010, the floating drilling platform Deepwater Horizon exploded killing 11 crew members and resulting in the biggest oil spill in US history. As well as the tragic deaths of men on the rig, long-term damage was done to wildlife in the region and to the way of life of fishing communities along the Gulf Coast. The total financial costs of fines and compensation are still to be calculated but in March 2012, BP reached a settlement with lawyers for 110,000 individuals and businesses along the Gulf Coast, totalling just under $14 bn for pay outs to people and firms whose livelihoods and health were damaged by the spill. The causes of this tragedy were complex but not unknowable. Investigations into the lessons to be learned have highlighted the importance of leadership within and between the many organizations involved as a key factor in managing risk in similar situations.

The first step in the chain of events that led to the disaster was a failure in the cement lining that was supposed to seal off the bottom of the well, prior to a manoeuvre where the Deepwater Horizon was going to be replaced by another production rig on the site. The cement job which failed was carried out by the oil services company Halliburton, and the rig was owned by deep water drilling specialists Transocean on behalf of their clients BP. The Presidential Oil Spill Commission set up in the aftermath of the disaster found that many people across the three organizations had access to individual pieces of the information jigsaw, and yet those pieces were not put together. Because of this, no one was looking at the big picture which may have shown that a blowout was likely to occur and later could have helped to avert a disaster once high pressure hydrocarbons started entering the bore hole. Reports from the Commission identified the causes as 'systematic failures of management rather than one-off technical problems', and at the heart was a failure of the 'many ambiguous dotted line relationships with and between the companies involved'.[1]

And it's not just safety which is at risk when information doesn't flow smoothly across an organizational boundary, long-term reputations are often put at risk too. When the UK Revenue and Customs department (HMRC) outsourced its data management to the IT services firm EDS and its internal postal service to the couriers TNT, it's unlikely that leaders imagined a risk scenario in which the combination of some unthinking actions by a junior official and a lost piece of internal mail would get senior officials and ministers on the front pages of all the papers. Yet all it took was a security failure in 2007, where two computer discs containing names, addresses, national insurance numbers and, in many cases, the bank details of all the Child Benefit recipients in the UK were put in an unregistered package and delivered by couriers TNT. The discs never turned up – and the ensuing scandal led to the resignation of the chairman of HMRC and even threatened to topple government ministers.

There are many reasons why risks like these, which are triggered by the actions of another party in a relationship, don't get identified and actively managed, but primarily it's because they're not under the control of any one organization. We call these 'relationship risks', and they are, by definition, complex and dependent on the nature, governance and operation of a collaboration. But crucially they are affected by the behaviour of the leaders involved and the culture of the working environment that they create for their people.

The paradox of shared control

Leaders considering how best to manage risk in a partnership or collaborative relationship face what we call the paradox of shared control. The traditional reaction of a leader to a sense of growing risk is to tighten controls across their organization. But in a partnership, the more a leader tries to control the details of their partner's work, the less likely that partner will be to take responsibility for the risks involved. If you end up with your contractor saying 'I was just doing what my client told me to' you are not going to create a robust risk management environment.

So the paradox is that creating more systemic control of risk across a collaborative relationship means individual leaders letting go of some individual control and developing a more open and trusting relationship with their partners.

Many of the early public–private partnerships tried to avoid this paradox by using the concept of risk transfer. The public sector contracting body (perhaps a local authority wanting to build a school, or the Health Service commissioning a new hospital) would transfer all the risks of managing the building work to a private sector company that in turn would set a price for the contract including some sort of risk premium. In simple terms the idea was that if the contract turned out to be less risky and easier to fulfil than expected, the private sector would come away with some additional profit. But if unexpected difficulties arose, the public sector would have to pay no more – the private sector partner was then responsible for the cost of overcoming the problems and delivering a fully working facility on time and on budget. The theory was that in multi-party arrangements the organization which was most experienced at managing particular types of risk would take responsibility for dealing with them and set a fair price based on their expert analysis of the risk involved. Of course the reality was far from that rosy picture. A report to the Public Accounts Committee in February 2012 showed that UK spending on Private Finance Initiative (PFI) projects, such as hospital and school building programmes, would add up to £131.5 bn but this vast expenditure would only deliver assets worth a quarter of that figure.[2]

The mistake was in thinking that you could hand over risks and their associated costs without being part of managing them. And it's not just the public sector that fails to get this right. Just consider the case of British Airways in-flight catering. BA outsourced much of its in-flight catering to Gate Gourmet, partly so that someone else could handle all the difficult industrial relations issues that were emerging as more and more catering jobs were being transferred out of the UK. Eight years later the relationships between managers and staff had got no better. In that summer of 2005, BA asked Gate Gourmet to take on extra workers to cover the holiday peak. This wasn't in itself a major problem – except that Gate Gourmet was also in the process of renegotiating pay and working conditions for its own staff. The workers took unofficial action in protest, and 670 people were summarily dismissed. The dispute snowballed and staff at British Airways walked out in sympathy. The result: 900 BA flights from Heathrow grounded during August, tens of thousands of holidays ruined and British Airways' reputation badly damaged.

These aren't isolated examples, many of the cost-overruns and missed delivery dates in partnership contracts like this occur because of the poor nature of interactions between one party and another. For example, if a client and a contractor don't trust each other, they both inspect every piece of work so they've got their own evidence of what was done in case of future penalty claims. Or, if as often happens, a client decides to change a specification just after their partner has taken delivery of the parts needed to build the original design, major frustrations will result. In both cases poor interaction between the parties involved leads to increased cost and delays all round.

As a collaborative leader you can't isolate yourself from risks that originate in your partner's business and you can't afford to try to control them all either. Successful risk management in collaborative systems is built on leaders who can share control – but that is a challenge that is often avoided by leaders who instead put their faith in some well-known but dangerous myths.

Three myths of relationship risk management

The reality of business interdependence means that leaders will find that some strategic risks lie at the boundary between organizations, or outside their own organization altogether. Collaborative leaders and their top teams must pay attention to these relationship risks and historically they have not been handled well. In many cases risk mitigation plans have been based on a belief in either the organization's own power and superior expertise or tightly defined legal contracts or partners they personally trust. However, these beliefs can sometimes be misplaced, rendering the confidence they engender a dangerous myth.

The myth of superiority

Big companies partnering with smaller ones or highly prestigious organizations partnering with suppliers of more mundane services can fall victim to the myth of superiority. Which could be stated as: 'If anything starts to really go wrong we can step in and take control.' Of course it's rarely as simple as that.

Looking in more detail at the events leading up to the BP Gulf of Mexico oil spill shows the risks of pursuing a new business strategy which is highly reliant on close relationships with technical partners. In the late 1990s, when the Board of BP first set a new strategic direction to become the number one in deep water oil exploration and production, they knew they had limited experience of drilling in deep waters – certainly not as deep as those encountered by the Deepwater Horizon rig drilling the Macondo well. Yet the Board believed that the company's size, power and superior expertise would enable it to direct its suppliers safely and successfully in these challenging conditions. BP were the client so they had the power to intervene but did they have sufficient knowledge and could they manage events that were changing minute-by-minute on a rig in the Gulf of Mexico from their HQ thousands of miles away? Halliburton had run some inconclusive tests which showed potential problems with the setting of the cement which was meant to seal off the bottom of the well. Transocean, the rig operators, had experienced a near miss with a similar incident on one of their deep-water North Sea rigs in 2009 and had even produced an internal presentation highlighting the 'what if' risks for their organization.[3] But these crucial pieces of information weren't pooled at the right time and, as we've seen, the lessons that might have been drawn from them weren't learned. BP may have thought they were the smart guys with all the power but they couldn't intervene to prevent the Deepwater Horizon disaster on their own.

The myth of the watertight contract

A reliance on tight legal contracts to remove all relationship risks is also a powerful myth but one that has been seen to fall apart on many occasions.

Look at the public–private partnership (PPP) contract that London Underground had with the Metronet consortium to maintain and upgrade large parts of the tube network. When that relationship failed London Underground and the taxpayer were left with a bill of up to £410 million according to the UK Parliamentary Public Accounts Committee.[4] The scale of the contract was enormous, it ran for many thousands of pages, and the lawyers' fees in drawing it up were similarly vast but in the end it couldn't protect the public sector client from picking up a large bill. Indeed, many commentators trace the causes of failure to the immensely detailed and rigid contract itself.

This is not to say that collaborative leaders shouldn't pay attention to contracts – a well-defined contract is a vital part of any good governance structure – it's just that you shouldn't expect a contract drawn up at the start of a relationship to be able to predict and legislate for all the issues that will come up during its lifetime. And a contract can rarely prevent the big relationship risks that can cause lasting damage to safety or reputation from occurring. The best you can hope for from the contract is a basis for some compensation after the event but by then the damage has been done and more often than not it's the leader that placed their reliance on the contract that has to carry the can – not the lawyers that drew it up.

The myth of personal trust

Some leaders fall foul of the myth of personal trust. They base their approach to handling relationship risk on trust in a specific individual in their partner's or potential partner's organization. Of course high–level interpersonal relationships are important, but in a complex world they are not enough; senior people move on and the organizations they manage are themselves complex and so reliance on the word of one individual is no guaranteed way to manage risk.

Furthermore, it may be the case that relationships at the top are good, but that the ticking time bomb is hidden several layers down the company with which you are planning to partner or acquire. If the sub-prime mortgage disaster teaches us anything, it is that hidden liabilities can have very far-reaching consequences. Who would have thought that lending decisions taken by small US banks would play such a key part in bringing down UK banks like RBS and LloydsTSB?

We'll perhaps never know all the details of the conversations that took place over a momentous few days in autumn 2008 between Eric Daniels (then CEO of LloydsTSB) and Prime Minister Gordon Brown over the terms of the Lloyds TSB take-over of HBOS and the subsequent government bail-out. But it's clear that whatever was said or what personal promises were given, the competition waivers granted to LloydsTSB were far from watertight in the longer term. Two years later a new Liberal Democrat Secretary of State for Business Vince Cable said 'My position is that the Banking Commission will operate from a clean sheet of paper and produce a set of proposals to make a safer banking system and provide maximum competition. If Daniels says he has an agreement, he's got to produce some evidence.'[5]

Personal trust is important but it can never be enough on its own as a means of managing relationship risk.

Beware the risk register

Perhaps in recognition of some of these myths, an industry has grown up around the formal recording and categorization of risk in the form of a risk register. Governance codes have been drawn up specifying where risk registers are required and how often they need to be reported to a Board or other governing body. But often compliance with the process can be a convenient distraction from the real task of managing the risks themselves. This seemed to be the case with RBS, which went from briefly being the biggest bank in the world in 2008 – as measured by the reported value of its assets – to being a complete 'basket case' which had to be taken over by the British government to prevent its collapse.[6] As Margaret Woods put it in the conclusion to her book *Risk Management in Organisations*, 'Using a highly quantitatively based system for risk analysis, RBS ticked all the right boxes but that was not enough.'[7] Their focus was on compliance with their own and the regulatory reporting requirements. Woods goes on to say 'the formal structures based around silos which reflect regulatory reporting systems ... indicate that compliance is the focus for the risk function in RBS rather than performance. As a result a massive and discrete risk bureaucracy failed to identify, communicate and/or mitigate the effect of both localised and aggregate risks in the bank.'[8]

Risk registers, with their red/amber/green coding for each risk, are the traditional way to categorize risks and plan how to mitigate them. They're certainly simple, but all too often they degenerate into simple-mindedness – a mechanistic box-ticking exercise with no roots in the reality of the collaboration. And when risks are coupled by trivial plans to mitigate them (for example 'insufficient sponsorship by leaders' being coupled with 'get sufficient sponsorship'), the alarm bells should start ringing.

One government department we know of dutifully produced a risk register with a huge list of around 150 elements. This labour of love was then consigned to a desk drawer where it languished for several months. To be honest, this probably didn't make much difference, as some of the ideas in the register for risk mitigation were entirely toothless – for example, one key figure in the partnership was known to be likely to leave, but the mitigation for this eventuality went along the lines of 'brief new Director' – it's not wrong but it's hardly a thought through strategy!

Risk registers can be a useful tool, but only if you make them so. There's no point in bundling every possible risk into one interminable document to which no one will ever pay attention. Instead a risk register should list a manageable number of risks and highlight a handful of the truly scary ones at any one time. 'I start by writing down the three things I'm worried about – and then see if they're on the risk register', says former Inland Revenue outsourcing chief John Yard. 'Then I look at the management information, and ask, "What does it feel like? Is it measuring the wrong things?"'

To do this, of course, you first have to know which issues to worry about – and that means keeping an ear to the ground. 'Failures are often because of an inability to see the warning signals', says oil industry leader Charles Jamieson. 'You need to tell people that if they make a mistake you want to know right now. Lots of people don't tell you bad news early enough.' Board adviser Kate Nealon goes further. 'When things get bad, staff start hiding things', she warns.

'Even if you try legitimising telling bad news, you still get fed stuff', says Julie Baddeley, a non-executive director on the Board of several major partnerships. 'And the Red Amber Green traffic light report just doesn't tell you enough. The very first time you see it switch to amber you need to go round asking questions – you have to go and ask people what's keeping them awake at night.'

Most importantly, leaders need to own the risk register. There's no point in sticking rigidly to one dreamed up at the start of a partnership, possibly by a different set of people, if it doesn't match what's going on day to day. And leaders certainly shouldn't delegate the responsibility for it. Creating and managing the risk register is a priority that collaborative leaders can't afford to duck.

Putting relationship risks on the risk register

Risks that originate in your partner's organization or risks that arise because of the interaction (or lack of interaction) between your two organizations need a place on a joint risk register. They also need to be watched carefully because relationship risks have their own peculiar characteristics that make them particularly difficult to manage.

Donald Rumsfeld was famous for his remarks about the risks of unknown unknowns – he was ridiculed in the press at the time about the reasons for going to war with Iraq. But there is a truth behind his words, conventional risks registers deal in 'known knowns' – risks whose impact and likelihood can at least be reasonably estimated. But when risks are being managed across an organizational boundary, things are never that transparent. It's difficult to interpret the potential warning signs that may be seen coming from within your partner's organization and in turn it's difficult for them to understand the signs from your organization. Trying to manage relationship risks brings us into the world of known unknowns and unknown knowns.

Known unknowns

By this we mean situations where you as a leader know your own organization has some dependencies and vulnerabilities to what your partner may do. But what is largely unknown is the likelihood of your partner triggering this risk by their actions. It's difficult to investigate the level of this risk without revealing to your partner your vulnerability to it – and this is something leaders are often reluctant to do.

And it's difficult for a leader of one organization to quickly pick up an informal gut reaction feel for the likelihood of risk in another – in the way you might in your own business or one you had known for years. This is particularly true when leaders are working across different organizational cultures. All the subtle cues that would tell them that something is wrong in their organization aren't there – and the informal networks of staff who they could ask about what is really happening on the ground aren't open to them either. When Carlos Ghosn first went from the French auto industry to Japan to join Nissan as its COO as part the Renault-Nissan Alliance he was surprised. He was sent there to help turn an ailing company around, but this partner that was supposed to be in a crisis felt calm and relaxed to a manager used to European factories. Although most of the Japanese workforce and middle management knew that there were problems in the wider organization there was no sense of crisis. The culture was to assume and indeed communicate to outsiders that each department was working optimally – if there were problems they were elsewhere and others would sort them out as they always had. But over the next six months Ghosn built up a series of cross-functional teams to analyse the real state of affairs and used them to create a Nissan Revival Plan which became the basis of Nissan's and the Renault Alliance's future success.[9]

Unknown knowns

Then there are the situations where as a leader you simply don't know what your partner knows. The unknown knowns. Situations perhaps where your partner has uncovered a problem or a potential risk and are working very hard to resolve that part of their process before telling you or anyone else about it. It might be something they consider and deal with every day – not a big issue but with unknown consequences in a larger system.

These may be risks that haven't been considered – issues that had not been conceived might ever be a problem. And from your partner's point of view these can look like risks that are contained totally within their own business. Things that are their responsibility to resolve with little or no knock-on impact on their partners.

Again the barrier is lack of transparency and an unwillingness for one partner to talk to anyone else about a problem or risk because they think they have it under control.

Trust and vulnerability

In both these cases of relationship risk the real source of the problem is fear. Fear on behalf of one organization that either by revealing their vulnerability or by raising their own mistakes, they will be punished in some way for it. It's a very natural fear and one that collaborative leaders need to work hard to overcome. Creating an environment where staff on all sides feel confident to share their organization's vulnerabilities to others and to confess to mistakes or recently uncovered problems is the difficult but critical collaborative leadership task.

One technique is to facilitate regular confidential risk workshops where senior leaders from all sides can talk openly about their worst fears for the joint enterprise and have a 'drains up' conversation about what they see as the danger signs in their own organization.

At this meeting, it's worth scheduling two or three key issues that you know are worrying people, and gathering survey data in advance of the meeting (for example, on staff morale and customer perceptions – both areas that provide leading indicators of future risks). But take care to devote at least part of the meeting to 'the things that keep you awake at night' – which may not be the obvious issues, and may well be vague and nebulous. Good risk management isn't always about examining the obvious – sometimes it's the subtle things that can trip you up.

A governance meeting for the partnership to rebuild the ticket hall at King's Cross Underground station threw up one such worry. Although each partner had developed their own plans for closing the Thameslink railway for maintenance over the Christmas period, none of the leaders had confidence that it would actually work. It emerged that some partners were worried about risks belonging to their partners – for example, whether King's Cross station could cope with the extra traffic generated by closing the Thameslink line. It was only by raising these half-formed worries that they started working together to check the interdependencies thoroughly – and to make the plans join up properly. Caring about each other's risk was essential in making the line closure go smoothly – which it did.

We've also seen workshops where teams have deliberately taken part in role reversal exercises and talked about risk from their partner's point of view, armed with the knowledge of their own organization. A conversation starting with a phrase like 'If I was standing where you are, I think I'd be worried about what we are doing in X ...' can be a useful way of beginning an important discussion about shared relationship risk.

Understanding different attitudes to risk

One of the difficulties in managing risk across collaborative relationships is that different parties may have quite different attitudes towards risk. This can be an advantage – in public–private partnerships the risk adverse public sector side can transfer risk to a private sector partner with more appetite for risk – and hopefully a greater ability to manage it. But as we know this risk transfer comes at a price – and as the scale of the risk rises there is a greater likelihood that in the worst scenario the public sector will still have to bear the ultimate cost of recovery and the impact on their reputation with the public.

However in order to build a resilient collaborative relationship – and to be able to explore the known unknowns and the unknown knowns – all sides need to be able to talk about their attitude to risk and to understand their own and their partner's risk profile. In our experience this goes far beyond a simple high, medium, low risk profile rating and means understanding more about your partner's business, its culture and its history.

All our attitudes to risk are informed by what we have seen going wrong in the past, the price we have paid for it and the lessons we have drawn from the experience.

Public sector and private sector expectations

There is a fundamental difference between the public sector and the private sector when it comes to expectations of risk management – which boils down to simple mathematics. Private sector organizations have the advantage of having a common currency to measure the performance of all their business activities – it's the money they make (or lose) by doing them. Public sector bodies do not.

If you are running a supermarket it's perfectly okay to offset losses in one area with excellent profits in another. If my losses from, say, sales of healthy fruit and veg are more than compensated for by soaring profits in sweets and chocolates then my shareholders are likely to be happy with my performance. But reverse the story to a school or a hospital and you see how ludicrous it becomes. A public sector leader cannot explain away failures in A&E by pointing out the excellent maternity results and trading off one against the other! The numbers simply don't and can never add up. The lack of a common currency and the inability to make trade-offs between different areas of performance is a major difference between ways of managing risk in public and private sectors.

This may appear to be so obvious as to be trivial, but we have seen the consequential difference in attitudes distort risk planning and mitigation activities across many public–private partnerships. Private sector partners may be baffled by their public sector counterparts' split focus on a very large number of targets and performance indicators – where they see a much bigger prize (or indeed risk) elsewhere in the operation. By focusing on different types of risks across the partnership, information can be mis-communicated, misinterpreted or ignored and greater risks to the whole joint enterprise may grow unnoticed.

Experience drivers

Within a private sector partnership the different drivers or risks may be less pronounced – but they are still there. If one partner has a history of being damaged by insufficient planning on past projects where another has been caught out by competitors grabbing market share by moving more swiftly, then they are likely to have different attitudes to what makes a good partnership planning process. Again that diversity can be a strength if leaders on both sides can discuss these differences openly. This will allow the parties to reach an agreed position on the degree of risk planning required to meet the needs of the situation they are in. But we've often seen these sorts of differences in attitudes to risk not shared with partners.

The solution comes back to the collaborative leaders' role in creating an environment of trust where all parties can raise their fears and concerns and where knowledge of the vulnerability of others is used by the leadership of the group to build a more resilient risk management regime for the whole enterprise. 'You can't predict the future, but you need to talk about it', says former Inland Revenue leader John Yard. But this isn't as easy as it sounds. To communicate effectively about risk, leaders must have the courage to admit potential shortcomings and vulnerabilities in their own organizations, well before they start causing problems.

Addressing relationship risk – areas for action

When it comes to addressing relationship risks and building a management framework for handling them successfully we use the same three-legged stool of governance, operations and behaviours that we have discussed in Chapter 3. Of course the amount of effort required in each will depend on the specifics of the situation you face, but a risk management plan that only addresses one or two of these areas will be less resilient than one that addresses all three.

Governance

The first step is to build relationship risk management into the formal governance process. All businesses have risk registers that should be periodically reviewed by the Board. But often these risk registers don't focus on the real worries and fears of the directors. Issues as complex as the relationship between organizations are rarely identified in these documents, so the whole Board doesn't get the chance to scrutinize this area of risk. If the future success of the business depends on building strong partnerships, then the UK Corporate Governance Code (see Chapter 9) provides a vehicle for Boards, during their annual Board evaluation process, to check that the risk register reflects the need to manage relationship risks inherent in the business's strategy.

Scenario planning can also have a role to play here with Boards regularly taking time out to look more broadly at a series of 'what-if' scenarios covering issues that could affect their partner's business.

Operations

Operationalizing the early warning systems is an important factor in successfully managing relationship risk. In your own organization experienced managers pick up signs intuitively (something just doesn't feel right), but between organizations these feelings are often dismissed. Data that could be a warning sign of growing risks across a relationship need to be collected and systematically analysed.

But what happens when warning signs start to emerge from such a system? Here it's important to have the right set of incentives and sanctions to hand.

In a complex technical environment such as oil exploration things may go wrong; equipment can fail, people can make mistakes. A robust relationship risk system will incentivize partners to identify these small failures and communicate them early to others – and also have a sanctions regime which notices when something is out of expected bounds and acts quickly to highlight it via a proportionate penalty.

The use of timely graduated sanctions is one of the design principles for the evaluation of collaborative systems described by Elinor Ostrom in the work which led to her being awarded the Nobel Prize in 2009.[10] She cites many examples of communities that have developed collaborative mechanisms for managing the risks associated with scarce resources which have shared use – such as irrigation systems, fishing grounds or alpine pastures – and the role of sanctions in the process. These are systems that have successfully managed shared risks for a long, long time. In the case of the Tribunal de las Aguas, which is responsible for irrigation in large parts of three regions of Spain, there are records dating back over 500 years to show how small fines have been levied against farmers who have taken more than their share of water. Fines that were large enough to show that their breaking of the rules had been noticed, but not too large as to push them over the edge. Again, small sanctions delivered swiftly are much more beneficial than the threat of punitive fines delivered long after the fact.

Behaviours

Formal risk governance and efficient operations such as joint safety management systems are essential foundations for good relationship risk management, but they are not enough in themselves. The behaviour of leaders plays a crucial part in setting the culture of the relationship and building its appetite to risk. Like any marriage, strong enduring relationships don't happen by accident and they have their ups and downs. Business relationships need tending carefully too. This means collaborative leaders must recognize the need to invest their own time and resources in building those relationships. And this can mean informal individual relationships as well as formal organizational ones. If there is a nagging doubt about a risk that may lie in your partner's business, it's much easier to start by having an informal conversation with someone you trust than tabling a new item on a risk register.

Because leaders are role models, the way they are seen to act establishes the culture of the relationship at many levels. Looking again at the Deepwater Horizon example, the Presidential Commission stated that 'a culture of leadership responsibility' had been lacking between all parties on the rig. They identified the need for a culture in which 'individuals take personal ownership of safety issues with a single-minded determination to ask questions and pursue advice until they are certain they get it right'.[11] This sort of culture needs leaders who demonstrate how to build open relationships, encourage upwards communication of 'bad news' and ensure that this same open communication happens with partners too.

Don't let risk management crush innovation

It's clear that collaborative leaders need to pay a lot of attention to risks across a relationship, but you can't let this focus on risk crush the creativity that comes from working with people different to yourself. You can't afford to let caution get the better of you. We've seen leaders so afraid of being out of control that they can't act when it matters, and won't let others either. They effectively kill all innovation. So if you're going to get the greatest value from collaborations, you have to foster creativity as well as effective risk management.

As we've seen, the greatest risks in a collaborative system are often found at 'the platform edge' – the points of high interdependence between different parties. Yet the greatest opportunities are often found at precisely the same points. Here, different organizations have to work closely together, and while that can be tricky, the friction can also be creative: people challenge each other's assumptions, ask apparently stupid questions that make people see in a new light, and posit different ways of doing things. And every so often breakthroughs are made.

Trusting your partners in those high-pressure, edge-of-the-platform situations is hard, but the point of greatest criticality is often the point of greatest creativity. And as Bill Joy, one of the co-founders of Sun Microsystems, is regularly quoted as saying, 'There are always more smart people outside your company than inside it.' The challenge is whether you can recognize what they have to offer if they speak a different language or bring with them a whole set of different assumptions about your business.

It's a balancing act – cultivating a healthy respect for risk, without letting it turn into a fear, and exploiting the opportunities of partnership without being reckless. In fact, the business world can learn from the voluntary sector when creating opportunity through collaboration. Voluntary sector organizations are often highly skilled at getting a lot done in tough circumstances and on a small budget. They understand only too well how joining forces can help them make a far greater impact. When nature conservation charity WWF agreed to a partnership with the world's biggest cement manufacturer Lafarge it seemed an unlikely collaboration and brought a high level of reputational risk. Accepting sponsorship is an implicit endorsement, and it would have been easy for WWF to be seen as a corporate collaborator (in the worst sense) by the rest of the voluntary sector. In fact at one point the partnership risked being derailed entirely by a conflict over a proposed Lafarge quarry in an area of outstanding natural beauty on Harris in Scotland.

For Lafarge, too, there were risks in entering the partnership. The company was publicly committing to stringent targets on rehabilitating quarries and cutting CO_2 emissions. There were plenty of critical voices within Lafarge complaining that the partnership was a waste of resources. Yet the opportunity – to create a partnership that really worked between a major corporate and a global NGO – made the very real risks worthwhile and created benefits for both parties. In the words of Luc Giraud-Guigues, Corporate Partnerships Manager at WWF, 'It's manageable, it delivers tangible results and from Lafarge's perspective it helps manage risk, whilst for WWF it speeds up delivery of our mission'.[12]

Collaborative leaders sometimes need to look beyond the obvious to find partners who can bring them innovative solutions whilst never taking their eye off the relationship risks involved in working with organizations significantly different from their own.

Chapter summary

Mind the gap

In collaborative relationships, risks multiply at the boundaries between parts of the system. That's true on London Underground where passengers have been warned for decades of the risk at the platform edge by the famous 'mind the gap' announcement. But it's true in organizational life too. The interfaces between different systems or different organizational cultures are the places where information can get lost or mistranslated and risks can be mismanaged or missed altogether.

We call this class of risks 'relationship risks' and they deserve their own place on a collaborative leader's risk register. In order to manage relationship risks leaders sometimes try to shelter behind a belief in the superiority of their own organization, the watertight contract they have negotiated or the great personal relationship they have with the CEOs of their partners. But in many cases these turn out to be dangerous myths which can lead to misplaced confidence in the resilience of a collaborative system.

In managing relationship risk, leaders need to watch for known unknowns – known potential vulnerabilities in your own organization but with an unknown likelihood of them being triggered by accidental actions of your partners. Also the unknown knowns – problems that your partners know about and are trying to correct without you finding out about them.

A risk management framework with the right governance, efficient cross-boundary operational systems and leaders who display open and trusting behaviours with their partners gives a stable foundation for a resilient relationship in a collaborative world.

But it's not all bad news. Just as risks are magnified at a boundary so is the potential for innovation. By opening up organizational boundaries to partners, suppliers and customers, collaborative leaders can increase the flow of ideas, and often generate creative ways of reducing cost or improving service that no one would have come up with on their own.

Lessons for leaders

- Leading across a collaborative relationship means you have to deal with the paradox of shared control. To create more systemic control of joint risk means that you need to let go of some hands-on control and develop an open and trusting relationship with your partners.
- To do this also means being prepared to admit to some vulnerabilities in your own organization and encourage your partners to do the same so you build resilient ways of managing risk together.
- Make sure relationship risks are explicitly addressed as part of a risk management process and that they have their own place on the risk register.
- Be aware of your own attitude to risk and what drives it. Does this fit with the risk profile of your own organization – and with that required by the situation you are in?
- Don't let overly prescriptive management systems crush innovation.

11
CONFLICT AND THE COLLABORATIVE LEADER

Conflict is inevitable

When the leaders of major collaborative ventures discuss their experience, they highlight the challenges they face and the lessons they have learned. Building relationships and sharing control are always mentioned but at the top of their list is often the need to handle conflict. It is often their number one concern at the start of a potentially difficult new partnership – how will they be able to deal with a serious dispute?

Fearing whether they can deal with it, many leaders see conflict as something to be avoided at all costs. Avoidance and collusion are common coping strategies: they tend to ignore the problem for as long as possible, and if that doesn't work, they pass it to others to resolve. The underlying fear is that relationships between the parties may break down – and possibly result in litigation, which is damaging for all concerned and often terminal for the collaborative venture.

However, conflict handling is not a talent limited to the few, all leaders can learn how to see the early signs of conflict as a useful warning, address the issues constructively and use the opportunity to take the relationship forward into new and more creative territory.

This is especially important for collaborative leaders – because in most collaborative ventures, some conflict is inevitable. And the success of a partnership is built on the level of trust between the parties no matter how comprehensive the contract. If conflict escalates and this trust breaks down, you can quickly get into a downward spiral of litigation, delay, and cost overrun – and the leaders will be held accountable. The saga of the new Wembley stadium and the long-running battle between the Football Association, its main construction contractor, Multiplex, and the steel work firm, Cleveland Bridge, over delays in the construction shows just how bad it can get. Cleveland Bridge originally took Multiplex to court back in 2004 alleging non-payment of some of the costs it was owed. Multiplex then issued a series of counter-claims totalling over £25 m. In February 2008, High Court Judge Mr Justice Jackson described the process as 'grim and ghastly', and said that he believed the whole row should have been sorted out years before. The judge sent the strongest possible message that 'once the principles in dispute are decided the parties should find a way to agree the quantum without recourse to the courts'.[1] But trust had been so damaged that the idea that the leaders could sort the dispute out themselves was long gone.

Individual leaders have to share control in any collaborative relationship. When a dispute arises within one organization, the leader can use personal authority or positional power to force through some sort of resolution, however painful or expensive that solution may be. In a partnership, however, the leader has given away some of that control, and if your partner doesn't like your solution, you have to look to different methods of dispute resolution. It takes a much more self-confident, mature leader to understand the limits of their personal control and realize the need to engage with others.

In addition, in a collaboration the leaders involved are likely to operate as peers in any debate. For example, in a road maintenance project carried out in-house by a local authority, a single director is ultimately responsible for resolving the outcome of any design disputes that occur along the way. But in a typical public–private partnership arrangement, there will be a partnership Board with a mix of public and private sector leaders representing the interests of different organizations. There is no one guiding mind, and although that difference of perspectives should in the end produce a better result, the process of getting there can create a lot of conflict.

Finally there are just more organizational interfaces and interdependencies in these complex situations – and each one is a potential source of friction and frustration and a place for high-quality collaboration. Well handled, these frictions can generate creative and resilient solutions to problems. Badly handled, they sow the seeds of eventual breakdown.

Handling conflict is the leader's priority

'Clashes between parties are the crucibles in which creative solutions are developed and wise trade-offs among competing objectives are made', says Jonathan Hughes, a partner at Vantage Partners, a consulting firm affiliated to the Harvard Negotiation Project.[2]

Hughes outlines 'three myths of collaboration': first, that giving people the skills to work in teams prepares them for collaborative working; second, that the right incentives guarantee collaboration; and third that the ideal structure makes it happen naturally – the collaboration spectrum, effectively used, should make this clear. These myths, Hughes believes, 'all overlook the central role of conflict in collaboration – the fact that collaboration requires actively engaging differences, that these same differences generate conflict, and that unless people and organisations are equipped to deal constructively with conflict, collaboration will break down'.[3]

For the collaborative leader this reality has a number of consequences.

Partnerships are multifaceted and long term, so you have to play the long game and find ways of making progress in some areas, while being in dispute in others. It's like a marriage, you can't change partners easily or without incurring major costs, so relationships matter and you have to be prepared to make compromises and accept some give and take. Not only do you need to see conflict as part of the process – you also need courage and sophistication in handling it.

Becoming competent and confident

As a collaborative leader, it's your responsibility to be able to handle conflict personally and directly in order to address disputes at the top of the organization and to provide a role model for the rest of the partnership. You also have to be able to help your staff and colleagues across the collaborative relationship build the capability to deal with conflict when it happens.

However, in our experience few leaders are well equipped to do this. Most of the skills for handling cross-organizational conflict aren't taught in conventional management development programmes. The common approach adopted by many managers to 'come down heavy' simply doesn't work, nor does marching in to solve other people's disputes. At the other end of the scale, leaders that over-stress alignment and harmony between partners can leave conflict simmering beneath the surface, storing up serious trouble for the future.

Some leaders are naturally more attuned than others when dealing with conflict. If you've had to cope with a lot of arguments in your early life, you may well have developed skills to defuse disputes effectively – or you might be terrified to start! However, for most leaders, dealing with conflict requires a set of skills and attitudes that have to be learned. At the heart of these is a strong awareness of self. You can't deal with conflict unless you truly understand how and why you're reacting to a particular situation.

In this chapter we look at the common causes of conflict in all sorts of collaborations, examine the best options to address conflict (building on our governance, operations and behaviour model) and identify the other attributes collaborative leaders need to develop. We don't cover legal resolution or litigation – such specialist areas are outside the scope of this book. However, if you have already called the lawyers, things are probably past the point of collaborative resolution anyway.

There's a caveat, however. Most of the necessary skills and attributes are best absorbed experientially – by practice, rehearsal and reflection on your feelings and responses to conflict. It's an area where training and coaching can really pay off. And if you're trying to build collaborative leadership capability within your organization, handling conflict development is an area well worth investing in.

Identify the reasons for conflict

In conflict situations the job of a collaborative leader is to be confident enough to stand back from the immediate situation and focus on the presenting problem.

This means understanding what's going on, who's involved and the impact of the conflict on others. In doing this the leader's contribution is to help people across the partnership address the causes of the conflict – not just the symptoms. If the leader simply reacts to what they see, taking sides and tackling actions without the full knowledge of the reasons for the conflict, they are likely to make the situation worse. In the sections below we look at four broad reasons for conflict. It's not an exhaustive list, but in our experience they are at the root of a large number of conflicts in partnerships, joint ventures and other collaborative arrangements.

Differences in objectives or values

Individuals and organizations can usually cope with different ways of working. There might be frustrations, but in these situations, serious conflict is rare. However, if there are real differences in objectives or values within a partnership, the ingredients are there for serious conflict. Unless those differences can be aligned satisfactorily, the collaboration risks implosion.

Take the example of public–private partnerships (PPP), you could say that at one level, every PPP has within it a fundamental difference in objectives. The private sector partner has objectives about profit and financial growth, while the public sector partner has to serve the needs of its political masters and deliver within budget. This can (and often does) lead to a degree of conflict. Too often considerable time and effort is focused on trying to align all the objectives of all the parties involved – this is likely to be impossible, better for all sides to align around a common purpose. In a public–private collaboration this common purpose is often to be found in the area of corporate reputation with the public and with the government paymasters. Identifying how reputations can be protected and enhanced through a successful public–private partnership will identify the objectives in common.

Differences in values between the parties involved in a collaboration tend to prove more difficult to deal with. A joint venture between a major US food manufacturer and a UK supplier is a case in point. The UK firm was somewhat paternalistic, with a long history of caring for its employees. Meanwhile, the American company had much more of a 'hire and fire' mentality. The leaders had discussed this at the outset and even drawn up some ground rules between themselves about the circumstances in which they would or would not dismiss staff. But when they hit competition from a totally unexpected source, they needed to move fast. With the UK supplier lacking the skills and equipment to change their products, the leadership team had a difficult choice to make – move production to a new site with a new workforce or buy in new equipment and try to train the existing staff. The American partners saw it as a simple business choice – a trade-off of time and cost. But for the UK leaders, it was a moral decision: how would they look after the interests of their staff, customers and shareholders? At that point, effective decision making broke down, conflict erupted in several areas and the whole venture was stuck for many months. The leaders were so involved in the content of the conflict, they were not able to stand back, understand the differences involved and manage things appropriately.

Differences in organizational culture

We know that organizational culture can be a frequent source of conflict. As we saw in Chapter 5, culture is a set of assumptions that defines how an organization habitually chooses to operate – different assumptions, then the ingredients for name-calling and conflict.

John Yard, former leader of the Inland Revenue's IT outsourcing project, recalls how the differences in character between the Revenue and technology services giant EDS were incubating conflict. 'EDS came in with a clear view – let's fix the problem', says Yard. 'But civil servants are very different in their approach. They get scrutinized and crucified by the press. They have to explain things – they can't just do them.'

His answer was to put in place a three-day process in which each side shared their perceptions of the other. In the first day EDS presented their feelings about the Inland Revenue to the Inland Revenue team. 'The rules of the process were that they didn't need to give evidence for their perception provided they felt it inside – and we couldn't respond', Yard recalls. 'So we were told we were bureaucratic, that we were covering our backs, and that we didn't believe in delivery.' The next day the Revenue staff did the same, explaining the anger they felt at overcharging for extras after an initial low bid, and complaining that EDS didn't listen. In the final part of the process, both teams went away together and spent the evening socializing. The following day they had to identify the differences and agree a set of actions. 'There were about ten areas and I nominated an EDS owner or a Revenue owner responsible for each', says Yard. 'You weren't allowed to say, "I can't do this because my partner won't do xyz", although if you wished you could blame the management. In the end we created a new culture where people started to believe that, as the leader, I was genuinely going to get people to work together.' The collaborative leader once again standing back from the conflict, providing a new vision for how the parties in the collaboration have to work together.

Differences in the leaders' personalities

Over the years, the business pages have been littered with lurid tales of personality clashes in the boardroom bringing down a company that was once a household name. These tales certainly make good copy, but there is also some truth that if the leaders in a collaborative relationship can't get on then the conflict that results can put the whole venture at risk.

The Daimler Chrysler merger was one of the biggest transatlantic mergers in history, and carried with it many sources of potential conflict, but the one the papers liked to focus on was the dispute between Thomas T. Stallkamp, the top American executive in charge of integrating Chrysler into its new German parent, and Daimler's chairman, Jurgen Schrempp. The joke went round the US media, 'How do you pronounce Daimler Chrysler? Daimler – the Chrysler is silent'. Eventually

Schrempp retired three years early and was replaced by Dieter Zetsche who was reported in the *Wall Street Journal* for being 'widely liked at Chrysler'. In a similar manner, when the AOL Time Warner merger was announced, the press saw the biggest source of risk as being the 'different personalities' of AOL's Steve Case and Time Warner's Gerald Levin, which were thought to personify the cultural differences between the two firms.

If two executives within a single organization don't get on, and this escalates to pose a threat to the performance of the whole company, then mechanisms exist to get rid of one (or both) of them. Shareholder pressure can be brought to bear and non-executive directors have the power to force executives out. But in a partnership, it's just not possible to sack the director of one of your partners just because you don't get on with them.

However, the quality of the personal relationship between the senior players often sets the tone for other relationships all the way down the partnership. If the people at the top are in conflict, leaders at other levels have a hard task on their hands to build an effective and trusting relationship between the different parties. And to that degree, the press have got it right.

Differences in resources

Finally there are resource conflicts – the stuff of major wars. And while partnerships don't generally come to grief over land, water or oil, other inequalities in the way resources are distributed can lead to fierce disputes. Resource conflicts can come in many forms, but we see three subjects crop up on a regular basis – critical skills, finance and technology.

Conflicts over critical skills are legion. After many years of relative decline, the UK rail industry is currently in the middle of a boom. Upgrades to the London Tube network, the construction of Crossrail, and a number of new light rail and tram systems around the country have led to a national shortage of railway signalling engineers. Conventional recruitment drives haven't filled the gap and so companies have often taken to poaching engineers from their competitors. But it's a small industry, and a competitor for one contract is likely to be a partner in another. If you have just poached a number of key signalling personnel from a company you are about to enter a partnership with, then the seeds of conflict are already sown.

Finance, of course, is a key factor in disputes. Perhaps the truth is that disputes about money are often a proxy for other conflict. But in a downturn where money gets tight, a lot of things in a partnership become harder to manage. Instead of being able to help your partner out of a short-term cash flow crisis, you have to delay paying invoices until the last minute. And instead of being able to take a risk and be generous in contributing towards your partner's R&D costs to investigate the potential of a money-saving idea, you may end up asking your partner to fund it all but still want to take a share of the savings. Money can oil the gears of a partnership, but when it's in short supply, the resulting conflict often highlights problems that were there all along.

Lack of technological resources can also cause serious problems. In one public–private partnership we know, the whole process of inspection and approval of a contractor's work could have been dramatically speeded up if the inspectors had remote access to the contractor's database of works-orders. However, incompatible technology got in the way, the hand-held PDAs used by one partner couldn't talk to systems used by the other, and what could have been a useful means of improving efficiency became a festering source of conflict at partnership meetings for months to come.

Addressing conflict

So the reason for the conflict might be clear, but as a collaborative leader, how do you tackle it? Sometimes a leader is part of the conflict themselves and they have the responsibility to make the personal change required. At other times they're outside it, but then their job is to ensure that the conflict is addressed and this might take personal involvement to mediate a successful outcome. The trick is to take time to choose the appropriate strategy with care. Many leaders wade into conflicts with the motivation to 'help' but the outcomes are often less than helpful!

We have discussed already that effective collaboration is built on three foundations – good governance, effective operations and the right behaviours. Addressing conflicts that have been created in a collaborative situation means focusing effort in the right area, for example, if the contract incentivizes the wrong behaviours, then perhaps the governance of the collaboration needs to be addressed first.

In all cases we believe there are six approaches that the collaborative leader can take when dealing with conflict in collaborative relationships:

* understanding the needs of groups
* finding the greater good
* holding difficult conversations
* mediating a solution
* putting the right governance in place
* making conflict-handling part of the culture.

1 Understanding the needs of groups

To understand the dynamics of the group of people involved in a conflict, the leader needs to know what stage of development the group is at. If people aren't getting their basic needs met at any point, conflict is likely to erupt. This is particularly relevant in a collaboration where different groups of people are thrown together and expected to 'get on and deliver' – fast. Missing out a necessary stage of group development will only make matters worse. The aim here is to build trust, but this takes time.

Will Schutz's work on the stages of collaborative group formation particularly strikes a chord with many of the leaders we work with. According to his model,

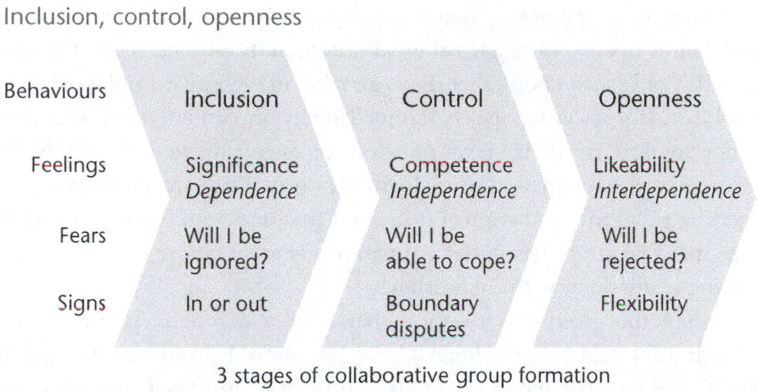

Inclusion, control, openness

Behaviours	Inclusion	Control	Openness
Feelings	Significance *Dependence*	Competence *Independence*	Likeability *Interdependence*
Fears	Will I be ignored?	Will I be able to cope?	Will I be rejected?
Signs	In or out	Boundary disputes	Flexibility

3 stages of collaborative group formation

FIGURE 11.1 Three stages of collaborative group formation

newly formed groups go through three distinct phases of development: inclusion, control and openness.[4]

In the first stage – inclusion – people are looking for legitimacy and significance. They need to know that they're noticed and accepted as part of the group. They're concerned about where they fit, and the unspoken fear is of being ignored or discounted. It may even bring back fears such as not being picked for a team in the school playground. And of course, you can't force a group to include you – they have to let you in.

So at this stage, the leader of the group needs to focus on ensuring that the right people are on board and everyone knows who is in and who is out. Key leadership tasks at this stage are things like getting the contract sorted out, running induction events and holding symbolic meetings where everyone can see that they're in the same boat together. If inclusion is mismanaged or left unaddressed too long, individuals may opt out of the joint enterprise – and the core group will blame this on the fact that they didn't fit in the first place.

Once people feel sure that they are part of the group they can move to the next stage and start addressing their needs for the right degree of control. In this second stage, people begin to assert their autonomy and independence. They need to establish what area of work belongs to them, and exercise control over it, with clear boundaries around their responsibilities.

In a collaborative system, this degree of separation isn't easy to obtain. During this stage, groups can spend a lot of time in disputes about boundaries and account-abilities. It can be healthy initially, but if they get stuck here, you see turf wars, fragmentation and sub-groups forming. As a collaborative leader you need to make some judgement calls about how much conflict is helpful, and to put energy into resolving the gaps and overlaps in accountabilities. The task is to help people to understand and accept where they need to be dependent on each other and where they can act independently.

The third stage – openness – is about people truly accepting their interdependence and being open with each other about their hopes and fears for the joint enterprise. It's only at this point that they can take off their guard and speak honestly, from the heart. But speaking openly has its dangers: the underlying fear at this stage is that they might have their views rejected, or even ridiculed. This is why there needs to be a strong foundation of inclusion (I know I'm part of this group and no one is getting rid of me) and control (I know I'm competent in my role and people recognize that I've got things under control in my area) before groups can take the risk of being really open with each other.

Only when the group has reached that degree of openness can it begin to wrestle with joint values and beliefs. These conversations can now be sincere and meaningful, because the members of the group have invested in each other and their joint future.

None of these stages can be rushed or skipped. They happen in this order, and every time someone new joins a group, each stage has to be repeated, albeit on a smaller scale. If people don't feel included, they won't take full responsibility for their areas of accountability. And if the leader is trying to sort out conflict over boundaries and competence issues from the second stage, they can't expect openness – the group hasn't got there yet.

Group dynamics is a big subject and we're only touching on one aspect here. But the progression from inclusion to control to openness is a key part of building a collaborative enterprise. As the leader, it is an omission if you fail to recognize the anxieties, skirmishes and full-blown conflict at each stage for what they are. The leader's job is to push the whole group involved in the collaboration through these three stages as quickly as they are able. Without this progress, relationships will not be created – and collaboration will suffer as a result.

Understand where you're at: inclusion–control–openness in action

Some years ago we worked with a leader in a bank that had recently outsourced its call centre operation to a third party. He was frustrated at the terrible dynamics in meetings of his new 'team' which included representatives from the call centre operation.

In a series of interviews with each member of the group, we used the inclusion-control-openness model to find out what might be driving their behaviours. It soon became clear that two people didn't feel part of the group at all.

Carol was representing the firm that now operated the call centre, although she had originally been part of the bank and had been transferred over when the outsourcing deal went through. Despite the fact that she'd known many of the individuals round the table for years, no one had really listened to her when she tried to explain her new role. Often she didn't get copies of the papers

ahead of meetings, because she was no longer on the bank's own email system. As a consequence, she felt she was there on sufferance, and contributed
very little in meetings.

Meanwhile, Brian was a member of the inner circle – but that was part of
his problem. Many of the old hands in the team expected him to sort
out operational problems, as he always had in the past. But under the new
outsourced arrangement he didn't have the power to do this any more. People
were always asking him to take on things he couldn't – and it put him on edge.
For Brian, meetings had just become a sparring match, and he now expected
nothing more from them.

Over a number of weeks we guided the team through the three stages.
We helped Carol to be more included by running sessions on the outsourcing contract where she could explain her role and others could talk about
what they needed from her. We also made sure everyone received invitations
and papers for all meetings well in advance. We then helped the team tackle
boundary conflicts by mapping accountabilities so people could see what they
could expect from their colleagues. Finally, with these foundations laid, we
ran a 'working together' session where the team talked about what helped or
hindered them in being open with each other.

It took time, but six months on, the management group had become more
collaborative and, as a consequence, more effective.

2 Finding the 'greater good'

In collaborative relationships the key to defusing conflict is often to help people to
find the 'greater good', or what Muzafer Sherif, the psychologist who did much of
the early work in intergroup conflict, calls the 'super-ordinate goal'.

If the leaders can be clear about what they are all trying to achieve, you can then
have a productive discussion with the parties involved about what may be getting in
the way of achieving it. Without that understanding, each party is reduced to 'trading' in an attempt to get the best deal for themselves. But this focus on transacting
makes little sense if the aim is to effectively collaborate. If these negotiations look at
face value like a great win for your organization, but you know that in the long term
your partner won't be able to afford it, you clearly haven't met your objective. But
it can be very attractive for the leader to think that they have won! Clearly such an
adversarial process can take its toll on the relationship – a serious problem when
building long-lasting relationships.

Instead, negotiations should aim to achieve 'win-win' outcomes over the longer
term, where each side obtains a useful result (though perhaps not the one they'd
originally hoped for). A process that resolves conflict by 'splitting the difference' is
an approach that satisfies neither party. As Jonathan Hughes from Vantage Partners
says: 'Trading offers and counteroffers may eventually produce agreement, but such

haggling rarely results in an effective exploration of each side's underlying interests, many of which therefore go unaddressed.'[5]

Looking for 'win-win' outcomes entails finding creative solutions to conflict by uncovering different interests, needs or objectives that can be used to reframe a possible solution. After exploring their individual interests, the parties can then explore multiple options for satisfying these interests — things like changing payment schedules, varying time frames, agreeing a solution contingent on performance in the future, or something completely different that none the less matters to each party. It is a sign of effective conflict resolution that the outcome could not have been predicted by either party in advance.

Partnerships simply aren't the place for hard-nosed negotiations of the old school. Aiming for win-win outcomes leaves relationships intact and able to continue for many years to come. After all, in any collaborative relationship there will be several occasions to address conflicts, possibly over many years.

Negotiating for the long term: an example from the oil industry

Leaders in the oil industry are used to working in partnership, but that doesn't mean that things don't go wrong. On taking over as leader of an oil company offshore operation, Robert discovered that the contract for the design and delivery of gas turbines for the offshore platform was out of control. His predecessor had not specified his requirements clearly enough, the design had changed, and the project was now late and $10 m over budget. Robert needed to address the situation and get an acceptable cost agreed.

As an effective collaborative leader, Robert realized that he had to engage his partner in detailed negotiations, but to do it in a manner that preserved the relationships for the future and found a result that everyone could live with. After all, the same company was contracted to maintain the turbines for their life on the rig.

Robert set up a clear negotiation process with the leader of the turbine company. Each company allocated time and prepared well. The meetings took place out of the office, and each party had time to explain their case and to listen in detail to the other views expressed. The process was tense at many points, but Robert ensured that there was plenty of time for each group to reflect and talk. He also ensured that the process had clear ground rules so that people behaved well throughout the negotiations.

With time, patience, tenacity and compromise, the parties found a mutually acceptable way forward that involved agreed delivery dates for the equipment at fixed costs everyone felt were reasonable in the circumstances. And more importantly, by the end of the negotiations, the parties wanted to work together again and indeed were already planning the next deal.

The lessons for the collaborative leader when negotiating are clear:

- A mutually acceptable 'win-win' outcome is even more important in collaborations where you will have to operate together in the future.
- The negotiation process must be agreed by all parties.
- The leaders must demonstrate the right behaviours if others are to follow.
- All parties must give the process time so that relationships can be protected throughout.

3 Holding difficult conversations

Some business conversations are just plain hard. Telling someone their work isn't up to scratch. Tackling someone who has persistently put you down. Having to disappoint someone when they rely on you. They're the kinds of conversations that trigger defensiveness and attack, blame and counter-blame. Sometimes they descend into bitter wrangling, or hurt withdrawal. And it's very easy to get them entirely wrong. No wonder that they have become known as 'difficult conversations'.

However, the inevitable conflict situations that arise in a collaborative situation demand the requirement to hold difficult conversations across organizational boundaries. This is a skill collaborative leaders need to cultivate. 'Being able to talk about what you feel is a key feature of people who are good at collaboration', says former Inland Revenue leader John Yard. 'We do it in our personal life, but it's harder to at work. It's all about trying to understand what someone is feeling. If you find out why people are under pressure and which triggers stress them out, you can empathise far better, and you have more chance of defusing the situation.' Perhaps we should use the term 'Crucial Conversations' as described by Patterson, Grenny, McMillan and Switzler in their excellent book by the same name.[6]

If you've built strong relationships first, you're better equipped to enter into this kind of conversation. 'You can't just do it by parachuting in', warns Julie Baddeley, a non-executive director on the Board of several major private and public sector organizations. 'If there's no relationship there already, it's hard to have difficult conversations. You need sensitivity and strong communications skills to have the conversation and come out of it positively, without everything falling apart.'

The techniques of conducting difficult (or crucial) conversations in a positive way have been researched extensively by Douglas Stone, Bruce Patton and Sheila Heen of the Harvard Negotiation Project, and their book, *Difficult Conversations*, is the best guide we know to recognizing the stumbling blocks and defusing the emotion in these situations. 'Delivering a difficult message is like throwing a hand grenade', say the authors. 'Coated with sugar, thrown hard or soft, a hand grenade is still going to do damage.'[7] Instead they map out a way of holding conversations more constructively, disentangling the intent from the impact and avoiding the painful process of blame and counter-blame altogether.

Fluency in these important interactions is a sophisticated skill and takes time – and practice – to master. But if you're to deal with conflict effectively, collaborative leaders can't do without it. And your personal life and friendships will benefit immeasurably too.

4 Mediating a solution

Sometimes relationships get stuck and need a third party from outside the system to help solve them. At this point it may make sense to use an external facilitator or mediator who is neutral about the outcome, but can steer each party towards some sort of resolution. If, as a leader, you stand outside the conflict, you may be well placed to play the role of a 'semi-independent mediator' or 'super-facilitator'. This role is possible so long as the leader is trusted by all parties, who see that they are able to intervene impartially because they care about the health of the whole system.

As a mediator you are responsible for making the conflict resolution process work well. Part of that is taking responsibility for providing a safe environment for the parties to come together and setting up the ground rules clearly. Leaders have to take care not to assume responsibility for the outcome or to negotiate for either side. Instead their role is to help the warring parties find common ground. They need to explore the issues and find creative ways to resolve the conflict, encouraging reciprocal gestures to get the process moving. A key role for a collaborative leader in these situations is to encourage honesty, challenging people if they're being less than candid and highlighting areas where unspoken assumptions are getting in the way.

Mediating is tough – but if as a leader you learn how to intervene effectively in other people's conflicts, you can reduce a considerable amount of grief, wasted time and escalating costs and quite possibly save your collaboration from the depressing fate that claims half of all alliances.

Mediation in a consortium breakdown

A central government department had entered into a ten-year technology out-sourcing deal with a consortium made up of the strongest players in the market. Shortly after the contract was placed, the department's leader, Susan, observed tensions between the members of the consortium. However, she felt these were teething problems that they needed to sort out themselves, so she left them to it.

As time went on, the tensions developed into arguments (some in meet-ings, some reported back by staff in the department), although day-to-day delivery suffered no significant setbacks. Looking to the future, however, Susan could see that the conflict would have an increasing impact on the partnership, inhibiting the open communication necessary to meet some challenging timescales. She raised these concerns with her counterparts in the consortium, but their initial reaction was to paper over the cracks and assure her that there was no serious issue. Susan pointed out that she was keen to make a contribution to resolve the problem if they wished, and left it at that.

A couple of weeks later Susan walked in on another real row between the partners, and offered to help them sort out the situation. She set up meetings with each individual and then agreed a process where members would air their difficulties and resolve a way forward. Her role (and her value) was that she was an outsider to the consortium but was trusted by all parties. They also knew that this wasn't altruism, Susan needed resolution of the conflicts that had an impact on the service her organization received from the outsourcers.

A plan of action was agreed, with Susan acting in a role of an on-going mediator when problems arose. This enhanced Susan's credibility with partners and increased her knowledge and engagement with the consortium. And while conflict didn't disappear altogether, relationships between all parties became considerably smoother.

The lessons for the collaborative leader in such situations are:

- Don't assume that other parties' problems don't affect you – they will in the long term.
- The collaborative leader is often in an ideal position to mediate in the difficulties of other parties.
- Make sure that the rules of the mediator role are clear to everyone and don't think that you have to find the solution for the other parties – your role is to manage a process and help the parties keep to their commitments.
- Be patient – it may take a long time to solve.

5 Putting the right governance in place

Acquiring the personal skills to deal with conflict in a healthy manner is a major part of keeping a partnership on the road. But in many conflicts, the personal skills of an individual leader are not enough. Remember the three-legged stool – an effective collaboration required more than good behaviour. Leaders need to make sure that you have the right escalation procedures and formal governance in place to deal with major disputes. Sometimes the arrangements that are set in place at the beginning of the collaboration are quickly proved to be inadequate in practice.

As we've seen, the starting point is to assume that conflicts will occur and to think through in advance the possible mechanisms for resolving them. Alternative dispute procedures should be written into the contract from the start (and revised with the benefit of experience), detailing how the partnership should recognize and escalate conflicts that cannot be resolved through the day-to-day operational channels.

The design of effective escalation processes is quite an art. They mustn't become too multi-layered, over-cumbersome or bureaucratic. Usually an important step is the formal mechanism to bring in a party from the parent organizations or a key stakeholder to mediate on a particular issue, before turning to legal intervention.

However, contractual dispute resolution should only be a weapon of last resort. If your first step is to call in the lawyers, the collaboration has zero chance of survival – and the costs of failure will escalate. Collaborative leaders need to build their own conflict resolution systems on top of the legalistic framework, allocating regular agenda items to issues of concern, creating enough space to air debates fully, being respectful with each other, examining the facts while separating them out from the feelings, and then coming to a decision wherever possible.

Remember too that collaboration requires a healthy dose of give and take. 'Once that decision is made', says Jonathan Hughes of Vantage Partners, 'part of collaboration means that everyone lines up behind the decision, even if they would have preferred a different outcome, and does their best to implement it successfully.'[8]

6 Making conflict-handling part of the culture

As a leader you can attempt too much conflict resolution as well as too little. Given that collaborations are likely to spark disputes at all levels, it's important that staff throughout the organization know how to resolve disputes themselves, instead of constantly referring them up the line. Not only does it save management time and effort, it also leads to better resolutions if conflict can be dealt with locally wherever possible. When managers step in to solve conflict below them, they're often not in possession of the full facts, or have been given a one-sided account of the situation. And sometimes different line managers end up attempting to solve things separately – creating a new conflict at a higher level.

So the leader's role is to create a culture of conflict management involving all those engaged in the collaboration. This might include training staff in some of the skills we've discussed above, so that they have the vocabulary and techniques to tackle conflict themselves, and is well worth the effort. And it's particularly useful if you can do this training in mixed groups with people from all organizations in the partnership.

When May Gurney – the infrastructure and services company – start up a new maintenance contract in partnership with a local authority, they run a series of joint development workshops in the first three months of 'mobilization'. In these workshops staff at all levels, from directors to gang supervisors, come together to discuss collaboration, conflict and their own habits when working with people who are 'not one of us'. They use tools like the Myers-Briggs (MBTI®) personality profiling questionnaire and the organizational partnering tool described in Chapter 5 to look at the differences between the different cultures and personalities, and to help them understand some of the potential causes of conflict. The workshops give people a safe environment to talk about their expectations of the relationship and about past experiences of similar situations, both good and bad, which may influence how they react. They also work through a number of simulation exercises and games about competition, collaboration and conflict, to build knowledge and skills of what to do when difficult situations arise.

Making conflict-handling part of the culture is enormously powerful. It doesn't prevent disputes from arising – nor should it. But it means that, as the leader, you have set an expectation that conflict will be addressed, rather than feared – and that means that you are much more likely to build a long-lasting and resilient relationship with your business partners.

Understanding your own relationship to conflict

As a collaborative leader, you will find yourself in many conflict situations and some of them will be aimed directly at you. For many people, this is stressful and unpleasant and it engenders intense and sometimes uncontrollable emotions. But to deal well with conflict the leader needs to be able to disentangle their reactions from the situation they are experiencing. And to do that, the leader needs to understand two things – first, how they habitually react to conflict, and second, how they behave under stress.

People's habitual behaviour in situations of conflict often is shaped by their past experiences, and especially by their early life. That informs whether they want to run away and hide, smooth things over and make everything all right, step in and square up to a perceived assailant, or use the situation to their advantage. These four reactions to conflict – avoidance, denial, aggression and manipulation – are the most common ones we see leaders demonstrate when facing conflict situations with their partners. But none are particularly healthy.

* **Avoidance**: If you recognize conflict for what it is, but strongly dislike it, you may find ways to avoid it – for example, not turning up at a meeting where you know there will be a dispute, exercising silence rather than openly disagreeing, or even agreeing to things when you have no intention of doing them.
* **Denial**: If you're afraid of the consequences of conflict, you may deny that it's taking place at all. For example, you insist that the team is really happy (despite what everyone says), because everyone goes to the pub together each week.
* **Aggression:** Some people react to conflict by going to war themselves in a bid to protect themselves from being hurt. If someone is in conflict with you, then it follows that you're in conflict with them – and you'll raise the stakes each time to prove it.
* **Manipulation:** Another reaction is to see conflict as a weakness that you can exploit in others. You're able to stay outside the conflict yourself, but can use this power to your advantage. It's a classic 'divide and conquer' tactic.

If, as leader, you adopt one of the first three reactions, you are effectively controlled by the conflict and allowing it to overwhelm your thinking brain, alienating colleagues and partners in the process. If you choose manipulation, you remain outside the conflict, but you risk losing people's trust if you're found out, and in the long game of collaboration, there's a lot at stake. You will probably seriously over-estimate your power to control the behaviour of others.

In fact, the healthiest reaction to conflict is to see it neither as good nor bad, but as an opportunity to get to the heart of the problem and make things better. Conflict may produce scenes of painful confrontation, but at least it's honest communication – even if people don't understand or can't articulate what's really bothering them, the feelings of frustration, disappointment and anger are genuine. And often it's the catalyst to getting things moving.

When leaders understand their habitual reaction, they can begin to clarify their motives and choose a better approach aligned with the objectives and agreed values of those involved in the collaboration. But leaders also need to know how they behave under stress – because that's when they start functioning well below their best.

At times of significant stress, individuals can unconsciously change character. They find themselves behaving in ways that they – and other people – don't recognize. If the individual is naturally flexible and laid back, they can become rigid and didactic. If they're logical and analytical as a rule, they can get tied up in emotion and start accusing others of lack of appreciation. If the individual normally grasps the big picture intuitively, they can start focusing exclusively on a few facts or details. It's almost as if the individual is taken over by a shadow of themselves – and not a very competent one. The Myers & Briggs Foundation, custodians of the Myers Briggs personality type tests, describe it as being 'in the grip'. You are suddenly in the grip of personality traits that you don't usually exercise – and unfortunately, you're not very good at using them. Just when, as a leader, you need to be at your best, you're suddenly at your least competent.[9]

If leaders are going to be able to address conflict situations, they will need to develop a conscious awareness of the triggers that can push them into a stressed state. And, as a leader, are you also aware of how your behaviour changes when under stress? With this information you will be in a stronger position to control your own actions in conflict situations, and of course you also need to be able to recognize the same things in other people too. To address the conflict you will need to use two of the core attributes of collaborative leaders – patience and agility.

Patience

So we know that working collaboratively creates conflict – and the more collaboration you need, the more conflict you're likely to see, at least until different parties have learned to build relationships, create trust and appreciate each other's differences. As a collaborative leader, you need to develop a combination of strong self-awareness and a thick skin if you're not to be overwhelmed by it all.

The risk is that you react quickly and become part of the conflict, and that your own reaction to the situation makes you less well-equipped to deal with it. But if you take your time and act with patience, you will be able to treat conflict as honest communication, rather than a personal attack, you can then begin to understand the causes of conflict and demonstrate your value as a collaborative leader.

Agility

While a jogger on a treadmill at the gym may see pain as something to be ignored or a barrier to break through, elite athletes are trained to see pain as their friend. It's a valuable warning sign of a flaw in technique, an imbalance in effort, or a training regime that has gone too far in one direction.

The same goes for attitudes to conflict in a partnership. When we are asked to do a health check for a collaborative venture, we are immediately suspicious if the senior players all report that there is no conflict anywhere in the system. That's because in any healthy collaboration there will be evidence of conflict being actively managed in different parts of the relationship or having been resolved in the past. We'll also see the leader aware of the emotional temperature of the partnership, ensuring that there is honest learning from any conflict, and knowledge of where the potential hot spots are for the future. And in the best of relationships, leaders ensure that this evidence and learning is available and used by all the senior people across the partnership.

It can be pretty obvious when conflict is brewing. Deadlines are missed. Communication gets strained – key individuals don't speak up, or don't even turn up to meetings. And meetings are characterized by bad behaviour, for example veiled or overt aggression.

Other symptoms are cynicism, silence, or withdrawal. People may find themselves making inappropriate jokes. At other times, conflict may be suppressed, with individuals strenuously denying that anything is other than perfect.

Leaders need to be aware when people start going back to their own territories and circling the wagons, making sure that no one invades their space. Sometimes this is accompanied by a profusion of identity building. Just before two organizations that were both part of the UK National Health Service (NHS) were due to merge, for example, we saw a massive outburst of business plans, mission statements, values statements and the like from each organization. The implications were clear. Neither side wanted to work with the other, and their defence mechanism was to create logos and symbols, stamping their identity on the areas they could still control. It was an unmistakeable sign that they felt out of control in everything else.

A key attribute of a collaborative leader is the ability to quickly recognize the signs of conflict and to find out what is going on behind the scenes. Whatever the presenting symptoms, underlying them all is some genuine source of conflict, which must be understood and handled if a partnership is to work effectively. The agility of the collaborative leader ensures that they can assess these complex situations, look for innovative solutions to the conflict that exists and engage others in working through solutions. However frustrating and time consuming, the leader will be unable to deliver the objectives of the collaboration without addressing any existing conflict – quickly and effectively.

Chapter summary

Handling conflict mustn't be avoided

Collaboration creates conflict – it is unavoidable. In fact, if you are not reporting any disagreement or dissent then you are probably avoiding the issue. This is often the hardest area for leaders to tackle in any collaborative situation and one of the most mature and significant skills for the aspiring collaborative leader. Failure to effectively address conflict situations will cost in lost time and wasted budget and damaged relationships. Leaders who demonstrate a confident and assured style when dealing with their own staff can become disabled in the face of conflict caused by clashes of different organizational cultures or different personalities of the senior players.

The tendency is for the leader to avoid, deny, fight or manipulate in the face of conflict. The starting point is for the leader to understand their habits, to think about the longer-term objectives of the collaboration and to choose an approach to address the conflict as soon as possible.

Remember that if conflict is unavoidable in a relationship then you need to set up the governance, operations and behaviours in advance in such a way that you can handle the inevitable and not get disabled by it.

Lessons for leaders

- Identify your own personal triggers – what tends to push you into bad behaviour? If your partner does something to trigger conflict, you may not always be able to prevent your initial reaction, but at least you can plan to deal with the consequences.
- Remember the other side of the coin too – understand what it is that you do that can trigger unhelpful behaviour in your partner and plan to avoid falling into those habits.
- Not all conflicts are equally important to the future of a partnership or other collaborative relationship and its business success. Identify the situations where conflict really matters and where it doesn't. Intervene fast in those places where conflict matters most.
- Seek to understand the motives of all concerned. What do they get from being in conflict at this point and what, therefore, might be their incentive to resolve it?
- As a leader, don't try to take the conflict away from those involved – it just creates an environment of avoidance or collusion. Make sure the people at the heart of the conflict are also at the heart of the work to find its solution.
- Teach others to manage conflict in a sustainable manner – share your own knowledge, and not just within your own organization. Your partners probably need to build their conflict-handling capability too.

12

THE FUTURE COLLABORATIVE LEADER

Since we published the first edition of this book in 2009, collaborative leadership as a term and as a concept has moved on considerably. Back then it was just an emergent idea arising from studies of leadership in joint ventures, business alliances and public–private partnerships. Now the language of collaborative leadership is in regular use in management journals and the business pages of newspapers. A Google search or news alert for collaborative leadership will show a daily stream of ideas and comment about the particular leadership challenges that collaboration brings.

But while the term is in much wider circulation it is still not well understood. In this final chapter we look back at the lessons learned as the discipline of collaborative leadership has developed over the last ten years and we reflect on some of the ideas that we have discussed in this book. We also look forward to explore three key trends that we believe will drive the demands on collaborative leaders in the future. But first a riddle:

What's the difference between an iPhone and a Betamax VCR?

Lessons from the past

No this is not the start of a bad technology-based stand-up routine but a serious question about collaborative leadership. The story of the commercial failure of the Sony Betamax home VCR is at first sight a familiar one of a technology superior product losing out to a rival system which had more manufacturers and better marketing behind it. But if you drill deeper there are some fascinating lessons for the aspiring collaborative leader.

The president of Sony in the 1970s was Akio Morita – he had had great success with the development of the Sony Trinitron TV and the first Walkman – products which paved the way for the first great consumer electronics revolution. In fact Steve Jobs described Morita as the inventor of the whole consumer electronics marketplace in a tribute delivered after Morita's death in October 1999.

So where did he go so wrong with the Betamax? With hindsight the key to this failure was Sony's attempt to go it alone with a standard they had developed and owned. When it was launched in 1975 Sony had a clear technology lead but they had to rely on enough film companies coming on board with pre-recorded video-tapes to make it a success with consumers. The idea of recording your own video material with cheap video cameras was in its infancy at that point. Their rivals at JVC realized that in order to compete they had to get a lot of other manufacturers lined up behind their VHS system and to flood the market with machines. This would, in turn, make the movie studios back the format by releasing new films on VHS and encourage video-hire shops to stock VHS because more customers had those players. They got Sharp and Matsushita (RCA in the US) to back their standard and by 1980 VHS players had 70 per cent of the US market and this scale of production enabled the manufacturers to bring the cost of the players down which in turn increased market share. Other manufacturers came on board and by 1984 there were 40 using the VHS standard. The film companies and video hire businesses just followed the trend – the availability of Betamax movies went down – and the cost went up. Eventually, in 1988, Sony accepted the inevitable and started producing VHS machines themselves.

Later Morita reflected on the lessons he had learned and said that he had 'made a mistake and should have worked harder to get more companies together in a family to support the Betamax product'.[1] JVC did try harder and was more effective at forming alliances to back VHS – and they and their partners won the day.

So much so obvious you might say – but if Steve Jobs was such an admirer of Morita, how does he address the big lesson of a high-profile failed product from his hero? And why was he able to succeed with products such as the Apple iPhone and iPad? These were ground-breaking designs which didn't share their operating systems or standards with anyone else – at a time when many of their rivals were getting together to adopt a common standard with the Android operating system. But the iPhone was a great success even though Jobs ensured that Apple went its own way, much like Sony. The stories of the Betamax VCR and the iPhone seem to lead to opposite conclusions about the business need for collaboration and collaborative leadership.

But digging a bit deeper these apparent contradictions can be explained using two of the collaborative leader's tools described earlier – the collaboration spectrum and the three-legged stool.

Choosing the appropriate amount of collaboration

In Chapter 2 we introduced the idea of the collaboration spectrum – ranging from highly collaborative almost symbiotic relationships, to transactional and customer–supplier relationships, with mutually beneficial partnerships sitting somewhere in

Amount of collaboration

High	Medium	Low
permanent team	partnership	customer supplier
symbiotic	*mutual*	*transactional*
close		*distant*
same objectives		*separate objectives*
loyal to the group		*loyal to my employer*
lots of time together		*little time together*
They're really one of us		*They give us a good deal*

FIGURE 12.1   The collaboration spectrum

the middle. The factor that determines where on the spectrum a particular relationship lies is the amount of interdependence between the players.

The greater the interdependence between your business and others the greater the amount of collaboration required.

When Sony launched the Betamax, Morita may have thought that he could capture the newly emerging home video market on his own. But crucial to that success was the availability of content for customers to watch on their expensive new VCR – and film companies weren't going to commit to risking a lot of distribution costs for pre-recorded video tapes until they were sure there were enough players out there. Sony had a major interdependence with content providers in its strategy, but partnering with some of its rivals to increase market share for the Betamax standard really wasn't in Sony's DNA at that point. JVC spotted this opportunity and had the collaborative leadership skills needed to bring rival manufacturers together and leap ahead of Sony. Morita for all his success as a leader either didn't see the need to build these relationships early enough or he lacked the skills to do so.

At Apple, Steve Jobs (in his second phase in charge of the company) decided that by concentrating on the quality of the consumer experience he could design new products that broke into new markets with little dependence on others and so little need for collaborative relationships. He found a strategy that worked for Apple's position in its market – at the transactional end of the collaboration spectrum. In fact, Apple is known for its control over its suppliers and to work with Apple you have to play by its rules. Now that works in situations where one company has all the power; power to specify contracts with suppliers and to make the decisions that will control its fate in its market, but this is a rare occurrence in our interdependent business environment. We see many more situations that are much more complicated for leaders – where no single organization can completely achieve its aims without being able to work with or influence others.

In these situations leaders need to balance an internal focus on product design or service excellence, with an external focus on building strong relationships and putting the right operating processes in place to link them efficiently to their partners. So in most situations leaders need to assess the levels of interdependence and the spectrum can help them choose the appropriate level of collaboration necessary.

The three-legged stool – governance, operations and behaviours

In Chapter 3 we explained how collaborative situations need much more than the parties 'being nice to each other'! Using the analogy of a three-legged stool we described the priorities that collaborative leaders need to balance – these are:

- **Governance** – the contracts, the accountabilities and the decision making.
- **Operations** – the joint processes and systems – the way progress is measured and information is shared.
- **Behaviours** – the way leaders behave as role models and people treat each other to produce joint results.

Just like a three-legged stool – if you take away any one of these legs you end up with something which is unstable – a resilient collaboration needs attention to all three elements. The relative amount of time and effort required on each element depends on how interdependent the parties really are and that can be discovered using the collaboration spectrum.

If the situation is more like the transactional approach used by Apple with their suppliers then the focus is on getting the governance right. However, the more collaboration that is required in a relationship the more attention needs to be paid to operations and, in particular, behaviours.

At the high-collaboration end of the spectrum in symbiotic situations, things are very different. Here the leadership focus has to be first and foremost on behaviours, finding common values and working to understand each other's culture. This helps to deepen the relationship and enables people to spot opportunities to join things up and create new business value in unexpected ways. This is what Akio Morita and Sony should have been doing with their rival video tape machine manufacturers but JVC and others proved more adept at responding to the collaborative leadership challenge and building these types of relationships with their partners and stakeholders.

Six capabilities of a collaborative leader

Put simply, collaborative leadership is the type of leadership required to get results across internal or external organizational boundaries. And that means the leadership required to get value from the differences (in culture, experience, or skills) that lie in the organizations that sit either side of that boundary. As we've emphasized this means leaders investing time to *build relationships*, being ready to *handle conflict* in a constructive manner and most importantly being able to *share control*.

As we saw from the examples of successful collaborative leaders in Chapter 7 there are many ways of doing this. There isn't a simple template to follow or one personality type to emulate, but successful collaborative leaders are pretty self-aware – they know their strengths and weaknesses and they understand that it's not all about ego and charisma.

Three critical skills and three essential attitudes

The capability of the collaborative leader is dependent on them having all the basic experience and skills of any leader, but it is also a set of skills and attitudes that is necessary to address these complex interdependent situations. There are three essential skills.

Mediation – Collaborative leaders need to be able to address conflict constructively and effectively as soon as it arises. This is a demanding skill. Evidence from many collaborative leadership 360° feedback programmes suggests that handling conflict and the associated mediation skills are often the number one leadership development priority.

Influencing – Collaborative leaders need to be able to share control and so choose the best approach to influencing their partners. This requires an understanding of the organizational culture and personality type of their partners as well as an objective analysis of the business situation to hand.

Engaging others – Collaborative leaders can't be successful without the skills of networking and relationship building. This means communicating with clarity, often in high stress situations, and involving others in decision making at the right time.

In support of these three skills, collaborative leaders can only be successful if they hold three additional essential attitudes.

Agility – These complex collaborative situations require a forward looking attitude of mind, coupled with an ability to quickly assimilate facts and ask incisive questions.

Patience – Managing relationships takes time and collaborative leaders need to be able to take a calm and measured approach, reflecting on new information and giving confidence to others.

Empathy – All the attributes of any collaborative leader must be underpinned by a willingness to truly listen and be open-minded to the views of others. Only with these attitudes can the leader develop the high degree of self-awareness necessary to accurately assess the impact of their behaviour on others.

In many ways Jobs' leadership style could be seen as the antithesis of what is required to tackle the collaboration challenges facing many leaders today – but remember that Apple has created a situation where collaboration with external parties is very limited indeed. For most collaborative leaders there may be more to learn from Akio Morita's more interdependent situation at Sony.

The impact of future trends

This is a time of great financial and business uncertainty but even now there are some emergent trends which will affect collaborative leaders in the years ahead.

We look at three of the most important of them here: the growth of collaboration technology, the impact of global power shifts from West to East and changes in workforce demographics.

The growth of collaboration technology

Collaboration is in the news – and this has been driven by the boom over recent years in collaboration technology. There has been phenomenal growth of websites such as Facebook® and YouTube® where millions of individuals are used to sharing all aspects of their social life on-line. This has led to a great deal of interest in how similar tools could be used to increase the sharing of information and the building of networks in a business context.

The potential market is huge for these technologies – the Forrester research group predicted the value of collaboration tools or what it calls 'social enterprise apps' would grow to become a $6.4 billion market by 2016.[2] Of course the scale of this market depends on what are defined as collaboration tools – people use the term to mean many things: video conferencing technology, document sharing and editing software, knowledge management tools, professional networking websites (such as LinkedIn), workplace blogs or cloud computing. And soon you can lose any sense of where this technology in going in a maze of buzzwords. But if we try to stand back and look at the longer-term trends, collaboration technology is really about three things:

- Remote collaborative working – helping specific groups of people to simulta-neously work together creating virtual teams.
- Managing user-generated content and knowledge – this is the Wikipedia or Trip Advisor of the business world, where large numbers of staff (or customers) can create and maintain bodies of knowledge about a product or service.
- Business networking – tools to enable people within an extended organization to make connections and to build relationships that might be useful to them in the future.

So as these technologies converge and allow access to this software and informa-tion on tablets and smartphones, there are new challenges (and opportunities) for the collaborative leader. In the future, organizational boundaries will mean even less, and new collaborations will evolve that are enabled by these technologies. These new collaborations will exist to exploit new business opportunities or to change how organizations work – for good.

Already leaders are finding new ways to implement these technologies and, at the same time, facing up to some new collaboration challenges.

Tesco – managing rapid growth far from home

Tesco has rapidly grown from its position as the largest retailer in Britain to being the third largest in the world – with most of this growth coming in markets far from the UK such as Turkey, South Korea and Thailand. The Tesco strategy depends on bringing together retail and logistics expertise from its mature markets with local knowledge from businesses it has acquired or staff it has recruited in its new markets – and doing all this quicker than its competitors.

Tesco has invested heavily in network technology and collaboration software as part of the package they bring to a new organization that they were buying or building in one of these markets.[3] Using this technology they set up tools for sharing written information such as blogs and wikis, and advanced video conferencing (or telepresence) suites for holding virtual meetings. After piloting various uses of the technology, and possibly because Tesco have a process–driven management culture, they incorporated these collaboration tools into a number of standard workflow processes for: stock planning, store layout, innovation and promotions.

This has meant that Tesco managers in their new markets could participate in the standard company operating model and learn from their colleagues without having to fly half way around the world – speeding up decision making and the integration of new stores into the Tesco business and culture. In this case the use of technology has enabled leaders to accelerate the sort of international collaboration they might have wanted to create anyway but it's made it a reality. However, the leaders know that the technology on its own will not deliver the benefits. Their tasks have been to re-think communication and decision-making processes in order to make the new collaborations work. Without these changes in ways of working, the leaders will miss the opportunity to deliver the benefits of new innovative collaborations.

Comic Relief project management

Comic Relief is an organization with a very different culture and we can see a different approach to using collaboration tools in a global setting. As well as fund-raising, Comic Relief staff have to work closely with organizations big and small across the world to ensure that the development grants that it awards are well used. This means people working together creating project plans and financial business cases on IT systems that are sufficiently secure, but also widely available and cheap and simple to use. You can't force your charitable partners to adopt an expensive corporate IT system or to send out a trainer to Africa to teach them how to use it.

For this type of collaboration, publically available web-based collaboration tools are a useful way forward, Comic Relief uses one called Huddle.[4] Any organization that is awarded a grant can buy a cheap user licence and, as long as they have a broadband or mobile access to the internet, can be given secure access to different sections of a Comic Relief filing cabinet. Groups can work together on plans – learning from similar projects elsewhere in the world and swapping ideas with others facing similar challenges. In this example the collaboration software is a neutral infrastructure which gives people secure access and a means of connecting groups but doesn't specify what they do with it – it's the leader's job to engage others in the potential benefits.

It's easy to get overwhelmed by the sheer numbers and scale of new collaboration tools and the speed of innovation in this area. One challenge for collaborative leaders is just to make sense of it all and to decide which new developments are important and which are not. Remember our message that effective collaboration does not come free; it will always take considerable effort to derive any real benefits from these new technologies. These technologies will require that people adapt their ways of working to make best use of the facilities that they bring. And making that happen is the real work of the collaborative leader.

Global power shifts

One trend that has gathered pace since the first edition of this book is the shift in power away from the old economies of the US and Western Europe towards markets in the BRIC countries (Brazil, Russia, India, China) and beyond. Originally this power-shift raised questions in the press about how established Western firms could exploit the increasing numbers of consumers in these markets and see off competition in their own countries from low-wage manufacturers. But this rather simplistic response was replaced by a more complex analysis highlighting the interdependence between global networks of suppliers, each with different customer needs and expectations. In terms of global power we appear to be moving away from the days when America was the only global superpower to a much more multi-polar world.

In business terms this means that for many well-established companies, a large percentage of their revenue is going to be generated far from their traditional markets. And at the same time much of their R&D and innovation as well as their product manufacture is also going to be happening a long way away from their home base.

Now in some ways this isn't new – but the traditional leadership response was to put in hub and spoke organizational models, with a central HQ (usually in the US or Europe) reaching out to regional centres each with a degree of local control over marketing and customer service. But in the future, if the majority of the business's revenue comes from outside your home market – leaders need to think carefully about where functions are based and where they draw talent from to staff their management teams.

Some leaders have tackled this by using matrix structures, with individual managers belonging to several different decision-making teams – perhaps a country-based sales team looking at the local market, a global product team looking at supply and production issues, and a regional talent pool for their own career development. This can get very confusing and decision making can slow to a crawl as different groups have power to review or block the decisions of others.

The temptation for leaders is to try to control – centralizing decision making again, but often that defeats the object. Collaborative leaders look to create decentralized decision making where authority for different types of decision is passed down to the appropriate level and there is a good understanding across a decentralized team of which stakeholders need to be consulted and when. This approach has the added advantage that local decision making can reflect the cultural norms of the people working in different parts of the world.

Of course the demands of a multi-polar world apply right at the top of organizations too. Boards and executive teams need to respond by becoming more diverse, representing the different parts of the world that they depend on for suppliers or customers. This global interdependence has major implications for the development of leadership talent and the selection processes for top teams. The question nominations committees on Boards need to ask themselves is: What are they doing to find and develop talented managers from across the full spectrum of regions in which they operate or have critical business relationships? The German manufacturing company Siemens has even gone as far as appointing a chief diversity officer to oversee this sort of work.[5] Only 30 per cent of its more than 400,000 employees are based in Germany and so having global processes for individual performance management, talent development and succession planning is vital if they want to recruit and retain the best people wherever they are located.

Shifts in global power mean that collaborative leaders will need to have a deep understanding of other cultures and the ability to work as part of very diverse senior teams. In organizational design terms, centralized control systems and organizational designs dominated by an HQ based in the old 'home country' are unlikely to succeed. Collaborative leaders will need to demonstrate that they can share some control by creating more decentralized structures and shared decision-making processes with different partners and different cultures.

Changes in workforce demographics

The fact that in the UK and most of the Western world we have an aging population is no surprise. Advances in medicine and greater awareness of the impact of lifestyle on health have combined to push up life expectancy and this trend is likely to continue. This fact, coupled with the decline of pension provision, has consequences for the workplace – one in five people questioned in a recent poll of UK employees said that they expected to work until they were over 70.[6] But having to manage the aspirations and needs of a significant number of older workers is not the only change that leaders will see in the workforce.

At the other end of the age spectrum the evidence is that young people are growing up with very different attitudes to work. Many graduates expect to spend some of their career working for a small business or indeed to set up in business for themselves as an entrepreneur. These IT literate young workers will carry this experience of a small and flexible workplace into the rest of their careers. Expectation of greater transparent access to information, instant results and rapid feedback on performance will not sit easily with the traditional styles of leadership. Some leaders are responding by bringing ideas from computer games into the workplace – in a so called 'gamification of work'. This can mean people earning reward points by completing tasks quickly and accurately. They can move up levels when they have reached a certain proficiency or have successfully worked with colleagues on team challenges. At the heart of the technique is using rapid on-screen feedback and competition (to beat your own high score or to beat your colleagues) in order to engage and motivate staff.

Using techniques borrowed from the gaming world may be useful when motivating some teenage workers but they are less likely to be a success in leading other segments of the workforce. An increasingly diverse age profile will call for diverse organizational approaches and a more collaborative leadership style.

Leading a future workforce which is more diverse is not just about addressing the age profile, the workplace is continuing to change in other ways too. There will be more female workers and more people employed on part-time contracts. Many office and knowledge worker jobs are likely to disappear as increased computing power makes it possible to automate standardized elements of these roles. But there are also skills shortages in areas such as medicine and engineering that have long periods of training and professional qualification. The most likely way to fill these gaps will be through more inward migration from countries with younger, educated populations.

The good news is that there is plenty of evidence that a diverse workforce has the potential to be more innovative and ultimately successful than a homogeneous one. In his book *Difference* Scott Page makes a very powerful argument for why diverse groups can outperform groups where all the members have similar characteristics. He uses some very elegant mathematics to show why – and in which situations – groups who have and can use that sort of diversity will outperform those that don't. But even without the maths his conclusion makes sense. To tackle tricky problems that have multiple causes and require innovative solutions, a group of similar people will find an answer they can all agree on and is the best fit to their common view of the world. But a more diverse group is likely to have people in it who will challenge that common view. This will force the group to explore other avenues which can eventually lead them to test a wider set of possible solutions - and if there is a better solution out there to find it.

For leaders, as the trend for greater workforce diversity continues, the question is how to get value from the differences that brings. And how to apply that value to problems where it really counts – problems that require innovative thinking and multi-party implementation. The ability of collaborative leaders to demonstrate agility, patience and empathy really comes into its own in these situations.

The consequences of these trends for collaborative leaders

Look back 20 years to a time when the internet and mobile technology were in their infancy and the BRIC economies had yet to grow, who would have predicted the business environment that we understand today? The trends that we have discussed are already having an impact – they cannot be avoided. We cannot fully predict the future business environment, all we can be sure of is that leadership will have to evolve to meet the challenges that these changes will bring.

A new kind of change management

First, there is the continuing need to manage the delivery of business change – often across a complex landscape of different business units and multiple external partners. The growth of collaboration technology is already a major driver of change. As the BRIC economies become more powerful players, consumer business models and organizational relationships will need to change. And the changes in the workforce will bring their own leadership demands. Traditionally change management has been seen by leaders as the 'softer side' of programme management – and something that can be planned and controlled with Gantt charts and programme Boards. In an interdependent world, leaders need to look beyond that programme model to more organic approaches to delivering change across a network of different organizations each with their own capabilities, traditions and constraints.

Understanding the different organizational cultures involved becomes an important skill as well as the ability to bring people together to create joint plans and common tools for managing the change process. Success often happens when, as a collaborative leader, you can create the environment where the different organizations involved can co-evolve, each organization learning from and reacting to the changes in the other as they move towards an agreed set of goals.

A new kind of organization design

In the future we envisage the need for leaders to design their organization to fit its own collaborative niche. This sort of organizational design work has often been seen as a technical task and delegated to HR specialists. But increasing globalization and powerful collaboration technology will mean that there are many more options for size, geographical base and organizational structure. Getting the strategic decisions right about which parts of the network you want to own, where you want to transact with others and where you want to collaborate is the responsibility of the leader. They then need to define the right governance structures, culture and accountabilities with regard to critical business decisions.

Building the right organization can be about designing dynamic roles rather than creating static structures. For example, when outsourcing an operation it's often the case that a team is left in the client organization to play a combination of 'inspection', 'supplier management' and 'intelligent customer' roles. But because the team is inevitably small, any allocation of individuals to static roles is going to leave tasks very under-resourced at key points in the contract lifecycle, especially when things go wrong. It's far better to have a group of staff who are trained to have a reasonable level of skill across the range of roles with expertise in a few. That multi-skilling, combined with some well-documented processes, means that the group can dynamically allocate its own time depending on need and the leader can oversee overall performance without having to get involved in regular re-organization and re-prioritization of work.

New kinds of business relationships

If the demands of organization design are an inward looking response to the three trends we discussed earlier, collaborative leaders need to make a similar response in the external world reaching out to engage wider groups of stakeholders. Resilient relationships with stakeholders seem to have been key to the long-lived success of many companies and we can only see that continuing as the world becomes more interdependent.

In his book *The Living Company*, Dutch business thinker Arie de Geus described a study he commissioned for Royal Dutch/Shell Group.[8] In a world where the average lifespan of a multinational company is between 40 and 50 years, Shell wanted to know what allowed some companies to weather fundamental change and survive for well over a century with their corporate identity intact. De Geus describes a number of traits that help companies build the constructive relationships that the study found to be vital to their longevity, but we'll focus here on just one, which he calls 'flocking' by analogy with bird behaviour. Blue tits, he noted, adapted remarkably over the twentieth century to tap the new food source of bottled milk delivered to doorsteps. Not only did they learn to siphon off the cream from the early topless bottles, but by the 1950s the entire blue tit population had also learned to pierce the aluminium caps of new bottles introduced between the wars. Apparently robins also learned the first step – but failed at the second. Although individual robins learned how to pierce the aluminium caps, the skill wasn't passed on to the species as a whole. What was causing the difference?

The answer is that blue tits flock for two or three months in the summer. Robins, meanwhile, are highly territorial, with fixed boundaries they won't allow others to cross. And the ability to flock is the determining factor that allows learning to be spread throughout the population. Birds that flock increase their chances of surviving and de Geus believes the same is true of organizations.

Collaborative leaders need to build their own and their organization's awareness of what other organizations and other leaders are doing. Understanding which relationships will support your long-term survival is essential. Some of the collaboration technologies can help this process by making the business of connecting to others and sharing knowledge easier to do. But learning from people in that wider 'flock' requires much more than technology, it needs the right attitude of mind and the skills of the collaborative leader.

A manifesto for the collaborative leader

Akio Morita at Sony was widely regarded as one of the most influential leaders of his generation and he certainly led the creation of some iconic consumer products, but perhaps the most lasting lesson of his leadership comes from near the end of his career when he learned that by failing to reach out and build relationships with his competitors at home and abroad he had made a strategic mistake.

Aspiring collaborative leaders need to keep learning – from their successes and from their failures – but most importantly learning from the other leaders who are their potential partners and collaborators. And this takes self-analysis and humility.

If collaborative leadership starts with *building relationships* and progresses through *handling conflict* of the sort that will inevitably arise when leaders with different objectives and cultures come together, it culminates with *sharing control* in a spirit of mutual trust. These are demanding challenges for any leader. In order to address these challenges, what follows is a ten-point manifesto for the aspiring collaborative leader distilled from all we have learnt in writing this book.

A manifesto for collaborative leaders

1. Seek out conflict early – address it openly and with confidence. And be prepared to mediate others' conflict in order to build relationships.
2. Don't expect your partners to have the same objectives as yourself – but look for common ground in shared values and in the things you can achieve together that neither of you could achieve alone.
3. Understand that collaboration is not a zero sum game – in an interdependent world your organization can only succeed through the success of others. If you want them to invest in your success you must invest in theirs.
4. Value and use diversity – both within your organization and between you and your partners. Apply the value of diversity to find innovative solutions to the most important and complex problems that need a new approach.
5. Only get as close and collaborate as much as the situation demands. Collaboration is not a moral choice but it is a business necessity in certain circumstances.
6. Look to the long term in relationships – and combine patience when sticking by your principles with agility in your actions to make tricky relationships work.
7. Listen hard – and then show that you have understood what you have heard. Get behind the face value of what your partners are saying to understand and empathize with their motives and fears.
8. Be clear where the significant 'points of interdependence' are in a relationship. Don't expect to eliminate them – you can't control everything – but get very efficient in your interactions at these key points.
9. Engage others in your mission to be a collaborative leader – one thing is for certain, you can never be a collaborative leader on your own.
10. Be authentic in all you do – people need to know that what they see is what they get.

We've been working in the fields of collaboration and leadership for much of our professional lives. Most of the fundamental lessons of what works and what doesn't work have remained constant over that time but the context in which these lessons are applied is changing rapidly. There is clearly more interdependence in the world but, perhaps more significantly, the nature of that interdependence is getting more strategic and the speed of the knock-on impacts is accelerating.

In the middle of all this, leaders are under yet more pressure to deliver and are judged harshly by their shareholders, customers or electorate if they are seen to be failing. Under this sort of pressure there is a risk that leaders turn to tribal behaviour – acting to serve the interests of their own constituency – looking within their own tribe and trying to isolate themselves from or defeat everyone outside it. And if we have learnt one thing in researching this book it is that this tribal approach simply will not work. Because if interdependence (financial, operational or reputational) is a reality then collaboration is a necessity and developing collaborative leadership capability becomes a vital activity for any business.

However there are opportunities as well as challenges in becoming a collaborative leader. By opening yourself up to different organizational cultures and working out how to collaborate with them effectively, leaders also increase their access to a diverse range of ideas, tools and opportunities. Out of this diversity collaborative leaders can create the innovative solutions necessary to both deliver results in today's difficult business environment and to enhance their own career.

That is the great promise of collaborative leadership.

NOTES

1 Interdependence and its consequences for leaders

1 Mervyn King, former Governor of the Bank of England, speaking on the BBC television programme *Back from the Brink*, broadcast 24 September 2009.
2 From para 607 to 613, 'The failure of the Royal Bank of Scotland', Financial Services Authority Board Report, December 2011.
3 'Tony Hayward: BP's straight-talking chief on evolution not revolution', *Guardian*, 4 February 2010, available at: http://www.guardian.co.uk/business/2010/feb/04/tony-hayward-bp-interview.
4 From 'Executive summary of the Chief Counsel's report to The Presidential Oil Spill Commission', 17 February 2011, available at: http://www.oilspillcommission.gov/.
5 http://www.guardian.co.uk/environment/2010/jun/23/dudley-manages-bp-oil-spill.
6 See, for example, *Daily Telegraph*, 8 May 2010: http://www.telegraph.co.uk/news/election-2010/7695794/General-Election-2010-Gordon-Brown-launched-telephone-rant-at-Nick-Clegg.html.
7 JFK public papers item #278, July 1962, available at: http://www.presidency.ucsb.edu/ws/index.php?pid=8756&st=&st1=#axzz1qElLtIFz.
8 See World Health Organization, Global Alert and Response Project: http://www.who.int/csr/sars/project/en/.
9 See: http://conversations.nokia.com/2011/02/11/open-letter-from-ceo-stephen-elop-nokia-and-ceo-steve-ballmer-microsoft/.
10 *Leading Change*, John P. Kotter, Harvard Business School Press, 1996, pp. 25–31: http://www.kotterinternational.com/kotterprinciples/management-vs-leadership.
11 Quoted in *Inside Apple*, Adam Lashinsky, John Murray, 2012.
12 'When to Ally and when to Acquire', J. Dyer, P. Kale and H. Singh, *Harvard Business Review*, July–Aug., 2004.
13 *Emergence: The Connected Lives of Ants, Brains, Cities and Software*, Steven Johnson, Penguin, 2002.
14 *Super Cooperators: Evolution, Altruism and Human Behaviour*, Martin Nowak with Roger Highfield, Canongate, 2011.
15 'The Tragedy of the Commons', Garrett Hardin, *Science Magazine*, 13 December 1968.
16 *Governing the Commons: The Evolution of Institutions for Collective Action*, Elinor Ostrom, Cambridge University Press, 1990.

17 Appendix 9.1 in *Working Together*, Amy Poteete, Marco Janssen and Elinor Ostrom, Princeton University Press, 2010.
18 For an overview see the UN 'Guidebook on promoting good governance in PPPs': http://www.unece.org/fileadmin/DAM/ceci/publications/ppp.pdf.
19 See, for example, the report by the Parliamentary Transport Select Committee into the London Underground PPP in March 2010: http://www.publications.parliament.uk/pa/cm200910/cmselect/cmtran/100/100.pdf.
20 'Launching a World-Class Joint Venture', James Bamford, David Ernst and David G. Fubini, *Harvard Business Review*, February, 2004.
21 'Grasping the Capability: Successful alliance creation and governance through the "connected corporation"', *The Point,* Volume Two, Issue One, Accenture, 2002.
22 'Launching a World-Class Joint Venture', op. cit.
23 See: http://blogs.hbr.org/hbr/hbreditors/2009/05/a_recession_casualty_trust.html.

2 The collaboration spectrum

1 From: http://www.civilservant.org.uk/numbers.pdf.
2 *Inside Apple*, Adam Lashinsky, John Murray, 2012.
3 *The Age of Paradox*, Charles Handy, Harvard Business School Press, September, 1995.
4 'Making Partnerships Work: A survey of UK senior executives', Ipsos Mori and Socia, February, 2007.

3 The three-legged stool – governance, operations and behaviours

1 'Making Partnerships Work: A survey of UK senior executives', Ipsos Mori and Socia, February, 2007.
2 Ibid.
3 'Laws of Logistics & Supply Chain Management', Alan Braithwaite and Richard Wilding, Chapter 4, pp. 249–59, *The Financial Times Handbook of Management,* 3rd edn (Editors: Ed Crainer and Des Dearlove), Pearson, London, 2004.
4 'Eight Ways to Build Collaborative Teams', Lynda Gratton and Tamara J. Erickson, *Harvard Business Review*, November, 2007.
5 Chief Counsel's Report to the Presidential Oil Spill Commission, February 2011, available at: http://www.oilspillcommission.gov/.
6 *'Tough Dialogue Pays Off: How Lafarge and WWF make their partnership work to help preserve the world's ecological balance,* Claudia Heimer, Roger Pudney, Jean-Paul Jeanrenaud, Luc Giraud-Guigues and Michel Picard, Ashridge Practitioner Paper, October, 2006.
7 Ibid., p. 3.
8 'Making Partnerships Work: A survey of UK senior executives', Ipsos Mori and Socia, February, 2007.
9 The Roads Academy: http://www.highways.gov.uk/business/31266.aspx.
10 'Child sweatshop shame threatens Gap's ethical image', Dan McDougall, *Observer*, 28 October 2007.
11 'In China, Human Costs Are Built Into an iPad', *New York Times*, 25 January 2012.
12 'Collaborative Advantage', Rosabeth Moss Kanter, *Harvard Business Review*, July–August, 1994.
13 *Together: The Rituals, Pleasures and Politics of Co-operation*, Richard Sennett, Allen Lane, 2012.
14 *Nudge: Improving Decisions About Health, Wealth and Happiness*, Richard Thaler and Cass Sunstein, Penguin, 2009.

15 'The Name of the Game: Predictive Power of Reputations versus Situational Labels in Determining Prisoner's Dilemma Game Moves', Lee Ross, Steven Samuels and Varda Liberman, *Personality and Social Psychology Bulletin*, Sept., 2004.

4 Measuring collaboration

1 *The Principles of Scientific Management*, Frederick Winslow Taylor, Harper and Brothers, 1911.
2 'Grasping the Capability: Successful alliance creation and governance through the "connected corporation"', *The Point*, Volume 2, Issue One, 2002.
3 Ibid.
4 Available from: http://www.nrls.npsa.nhs.uk/resources/?EntryId45=61830.
5 'Project management at Heathrow Terminal 5', Christian Wolmar, *Public Finance*, 22 April 2005.
6 *Alliances and Joint Ventures: Fit, Focus, and Follow-Through*, KPMG International, 2005.
7 See for example: *The Balanced Scorecard: Translating Strategy into Action*, R. Kaplan and D. Norton, HBR Press, 1996.
8 'The Right Role for Top Teams', J. Katzenbach and R. Cross, *Strategy + Business*, February, 2012.
9 Independent review of RIDDOR reporting by Network Rail and its contractors, available from: http://www.rssb.co.uk/.
10 Home Affairs Committee report HC 58-I, Fifth Report of Session 2007–08, Volume I: The Stationery Office, July 2006.

5 Analysing different organizational cultures

1 Armne Yalnizyan, Canadian Centre for Policy Alternatives: http://www.policy alternatives.ca/publications/monitor/21st-century-globalization.
2 Armne Yalnizyan, ibid.
3 *Toronto Star*, 27 March 2011: http://www.thestar.com/business/article/786135-clash-of-cultures-blamed-in-vale-inco-strike.
4 *User Guidebook on Implementing Public–Private Partnerships for Transportation Infrastructure Projects in the United States*, US Department of Transportation, July, 2007.
5 'Making Partnerships Work: A survey of UK senior executives', Ipsos Mori and Socia, February, 2007.
6 *The Character of Organisations*, William Bridges, Davies Black Publishing, 2000.
7 The Myers-Briggs Type Indicator® was developed in the early 1940s by Katharine Cook Briggs and her daughter Isabel Briggs Myers. Based on Jungian archetypes, it is widely used for personal and team development in business settings.
8 *The Character of Organisations*, op. cit.
9 Ibid.
10 'Changing culture in the Royal Parks', *HR Director*, February, 2008.
11 *Together: The Rituals, Pleasures and Politics of Co-operation*, Richard Sennett, Allen Lane, 2012.
12 'Collaborative Advantage', by Rosabeth Moss Kanter, *Harvard Business Review*, July–August, 1994: 94.
13 *Business Week*, 17 September 2001, available from: http://www.businessweek.com/magazine/content/01_38/b3749001.htm.
14 *Business Week*, 29 March 1999, available from: http://www.businessweek.com/1999/99_13/b3622227.htm.
15 Quoted in 'Renault-Nissan the paradoxical alliance – European School of Management and Technology case study', ESMT 305-0047-1: https://www.esmt.org/fm/479/ESMT-305-0047-1M.pdf.

16 *Automotive News*, 5 April 2004: http://www.autonews.com/apps/pbcs.dll/article?
AID=/20040405/SUB/404050845.
17 *Financial Times*, 7 April 2010.

6 The partnership roadmap

1 http://www.neccontract.com/news/article.asp?NEWS_ID=782.
2 'When to Ally and When to Acquire', Jeffrey H. Dyer, Prashant Kale and Harbir Singh, *Harvard Business Review*, July–August, 2004.
3 'The PPP is Gordon's fault', Christian Wolmar, *Evening Standard*, 17 July 2007.
4 'Health officials say IT scheme has enough scrutiny in response to technical audit call', Tony Collins, *Computer Weekly*, 18 April 2006.
5 *Managing Transitions*, William Bridges, Nicholas Brealey Publishing, 3rd edn, December 2009.
6 'Launching a World Class Joint Venture', James Bamford, David Ernst and David G. Fubini, *Harvard Business Review*, February, 2004.
7 'Making Partnerships Work: A survey of UK senior executives', Ipsos Mori and Socia, February 2007.
8 Partnership Contract for Recycling, Waste Collection, Street Cleansing and Related Services. Royal Borough of Kensington and Chelsea: http://rbkc.gov.uk/yourcouncil/foicontracts/wm_foi_partnershipcharter_main.pdf.
9 http://www.itgovernance.co.uk/capability-maturity-model.aspx.
10 *Creating Resilient Supply Chains: A Practical Guide,* Cranfield School of Management, 2003: www.som.**cranfield**.ac.uk/som/dinamic.../57081_Report_AW.pdf.

7 Secrets of success – conversations with collaborative leaders

1 Quoted in *Psychology Today*, 'Leadership Style and Employee Well-Being', Dr Christopher Peterson: http://www.psychologytoday.com/blog/the-good-life/200809/leadership-style-and-employee-well-being.
2 Quoted in *McKinsey Quarterly*, June 2012: https://www.mckinseyquarterly.com/Leading_in_the_21st_century_2984.

8 Why some collaborative leaders fail

1 'When to Ally and When to Acquire', Jeffrey H. Dyer, Prashant Kale and Harbir Singh, *Harvard Business Review*, July–August, 2004. The authors studied 1,592 alliances that US companies formed between 1993 and 1997.
2 'Procuring through partnerships', Audit Commission research report produced by Rob Abercrombie, Ana McDowall and Stuart Bailey, January 2008, as evidence for the Audit Commission 'For Better For Worse' study, available at: http://www.audit-commission.gov.uk/nationalstudies/localgov/forbetterforworse/Pages/Default.aspx.

9 Collaborative leaders in the boardroom

1 Report of the New York Stock Exchange Commission on Corporate Governance, September, 2010.
2 The True Purpose of the Board, June 2008, at: http://www.nikosonline.com/wp-content/uploads/nikos/TheTruePurposeoftheBoard.dot.
3 The UK Corporate Governance Code, Financial Reporting Council, June, 2010, see: http://www.frc.org.uk/Our-Work/Codes-Standards/Corporate-governance/UK-Corporate-Governance-Code.aspx.

4 'The Failure of the Royal Bank of Scotland', FSA Board Report, December, 2011: http://www.fsa.gov.uk/rbs.

5 'Apple enhances corporate governance', March, 2003. Available from: http://www.apple.com/pr/library/2003/03/20Apple-Enhances-Corporate-Governance.html.

6 'Apple faces scrutiny', *Wall Street Journal*, 7 October 2011. Available from: http://online.wsj.com/article/SB10001424052970204294504576615381967617082.html.

7 'Al Gove praises Apple Board', October, 2011. Available from: http://www.tuaw.com/2011/10/22/al-gore-praises-apple-board-at-all-things-d-conference/.

8 'Apple Board needs to step up to new era', Reuters, 6 October 2011: http://www.reuters.com/article/2011/10/06/us-apple-board-idUSTRE7957C520111006.

9 'Apple announces changes to its Board', Engadget, November, 2011: http://www.engadget.com/2011/11/15/apple-announces-board-changes-arthur-d-levinson-named-chairman/.

10 See the full report and the archive of papers that led to its creation at: http://www.jbs.cam.ac.uk/cadbury/report/index.html.

11 See the 'Greenbury Report', also at: http://www.jbs.cam.ac.uk/cadbury/report/furtherreports.html.

12 'Review of the Role and Effectiveness of Non-Executive Directors', Higgs Report, DTI, 2003, see: www.dti.gov.uk/cld/non_exec_review.

13 'Walker Review of Corporate Governance of UK Banking Industry', available at: http://webarchive.nationalarchives.gov.uk/+/http:/www.hm-treasury.gov.uk/d/walker_review_261109.pdf.

14 'The UK Corporate Governance Code', Financial Reporting Council, June, 2010. Available at: http://www.frc.org.uk/Our-Work/Codes-Standards/Corporate-governance/UK-Corporate-Governance-Code.aspx.

15 New York Stock Exchange, see: http://www.nyse.com/press/1285236224629.html.

16 'The Behavioural Drivers of Board Effectiveness: A Practitioners' Perspective', MWMConsulting:http://www.mwmconsulting.com/downloadables/Board-Behaviour-Summary-Research-Findings.pdf.

17 'The UK Corporate Governance Code', Financial Reporting Council, June, 2010. Available at:http://www.frc.org.uk/Our-Work/Codes-Standards/Corporate-governance/UK-Corporate-Governance-Code.aspx.

18 See the PRINCE 2 standards at: http://www.prince2.com/prince2-structure.asp.

19 'Making Partnerships Work: a survey of UK senior executives', IPSOS Mori survey for Socia, 2007.

20 'Good Governance: A Code for the Voluntary and Community Sector', The Charity Commission 2010, available at: http://www.charitycommission.gov.uk/Library/guidance/good_governance_full.pdf.

10 Relationship risk

1 Presidential Oil Spill Commission Chief Counsel's Report, February 2011, available from: http://www.oilspillcommission.gov/.

2 *Independent*, 7 February 2012, available at: http://www.independent.co.uk/news/uk/politics/treasury-under-fire-as-spend-now-pay-later-tactic-stores-up-a-200bn-tax-bill-for-the-next-generation-6612064.html.

3 'Lessons not Learned', *The Economist*, 6 January 2011, available at: http://www.economist.com/blogs/newsbook/2011/01/bp_and_deepwater_horizon_spill.

4 See PAC 14th report, February 2010, available at: http://www.publications.parliament.uk/pa/cm200910/cmselect/cmpubacc/390/39005.htm.

5 *Daily Telegraph*, 7 August 2010, available at: http://www.telegraph.co.uk/finance/financetopics/profiles/7932095/Eric-Daniels-on-HBOS-We-did-the-country-a-great-service.html.

6 http://www.guardian.co.uk/news/datablog/2009/mar/25/banking-g20.

7 *In Risk Management in Organisations: an integrated case study approach*, M. Woods, Routledge, 2011, p. 162.
8 Ibid.
9 Ghosn, Carlos, 'Saving the Business without Losing the Company', *Harvard Business Review*, January, 2002.
10 *Governing the Commons: The Evolution of Institutions for Collective Action*, Elinor Ostrom, Cambridge University Press, 1990.
11 Presidential Oil Spill Commission Chief Counsel's Report, February 2011, available at: http://www.oilspillcommission.gov/.
12 'Tough Dialogue Pays Off: How Lafarge and WWF make their partnership work to help preserve the world's ecological balance', Claudia Heimer, Roger Pudney, Jean-Paul Jeanrenaud, Luc Giraud-Guigues and Michel Picard, Ashridge Practitioner Paper, 6 October 2006.

11 Conflict and the collaborative leader

1 'Multiplex court case a "grim and ghastly" saga', *Contract Journal*, 20 February 2008.
2 'Want Collaboration? Accept and Actively Manage Conflict', Jeff Weiss and Jonathan Hughes, *Harvard Business Review*, March 2005.
3 'Collaboration Advantage: An Interview with Jonathan Hughes', *Effective Executive*, March 2008.
4 *The Truth Option*, Will Shutz, 10 Speed Press, 1984, pp. 244–51.
5 'Negotiation, The Better Way', Jonathan Hughes and Jeff Weiss, *InSpine*, 1 October 2005.
6 *Crucial Conversations*, Kerry Patterson, Joseph Grenny, Ron McMillan and Al Switzler, McGraw-Hill, 2011.
7 *Difficult Conversations: How to Discuss What Matters Most*, Douglas Stone, Bruce Patton and Sheila Heen of the Harvard Negotiation Project, Penguin Books, 2000.
8 'Collaboration Advantage: An Interview with Jonathan Hughes', *Effective Executive*, March 2008.
9 *In the Grip*, Naomi L. Quenk, CPP Inc., 2000.

12 The future collaborative leader

1 Quoted in 'Sony Betamax', Ecole Polytechnique Fédérale de Lausanne Case Study, January 2007.
2 'Social Enterprise Apps Redefine Collaboration', Henry Dewing, Forrester Research, November 2011.
3 See: http://www.cisco.com/web/about/ac79/docs/success/Tesco_Success_Story.pdf.
4 See: www.huddle.com.
5 'Managing in a multipolar world', Paolo Pigorini, *Strategy + Business*, May 2012, available at: http://www.strategy-business.com/article/00112?gko=855a7.
6 'Work: Life UK: Making plans for an ageing workforce', *Guardian*, 22 November 2011, available at: http://www.guardian.co.uk/worklifeuk/making-plans-for-an-ageing-workforce.
7 *The Difference: How the Power of Diversity Creates Better Groups, Firms, Schools, and Societies*, Scott E. Page, Princeton Press, 2008.
8 *The Living Company*, Arie de Geus, Nicholas Brealey Publishing Limited, 1997.

INDEX

Page numbers in **bold** refer to figures, page numbers in *italic* refer to tables

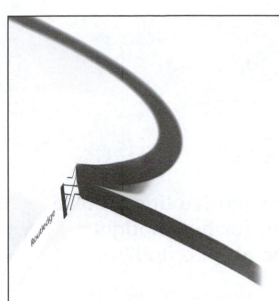